the Weather-Wise Gardener

A Guide to Understanding, Predicting, and Working with the Weather

CALVIN SIMONDS

Rodale Press, Emmaus, Pennsylvania

Printed in the United States of America on recycled paper, containing a high percentage of de-inked fiber.

Book design by Anita Groller
Art direction by Karen A. Schell
Illustrations by Mark Schultz

Library of Congress Cataloging in Publication Data

Simonds, Calvin.
  The weather-wise gardener.

  Bibliography: p.
  Includes index.
  1. Weather. 2. Gardening. 3. Gardening—United States. 4. Crops and climate—United States. 5. United States—Climate. I. Title.
SB454.3.W43S55 1983   551.5′024635   82–18066
ISBN   0-87857-428-X   hardcover

      2 4 6 8 10 9 7 5 3 1   hardcover

To all the people who have helped and encouraged me to write, this book is dedicated with the profoundest gratitude.

CONTENTS

INTRODUCTION
THE GARDENER
AND THE WEATHER

Over the years, I have come to think of my garden as more than just the place where I grow vegetables. More often I think of it as an arena where I grapple with nature. A gardener's perspective on nature is a very special one. Most people experience nature as spectators: they gaze out a window at an ocean view, a spectacular rock formation, a sunset, or they watch the TV news to learn of an earthquake in California or a fearful blizzard in the Midwest. Only occasionally does nature actually intrude on their lives. But gardeners experience nature right along with their plants, every day of the growing season. They luxuriate in sunshine, shrivel in a dry wind, relax in anticipation of rainfall, wilt in the cold. Through their relationship with their plants, gardeners come to know the natural world as few others do.

An Understand-It-Yourself Book

One morning a while back, when my teenaged son came down to breakfast, I had the kitchen table covered with do-it-yourself gardening books. I was trying to figure out how to rotate crops in my garden. My son cleared a little corner for himself at the edge of the table and sat down to eat, while I continued to flip pages and take notes. When he finished his bowl of cereal he looked at me quizzically and said, "Dad, I don't get it. How come you have to read five different books to find out how to do something?"

It was a good question. The more I thought about it the more I realized that I don't use do-it-yourself books to find out what to do. I use them to understand how something works. By comparing the instructions in different garden books about how to rotate my garden, I was developing a real understanding of how **vii** garden rotation worked. I was not actually going to do what any of the do-it-yourself books suggested; I was going to invent my own garden rotation system on the basis of what I learned from the do-it-yourself books.

So, why didn't I read a textbook on farm management, or crop rotation practices, and learn the principles directly? The fact is, I don't find textbooks very helpful. They give me abstract academic principles but they don't share experience. The nice thing about do-it-yourself books is that I can practically smell the garden dirt on the pages. (In fact, my copies all have garden dirt on the pages because they often end up out in the garden with me.) The learning I get from do-it-yourself books is more pleasurable and more permanent because it is learning which is all tangled up with experimenting in the garden, and smelling, and feeling, and seeing how the experiments work.

After I had thought about my son's question for a couple of weeks, I began to feel that there was a need—for gardeners like me, anyway—of a new kind of book about gardening and related things. This sort of book would be an "understand-it-yourself book." Instead of striving to give the reader the last word on how to *do* something, such a book would give the reader such a thorough understanding of how that something works, that he or she would be able to devise his or her own ways of doing. In the long run, such an understanding would be more useful than the learning of specific techniques. It would stay with the reader for years after the book that provided it had been long out of print. Unlike a text, the book would be written from close to the garden, by somebody with garden dirt under his fingernails. The language would be clear, simple, direct, and to the point.

Not long thereafter, I was given the opportunity to prepare a book about weather for gardeners by Rodale Press. I have been an organic gardener for twelve years, and a professional natural historian for nearly twenty, but my first love since childhood has always been weather. To be in love with the weather is to live in a slightly different world from that lived in by other people. The dark roll of cloud that marches across the sky some summer afternoons is not just a shower; it is a cold front, a contested boundary between two regions of the atmosphere. The feathery band of cloud stretching across the sky on a cold winter afternoon is not just mare's tails; it is actually flotsam borne on a jet stream, a river of air five or six miles away in the sky. Life lived as a weather-lover is life led on a grand scale.

The way a weather-lover looks at weather is a little like the way a gardener looks at dirt. Before I became an organic gardener, I perceived "dirt" as the opposite of "clean." Dirt was something to be washed off things: washed off clothes, washed off cars, washed off blacktop driveways, washed off my hands. After twelve years of intense gardening, "dirt" is now synonymous with "life." A handful of dirt is not a potential contaminant so much as it is a place where thousands of interesting things are going on. Little animals are crawling about, microbes are gobbling up things, and complex chemical reactions are taking place. Life is being created. Mind you, I still wash the dirt off my spinach. My behavior has not changed all that much. But I *see* dirt differently.

It actually looks like a different sort of substance to me than it did twelve years ago when I began my gardener's career.

The purpose of this book is to share with my fellow gardeners a weather-lover's perception of weather. To most of my gardening friends, I suspect, weather is like dirt to a nongardener. Weather is a necessity, weather is an encumbrance, weather is the balky and unpredictable context in which they must carry out their gardening. I want to change these friends' view of weather in just the way a decade of gardening and reading gardening books has transformed my perception of dirt. This book is a gardeners' understand-it-yourself book about weather. It is not primarily designed to give readers the last word on gardening and the weather—although, where I have some tips or techniques I will certainly share them. On the contrary, it is designed to open the subject up for you . . . to be the first word, so to speak. I hope this book will change gardeners' perceptions of the weather from just the source of rain or frost or other necessities and irritants to the grand show it really is. I hope to leave readers in the same state of constant bemusement and curiosity about the weather that I find myself in every day of my life.

Leave It to the Experts?

But isn't weather science too complicated to be read or written by gardeners like you and me? I do not think so. All scientists like to puff themselves up. Weather scientists are no exception. Their maps are full of little symbols so complex and cabalistic as to suggest the occult. Their language—highs, lows, fronts, occlusions, troughs, ridges, convergence, divergence, and the like—suggests a world beyond the sense of ordinary people. But the reality of weather science is much more homely. In essence, professional weather observers do what we ourselves do when we go out in the morning to sniff the wind. The complicated symbols simply make it possible for the professional to write in a compact space a message which in content is essentially the same as: "It's a beautiful day today; the sky is completely clear except for a few puffy, white clouds. The temperature is cool, the barometer is high and rising, the air is dry, the winds are light, and you can see for thirty miles."

The meteorologists who draw weather maps do something equally commonplace. They proceed essentially as we do when we fit a jigsaw puzzle together. They put together all the places with cool, dry weather and call them the cool, dry region, and then they put together all the places with hot, humid weather and call them the warm, humid region. Then they draw a boundary between these two regions and call it a front. Before long, they have a weather map.

When I was a child of ten growing up in Ipswich, Massachusetts, I tried to form a neighborhood weather club. At first, I made good progress with my friends. I convinced them that we should all get up at the same time each morning and write down the temperature and note the wind direction and what kind of clouds were overhead and whether it was raining or not. I got them to join the club by promising them that I would teach them all the *codes*. Then I let them look for just a moment at all the intriguing little squiggles and mysterious numbers that cover the surface of a weather map, before I folded it up and snatched it away.

For a while, this recruitment technique was very successful. We converted an old horse stall in the barn into a clubhouse, and put pictures of clouds all over the walls and a table in the middle. The club members cadged thermometers from our parents and made improvised wind direction indicators and began to make our observations. But then, of course, I had to make good on my promise to teach them the codes. We all convened one Saturday morning. My colleagues were in a very conspiratorial frame of mind and insisted on bolting the door of the stall and covering up the little window that the horse had had to look out of. It was so dim that we could barely see the map as I spread it out on the table.

The club members were very impressed. They crowded around the map and said things like "Wow," and "Hey, look at this," and "This is neat." Members eagerly pointed their fingers at different symbols and read the meanings: things like "veil of cirrus covering the entire sky," or "nine-tenths of sky overcast," or "sky overcast with breaks," or "moderate thunderstorm with rain and hail," or "dust devils in progress."

But then one of the club members made a very penetrating observation. He had been one of my most reluctant recruits. He was a baseball fanatic and was much more interested in establishing a Ted Williams fan club than a weather club. He said, "Hey, this code is *dumb*. You can only talk about weather with this code. What are we going to do, sneak around with secret messages about the temperature? Who wants to have a secret club about that?"

So ended the Ipswich Weather Society. The rise and fall of the Ipswich Weather Society portrays a fundamental ambiguity concerning science. One of the great pleasures of being a scientist is the feeling of belonging to a club. Members of the club communicate with one another in special languages and special codes which are difficult for nonclub members to understand. On the other hand, the club's subject matter deals ultimately with the real world. You do not have to be a member of the club or speak the club's special language to know a great deal about the real world. Thus the layman may speak in a different language from the scientist, but the two ultimately speak of the same things and their languages must be mutually translatable, one into the other.

I would be the last to deny weather scientists their special languages. I am a kind of scientist myself, and when I deal with my scientific colleagues I readily fall into the jargon of our specialty. Not only does the language confer on us the pleasures of club membership, it helps us to convey precise meanings. Two gardeners talking long distance on the phone one hot, humid morning might have a difficult time agreeing which of them had the muggiest weather. But no two weather observers would have any difficulty agreeing which of them was measuring the highest dew point.

But the essence of being a scientist is not understanding codes and talking in obscure languages. From a gardener's weather experience to a scientific understanding of the weather is not as big a step as you might suppose. The essence of being a scientist is being excited and curious about some part of nature. The fact is that anybody who spends a lot of time outdoors, who keeps an eye to the sky, and who regularly taps his barometer, is well on the road to being a weather scientist. The more such a person thinks about his or her weather experiences, the more he or she demands explanation, the more the curious codes and languages of the weather scientist appear to make sense. Hence, this book begins not with the weatherman's lingo, but with your everyday experience of weather in your garden.

This gardeners' understand-it-yourself book about the weather comes in three parts. The first puts together the basic principles of meteorology from everyday, garden-variety, weather experiences. This first section is designed to give a fundamental understanding of weather that will lend depth to the rest of the book. The second section shows how these principles conspire to make the weather that prevails in different parts of the country and at different times of the year. The third section shows you how you can apply your understanding of the basic principles to anticipate weather emergencies and cope with the effects of weather on yourself and your garden. Finally, in the conclusion I want to share some thoughts with you—many of them uneasy thoughts—about the future of our weather. The book is designed to be read from chapter 1 to the end. But if you want to jump around in it, you can do that, too.

So let's begin. Imagine you are out at the end of your garden one late fall afternoon. Your crops are harvested except for those hardy plants like Brussels sprouts and carrots which are very frost-resistant or sheltered in the ground. It is a time of reflection. You walk around the garden mulling over the season past and your hopes for the next. There is a fitful, chilly wind blowing and the sky looks like a fuzzy grey blanket. "Why is the wind increasing?" you wonder. "What does this funny sky mean? Something's happening with the weather. I wonder what?"

Part One

WHAT YOU NEED TO KNOW TO UNDERSTAND THE WEATHER

1

THE CYCLES
OF THE WINDS

Even without reading a weather book, most gardeners are pretty fair forecasters of the weather in their own gardens. Take me, for instance. Let's say it's a bright August morning and a gusty northwest wind is rummaging through the stalks of my corn and making their broad leaves lash and clatter together in a most disconcerting manner. Without turning on the radio or reading the morning paper, I know with a hundred percent probability that:

—No general rainfall will occur during the day.
—No rain at all will fall overnight.
—The wind and clouds will increase toward midday and taper off by dark.
—Tonight and tomorrow will be less windy and cloudy than today.
—It will be very chilly tonight.

I know these things with absolute certainty, even though I have no radar, no satellite photographs, no mast covered with weather instruments, and no rattling teletype. I know them, even though I have not even looked at my barometer or my thermometer. I know them, because I have something better than all these kinds of equipment. I have the kind of experience that every gardener has with the weather in his or her garden, and that experience tells me that certain kinds of weather follow other kinds of weather as daylight follows sunrise. It is just that simple.

That experience tells me that the weather passes by in a three- or four-day cycle. Like all cycles, it is a bit hard to describe because to describe it you have to *begin* somewhere, and that of course violates the most essential element of a cycle. Let us break into the cycle on the morning of an exceptionally cool and invigorating August day: the kind of day when the sun rises on a crisp and well-defined horizon, when the winds are gentle from the northwest and the barometer is high and rising slightly, a day when only the flimsiest clouds mar the intense blue of the sky. In the garden, the soil dries out rapidly and each plant reacts in its characteristic way to the intense radiation of the sun. Some seem to grow eagerly, while others, the more succulent perhaps, hang back, look sullen, wait for more humid air. Let us call this *Day One* of our cycle.

Day Two dawns pretty much the same. But when I come into the kitchen in the morning and look out over the garden I notice that the western sky near the horizon is full of a matted network of mare's tails and vapor trails. As the sun rises in the east, so do the clouds in the west, and before noon the sun has slid behind the clouds. They dim its light, but its heat is still intense. The wind is indecisive all morning, but when I go out to pick some lettuce for lunch, I notice that it has swung around and is blowing just a bit east of south. The air is still dry and the plants in the garden long for rain. By nightfall, rain looks certain. Grey and purple clouds mask the sunset, and a soft south wind is blowing. During the evening I notice that the barometer is falling. As I climb into bed around midnight, I hear the rain begin. At first gentle, it gradually comes down more heavily. Lying on my back in bed, I consider whether I must close the windows. The wind is a bit west of south now and strong enough to blow a bit of mist on me as I lie near the south windows. The rain eases up. Too bad for the plants in the garden, I think, but good that I do not have to close the windows. I doze off, listening to the trickling of the last water in the gutters.

Day Three is a stinker. The barometer is sharply down from the night before. The air is sticky with moisture. Haze and overcast overhang the valley. My trouser legs adhere to my skin as I try to pull them on. I get myself a bowl of cereal and wander about the house looking for a cool place to eat it. By ten A.M. the sun's warmth can be felt through the overcast and by eleven, the overcast breaks into indistinct clouds moving across the sky from southwest to northeast. In the garden, the air hums with insect life. The plants are growing so fast you can practically hear them. Squash vines clamber around among the rows of corn. The corn leaves rustle in a brisk southwesterly breeze. The dog lies under the arborvitae on the north side of the house and his panting can be heard from deep within its branches.

About four P.M. the western sky darkens first grey, then blue, and finally almost to a green. Distant thunder can be heard. The dog comes out from his shelter and begins to follow me about as I make ready for the storm. The barometer, which has been mostly steady all day, now begins to fall again. The thunderstorm comes on fast, with lightning, thunder, a lot of rain, a little hail, and gusts of cold wind from the west. The rain gauge in the garden collects an inch of rain in a half hour. Several cucumber plants blow off their supports and I have to thread the vines back through the chicken wire when the rain subsides.

After the storm, the air goes still again. It is almost as if the thunderstorm never happened. But when I go out for a last look at the weather just before I go to bed, I notice that the air is distinctly lighter, and as I come around to the west side of the house, I notice that a breeze has picked up from the northwest. Looking up, I can see bright stars winking on and off as small clouds hurry across the sky from the northwest.

Day Four dawns crisp and breezy. The horizon is distinct once more, the sky is again blue. The barometer is rising steeply. The garden looks a bit wind-whipped but is grateful for the rain. By midmorning, puffy white clouds are drifting across the sky and by afternoon their undersides are black. Up the valley, a grey veil below a particularly large cloud shows that the next town north is getting a shower. But this shower will pass my garden by. By nightfall, the sky is clear once more. The stars are bright. Perseus rises in the northeast and we look for meteors. Tomorrow will be a wonderful day, much like *Day One*.

This cycle, from northwest to south-southeast to southwest and so back to northwest again is a very common cycle during the growing season in New England. Notice that it is a clockwise cycle; that is, the winds move around the compass in a clockwise direction as they pass from the east and the west half of the compass. There is another cycle of the winds, a counterclockwise cycle, that we get more commonly outside the growing season. But we do get it sometimes during the summer. It begins like *Day One* of the other cycle. A beautiful, dry, clear day with light northwest winds.

But *Day Two* dawns differently. There is the same dense net of high clouds as in the other cycle, but it is concentrated in the southwest and south, rather than the west. The sun rises amid a raft of ragged grey cloud drifting out of the east. Winds are from the east, or perhaps just a little south of east. As the sun rises, so do the high clouds in the southwest and the low cloud in the east. For a while, the three vie for control of the sky, and then the low clouds win out. By bedtime when I go outside to give the dog a run, the air has a maritime feel to it. The clouds hang very low overhead. Where they are illuminated by the lights of the little village to the north, I can see that they are moving busily from east-northeast to west-southwest across the sky. Inside, before going up to bed I tap the barometer. The needle jumps lower on the scale.

Morning of *Day Three* dawns not very summery. The sky is grey and ragged and low. The distant hills are indistinct in mist and drizzle. A restless northeast wind pries at the windows and whistles through the crevices of the house in a manner that is distressingly like winter. The barometer has fallen sharply overnight. From time to time, the drizzle increases to a steady rain and even to a downpour. Puddles form in the driveway and on low points in the garden. Their surfaces jump with the impact of the raindrops. Blanched worms litter the ground. Seen from the window of the house, the garden begins to take on a drowned look. Temperatures fall to the low sixties. The house is clammy. Feeling a bit foolish, I run the furnace for fifteen minutes to get the chill off the house.

About noon, the rain lets up, the wind calms down, and the overcast lifts and lightens a bit. The barometer, which has been falling all morning, now levels off. Outside, in the garden the birds begin to sing as if it were dawn. The robins come to strut on the rain-soaked lawn. But when I go out later to pull some carrots for dinner, I notice that the clouds have begun to lower and thicken again and the wind has again begun to pick up, now from the north. When I go back inside, I check the barometer and discover that it has begun to rise. Later, before climbing into bed, I notice that the wind is again prying at the windows of the house, but this time on the north. I turn out the lights and look out the windows and see low clouds rushing across the sky from north to south. Between them an occasional star winks on and off as they rush by.

Day Four dawns chill and blustery. The sun rises over a flock of blobby blue-grey clouds rushing southward on the eastern horizon. Stragglers from this flock dot the sky here and there. The barometer is rising rapidly. It seems like it is going to be a raw day. The garden looks listless and beaten, waiting for warmth. As the day wears on, the sun pulls itself free of the clouds in the east, and the wind slides from north-northwest to northwest. Now puffy white clouds form here and there; some are large enough to have dark bottoms and may yet give us a shower. But the air is drying out rapidly and I know that tomorrow will be a beautiful day, much like *Day One.*

Summarizing the Cycles

These are the two basic cycles of the winds. They occur in my garden nearly a hundred times a year and if you live anywhere in the U.S. or Canada, they occur regularly in your garden as well. As an aid to recognizing the cycles, think of the compass as divided in half along a line running from northeast to southwest. We will call the right or east half, "the foul weather half"; we will call the left or west half, "the fair weather half." Both cycles begin when the wind crosses the compass from the fair weather to the foul weather half and the barometer begins to fall. In one of the two cycles the wind returns toward the northwest in a counterclockwise direction and the weather is dull and chilly; in the other it returns in a clockwise direction and the weather is muggy and showery for a time. Both cycles end when the wind enters the fair weather half of the compass and the pressure starts to rise.

In winter, the cycles of the winds are the same, but they bring different weather. The winter clockwise cycle rarely brings thunderstorms, but it brings balmy southerly winds that gobble up the snowcover. The counterclockwise cycle, on the other hand, brings the most ferocious snowstorms with gale-force northeast winds that drive the snow right through the windows of our old house, windowframes, storm windows, and all. But even though the weather is different in winter, the pattern is the same: an excursion to the east followed by

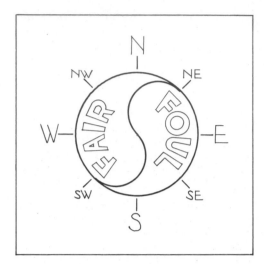

The fair and foul weather halves of the compass. Bad weather usually begins when the wind moves to the foul weather half and improves as the wind moves back into the fair weather half.

a falling barometer. Then a gradual shifting of the wind around the compass toward the northwest, accompanied finally by a rising barometer and better weather.

Of course, there are variations. Sometimes as the barometer begins its fall, the wind does not jump so far east: it may only go as far as northeast or as far as southwest before it begins its return trip. On these "short" cycles, however, the barometer does not usually fall so far, winds are lighter, and the bad weather is usually less intense. Sometimes the wind gets stuck in one position for long periods. In January, around here the wind can get stuck in the northwest and give us days or even weeks of ferociously cold weather. In July it gets stuck in the southwest and we have temperatures in the nineties day after day after day. One June, I remember it got stuck in the east and we had three weeks of drizzle and chilly air. My tomato plants practically lay down on the soil and wept. It was so cold that even the peas refused to grow.

Noticing the Cycles

Once you start to look for them, the cycles of the winds around your garden are easy to observe. If your house sits in an exposed location and you have a weather vane and a barometer, then spotting the cycles of the winds will be a cinch. But even if you do not have any of these advantages, you can spot the cycles of the winds. A little plastic streamer attached to a lightning rod or a TV antenna will make a perfectly acceptable weather vane. Or, if your house is too sheltered to catch the wind, keep an eye on the weather vane on the steeple of a nearby church, or the flag on a public building. You can even observe the cycles of the winds while commuting to and from work. Tall smoke stacks make excellent weather vanes. Just make a note each day, as you pass the stack, of the wind direction and the weather. Somewhere along your route, there is bound to be one of those digital bank clocks which shows the temperature. Note that down as well. One way or another, it will not be long before the cycles of the winds will stand out like two sore thumbs.

The chances are the cycles of the winds in your garden will be pretty much like the cycles of the winds in mine. You will probably find that there is a fair weather half of your wind compass and a foul weather half, just as there is on mine. Chances are that wherever you are the foul weather half circle will be mostly on the east side of the compass. The fair weather half circle will be mostly on the west.

Foul Weather Winds and Fair Weather Winds

In 1903, the U.S. Weather Bureau published maps which show the rain winds for different parts of the country. A rain wind is a wind that reliably precedes rainfall by some number of hours, say eighteen to twenty-four. In most places in the country, except in some of the drier parts where rain is the result of very special meteorological situations, the rain winds are concentrated on the east side of the compass. In most places, the foul/fair line is "tilted," just as it is where I live. A north wind, even a north-northeast wind, is a fair weather wind in a great many places, whereas a south wind, or even a south-southwest wind, is a foul. So if you wanted to have a general rule to take with you to apply all over the country, it would probably be that winds from the southeast half-circle of the compass suggest that rain is on the way, and that winds from the northwest half-circle suggest that improving weather is on the way.

Being familiar with the cycles of the winds in your part of the country will make something of a weather forecaster of you. You will know, for instance, that if the barometer is low and rising and the wind is shifting toward the northwest, you can be hopeful for some good weather. You will know, also, that if the wind crosses the compass to the east and the barometer begins to fall, you should be on the lookout for bad weather. Finally, you will know that if the winds start their return trip in a counterclockwise direction, you should be on the lookout for cloudy, damp, cool, drizzly, and rainy (or snowy) weather. If they start their return trip in a clockwise direction, then you should be on the lookout for a showery or rainy period, followed by a muggy, warm period, followed by a briefer period of showery weather, followed finally by a return to cool and dry weather.

Winter

Summer

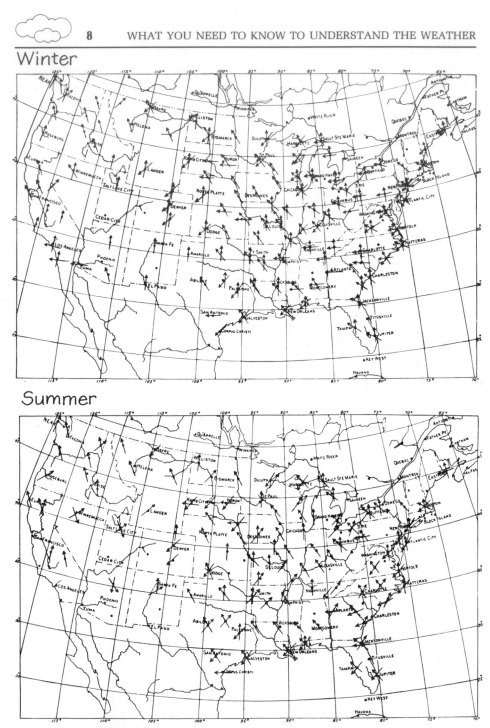

The rain winds of North America in winter, top, and summer, bottom. A rain wind is the wind direction that typically precedes rain or snowfall at a given location. Reprinted from Edward B. Garriott, Weather Folk-lore (Washington, D.C.: USDA, 1903).

Why Do the Winds Come in Cycles?

It is one thing to be able to predict the changes of the winds, quite another to understand them. That north winds bring cold weather and south winds warm weather is easy to understand. Each of these winds comes from a place that is "like" the character of the wind itself. But why should an east wind be foul and a west wind fair?

I was raised near the Atlantic Ocean, and I believed for a long time that southeast winds were foul because they blew off the ocean, and the northwest winds fair because they blew off the dry land. When I grew up and started to travel around to different parts of the country, I soon discovered that a southeast wind is foul in a lot of places where the ocean is not very near, like Cleveland or Chicago, for instance. In fact, I could fly in a plane from Washington to Chicago, leaving Washington clear and dry and arriving in Chicago with rainy weather and a strong east wind. Surely if Chicago were importing its weather from sunny Washington on easterly winds, then Chicago should be sunny, right? Wrong!

But the clincher was when I moved to San Francisco. San Francisco has more than 5,000 miles of ocean to the west of it, and 1,000 miles of desert to the southeast. Still, the winter rain wind in San Francisco is a southeast wind. Clearly there is something about the fairness of a west wind and the foulness of an east wind that is quite apart from where they are blowing from.

There are other puzzles. Why does the barometer begin to fall as the winds go easterly and rise again as they finish their return to the west? A barometer measures the weight of the air over it. When a barometer "falls" it indicates that there is less air over it; or perhaps to speak more precisely, that the density of the air above it is less. The changes in the weight of the air which accompany most weather changes are very small, rarely much as 10 percent of the total and usually 2 or 3 percent at most. Why should changes of a few percent in the weight of the air tell us so much about what the weather is doing?

And why the *cycles* of the winds? Why does the wind first shift to the east as the weather begins to get bad, march westward as it gets worse, and continue westward as it improves again?

Even though we know a lot more than we did a few pages ago, still the question of what sort of a something it is that causes the cycles remains a puzzle for us to solve. What if I could devise a way of seeing the weather all over the country at just the instant the cycle of the winds is starting at my farm? Then perhaps I could see the "something" coming and see where it goes after it passes me by. In the next chapter, we'll work out a method of taking a sort of picture of the thing that makes the cycles of the winds, just as it lurks on our doorstep.

An Explanation
for the Cycles of the Winds

When scientists are puzzled, they often invent what they call a "model." Scientific models often seem a bit frivolous, but they always summarize the relationships that the scientist has discovered. What if we were to invent a model to explain the cycles of the winds? Such as:

The Rain Train Theory
of the Cycles of the Winds

Northwest of my location and southeast of my location are two straight railroad tracks, running from northeast to southwest. On these tracks run trains which pull only two cars. On one car is a giant water tank; on the other is a giant electric fan. As the train passes by me from northeast to southwest, workmen on the fan car labor mightily to turn the fan so that it is always directed at me. As the fan comes abreast of me, I am closer and closer to it so that the wind is stronger and stronger. On the second car, workmen labor to direct a jet of water from the water tank into the fan. As the train gets closer, that water reaches me as rain. If the train passes me on the track which runs to the northwest of me, then my winds change in a counterclockwise direction northeast to north to northwest as the train passes by. If the train passes me on the track which runs to the east of me, then the winds change in a clockwise direction southeast to south to southwest to west as the train passes by.

Silly as the rain train idea is, it does explain why the winds increase and move around the compass as the rains come and go. The model asserts that these events occur because something approaches from the east and passes by headed west. This something brings the rain and wind.

Apart from its frivolity, this model has at least two crucial flaws: first of all, it doesn't explain why the barometer falls as the weather worsens. Second, it doesn't explain the way in which high clouds behave before a storm. Once you are familiar with the cycles of the winds in your area,

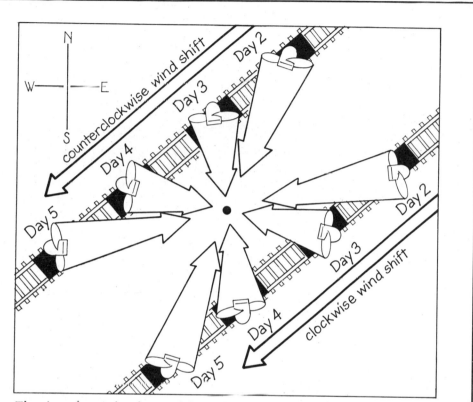

The giant electric fan theory of the cycles of the winds.

take some time to look at the high clouds in the sky as the cycles come and go. You can tell that clouds are high because they appear to be beyond the lower clouds and because their features seem smaller and more detailed. High clouds before a storm usually come from the *west* part of the compass. Why is it that the high clouds approach us from the west, when the cycles of the winds suggest that bad weather approaches us from the east?

2

THE THING THAT MAKES THE WINDS GO 'ROUND

How could I settle once and for all what sort of a "something" it is that makes the cycles of the weather? Let us imagine that I got in touch with all the organic gardeners in the United States—preferably in the off-season when they are not too busy. And let us say that I asked each gardener to go out to the end of his or her garden at precisely the same time and take note of the wind direction, the clouds, whether rain or snow is falling, what the temperature is, and any remarkable characteristics of his or her weather. And then, let us say, the gardeners all went directly into their houses and tapped their barometers and noted the air pressure and whether the needle "rose" or "fell." And what if, then, I called them all on the telephone and asked them what they had observed? Perhaps, by putting all their observations together I could form a portrait of whatever it is that makes the cycles of the winds.

So, I wait until a morning when the cycle of the wind is beginning at my farm in Massachusetts. The wind is from the southeast, the barometer is high and starting to dip, and there are high clouds in the southwest. I eagerly look forward to the reports from my gardener-observers.

The first report I get is from the gardener at Albany. The weather at his garden is very like the weather at mine. The sky is partly covered over with high clouds, the wind is southeast. The differences are that the cloud cover is a bit heavier and his barometer is lower. So, I look farther west. The gardener at Buffalo continues the trend. Her wind is 15 miles per hour from the southeast, the temperature is 29 degrees. Her barometer is quite low, only 29.68, and she reports that it is falling rapidly. The further west I go, the further along is the cycle of the winds and the worse the weather is. I suspect that some weather drama is taking place in the Ohio River Valley. My suspicion is confirmed when I hear from the gardener at Detroit. He has a 25-mile-an-hour northeast wind, heavy snow, and a barometric reading of only 29.44. It has been snowing there for nine hours, and the temperature has been falling for the last three. The snow is beginning to blow and drift. He notes with some relief that the barometer has stopped falling and begun to level out, perhaps even to rise a bit.

Continuing westward, the gardener at Milwaukee reports a biting 15-mile-an-hour north wind, temperature of 16 degrees, and clouds that are "spitting" snow; a most unpleasant morning. She adds, however, that the western sky is lighter than the east and that her barometer is rising sharply. She thinks the weather is improving. The gardener at Des Moines verifies her prediction. The sky at Des Moines is clear, except for a few wispy clouds, and the wind is north-northwest. The temperature is only 2 degrees and the pressure is back up to 29.97 and still rising.

As I hang up the phone, I note that in passing westward along a line from New England to Iowa, I have recapitulated the weather changes of the counterclockwise cycle of the winds just as they occur at my farm: first southeast, then northeast, then northwest, with the weather first deteriorating, then improving. How interesting!

I turn my attention southward. The gardener in a suburb of New York City reports a southeast wind, light snow, a temperature at freezing, a pressure of 29.91, and a falling barometer. Her report is sort of like the one I got from a gardener at Buffalo, except the pressure is not so low and the temperature is higher. Further south and west, near the organic farm in Emmaus, Pennsylvania, the gardener reports a southeast wind, a temperature of 34 degrees, and rain. The pressure is still lower at 29.77.

But 300 miles beyond in Charlestown, West Virginia, the weather is like the weather in another world. The sky is only partly cloudy, the winds are 15 miles per hour from the southwest. And it is *warm*. The sun is peeking through the clouds. The air has a humid, balmy feel to it, like spring is on the way. So I push on to Nashville. The gardener tells me that until recently, the weather has been very mild, like the weather in West Virginia. But in the last hour it has changed dramatically. The wind, which had been steady from the west-southwest all night, has shifted and is blowing fitfully from the south-southwest. The temperature has taken a dip and a cold rain has started to fall. Black clouds are looming on the western horizon and the barometer, which had been steady all night, has started to fall again. The Nashville gardener says she does not like the look of the weather, at all.

Her worst fears are confirmed by the Memphis gardener only a hundred miles south and west. He reports a black, ugly, wintery-looking sky, a west-northwest wind of 15 miles an hour, light snow, and a temperature of 33 degrees. The weather at Little Rock, Arkansas, is even colder. The temperature is only 22 degrees, the sky is partly cloudy, and there is a snowshower in progress. The wind is from the northwest and the barometer is rising steadily.

Reviewing the information I have gathered from the gardeners from New York southwestward to Arkansas, I realize that this time I have recapitulated the clockwise cycles of the winds, including the falling barometer and the period of mild, sunny weather between two periods of rainy weather.

There are many puzzling things about the reports I have. The most striking is the difference between the weather at Detroit and the weather at Charlestown, West Virginia. These two gardeners live only 300 miles apart but their weather is about as different as weather can be. Their winds are opposite. The weather in one place is sunny and mild; in the other, cold and snowy. And yet their barometers are not very different, certainly not as different as one might expect, given the difference in their weather. Strange doings in the Ohio Valley!

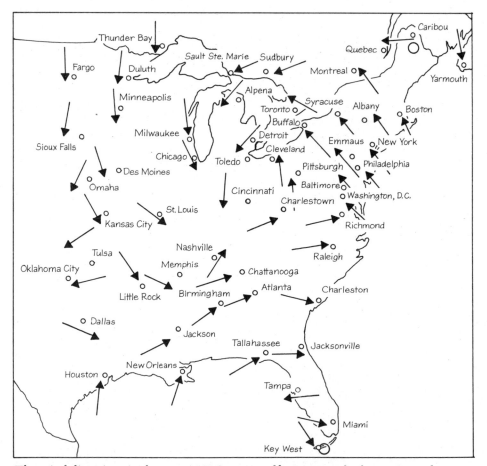

The wind directions in the eastern U.S. reported by a network of organic gardeners.

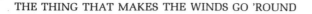

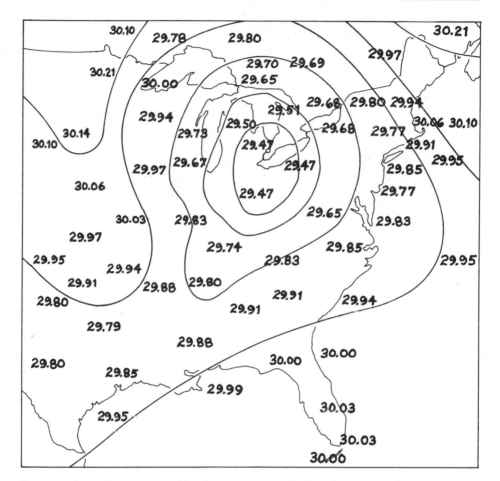

Barometric readings reported by the same network of gardeners.

The more I learn from the gardeners around Ohio the more confused I get. Cincinnati, which is 200 miles west-northwest of Charlestown and about the same distance south-southeast of Detroit, has a 20-mile-an-hour north wind, heavy snow, a temperature of 32, and a barometer which is very low (29.47) but which has begun to rise. Pittsburgh, on the other hand, 200 miles north-northeast of Charlestown, has a 20-mile-an-hour south wind, light rain, and a barometer of 29.56 which is still falling. Whatever is going on in Ohio is producing dramatic contrasts in the weather over very short distances.

One thing is clear. I am not going to get very far understanding what's going on if I keep trying to interpret, item by item, all the information I am getting from my gardeners.

Perhaps if I put all the information on a map, then some patterns will emerge. Let us start with the wind directions. Look at the map of the eastern

United States on page 14 marked with all the wind directions reported by my network of gardeners. Each wind direction is drawn just as if we were looking down on the gardener's wind vane. (Where there is no wind, I have drawn a circle to indicate calm.) The arrows make a dramatic pattern. All the winds on the map seem to be rotating around a common point: Toledo, Ohio, roughly speaking. Over the northeastern states, the winds are blowing from the southeast; over the upper midwest, they are blowing from the north and northwest; and over the south they are blowing from the southwest. Whatever else might be said about the thing that makes the cycle of the winds, it is a *rotating* sort of a thing.

If I plot the pressures on a map, I get the same sort of circular pattern. It is a little hard to see, so I have put some lines on the map to emphasize the pattern. To make the lines I started by estimating where the pressure would be 29.50. For instance, the pressure in Detroit is 29.44; in northern Michigan it is 29.62; 29.50 should be about a third of the way from Detroit to northern Michigan. So I made a little dot on the map at this point and tried to look for other places where the pressure was 29.50. The pressure is 29.47 at Cincinnati, so I put a dot just to the south of Cincinnati. When I had made several such estimates I then connected all the dots with a line. Next I estimated where the pressure is 29.65 and connected all those points. I did the same with 29.80, 29.95, and 30.10. These "lines of equal pressure" make a circular pattern just like the circle of the winds, and like the center of the circle of the winds, the center of the circle of barometers appears to be just over Toledo, Ohio.

When I compare the circle of the winds with the circle of pressure measurements, I find that the wind direction is always "toed in" a bit. It is as if instead of blowing around in a precise circle, the winds are spiraling inward toward the center of the circle. This fact makes a useful constant relationship between the wind direction and the center of the circle. If I stand on my farm in Massachusetts and face into my southeast wind, and hold my right arm straight out and a little behind my body, then I will be pointing roughly toward the center of the circle. The same is true for every gardener around the circle. It is true for the gardener in Chicago who faces into the north wind and points east toward Toledo. It is true for the gardener in Charlestown who faces west-southwest and points northwest toward Toledo. The relationship is only approximate, but with some variations the center of the circle of the winds is always on the right hand and usually a bit behind an observer who is facing the wind.

When I turn to the temperatures reported to me by my gardeners, another pattern emerges. As with the pressures the numbers on the map do not themselves readily make a pattern, and so I put lines of equal temperature on the map analogous to the lines of equal pressure on the barometer map. Here, another pattern emerges, an S-shaped pattern. Temperatures are relatively low on the west side of the map and relatively high on the east side of the map. The upper curve of the S is just about where the center of the circle is on the barometer and wind maps. It almost looks as if the atmosphere is rolling around that center: the cold air on the west is sweeping down around the center toward the southeast while the warm air on the east is sweeping up around the center to the north.

The same sort of lazy S-shaped pattern is formed in the shape of the area which is receiving rain or snow. That area is widest in the area around Toledo where the upper part of the S curve is found. The heaviest precipitation occurs in the top part of the S, particularly around the top loop of the S.

If I plot all the different kinds of information on a single map, then we can get a composite picture of what it is that makes the cycles of the winds. To get all the information on the map at once, I have had to do some simplifying. I have left out the numbers and represented the temperatures and barometer readings as lines of equal temperature and pressure. I have also left out the

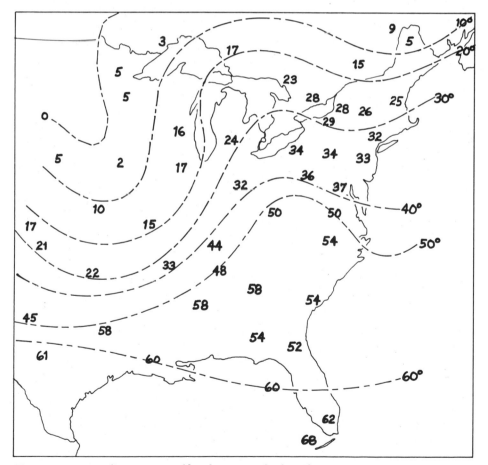

Temperature readings reported by the network of gardeners.

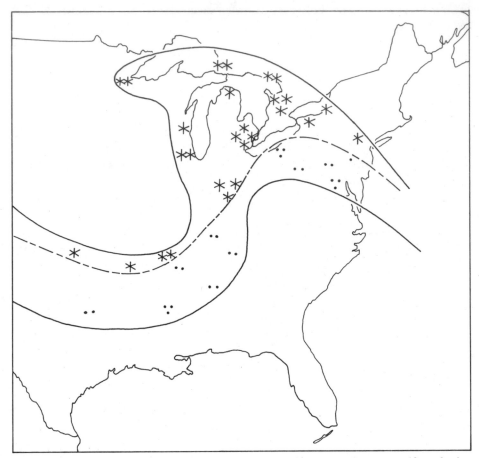

The shape of the areas receiving precipitation from the storm, determined by which gardeners are reporting rain or snow.

individual precipitation reports and simply shaded the area where precipitation is falling: dark shading for snow, a lighter shading for rain.

The map is a little confusing at first, but if you study it some features begin to stand out. Running across the map from the lower left-hand corner to the middle of the right side is a region of the map where much of the action seems to be taking place. This region is marked with a dark black line studded with triangular and semicircular shapes. A lot of the most intense precipitation occurs along this line. On either side of the line there seems to be a wind shift. The lines of equal temperature get closer together near this line and the circle of the barometers seems sometimes to bulge out along it, meaning that the pressure along the line is a bit lower than on either side of it. The line seems to form a sort of boundary between warmish air in the south and southeast and cold, blustery weather in the north.

Meteorologists call this sort of a boundary a "front." The part of the front on the south and west of the center where the cold northwest winds are blowing against the western edge of the warmer air, they call a "cold front." The part on the east where the warm winds are blowing against the cool air to the north and east, they would call a "warm front." A cold front is represented on weather maps by putting sharp protrusions on the front in the direction it is moving. A warm front is represented with round protrusions. Sharp = cold; round = warm. The whole circle of the winds, meteorologists would call a "frontal cyclone": "frontal" because it has fronts; "cyclone" because the winds swirl around the center in a counterclockwise circle.

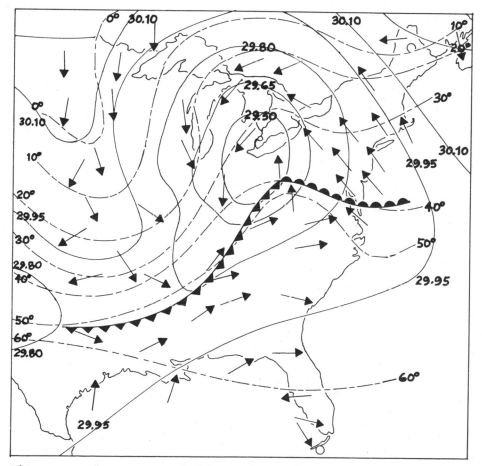

This map provides a summary of all the weather conditions reported by our network of gardeners.

Tracking the Movement of the Cyclone

Suddenly, the falling barometer, the gentle southeast wind, and the thin, high overcast at my farm take on a whole new dimension. I am standing just at the outer edge of a great whirlpool of winds that is transporting huge quantities of air around the country: frigid air southward, balmy air northward. This whirlpool is accompanied by rain and snow and buffeting winds. Reviewing the notes on my conversations with my fellow gardeners, I discover a disconcerting fact. The gardeners from west and south of the center of the circle all reported steady or rising pressures; the gardeners from northeast of the center of the circle all reported falling pressures. These changes cannot go on for long before the center of the circle of the barometers will have moved north and east. And with that circle will presumably come the winds, and rain and snow, and everything that goes with it. Not only am I standing at the edge of a big whirlpool of air, but that whirlpool is coming my way!

As the day wears on, I watch the weather apprehensively. The wind veers slightly toward the south. The temperature rises slowly, and the clouds lower. At about one in the afternoon, it begins to sleet gently, but by three in the afternoon the sleet has changed to drizzle, and finally to light rain. The clouds continue to lower until by sunset they are draped over the tops of the low hills to the west.

Coming inside to fix dinner, I note that my barometer has fallen. Comparing my current weather with the map I made at nine A.M., I get the impression that my farm has been transported southwestward to Pennsylvania; but of course the reverse must be true; the circle of the winds must have moved toward me just about as far as the distance from Massachusetts to Pennsylvania. I also can guess where the center of the wind is. Standing facing into the south-southeast wind at my farm I point my arm almost due west. The storm must be somewhere out over Lake Ontario, east of Toronto and west of Montreal. I call the gardener in Syracuse.

"No storm here," he says, "stopped a few hours ago. For a while I thought we were going to have a real snowstorm, but then it warmed up and rained a lot. But now it's not doing anything. A little drizzle. The barometer's real low, though," he adds, as an afterthought. "How low?" I ask. "29.25," he replies. This is the lowest reading I have seen yet! Something strange is going on.

The curiosity is more than I can stand, so when dinner's cleaned up and the house has settled down I get on the phone and call all my gardener-observers and ask for their nine P.M. weather.

The Charlestown gardener tells me philosophically that all morning she was thinking about putting in the peas. However, about two P.M. great, black clouds rolled in from the southwest, the wind began to howl, and the temperature to fall. There was even a rumble of thunder and some lightning. For about ten minutes, it snowed so hard you could barely see across the street. The barometer, which had started to fall when the sky looked bad, leapt upward as soon as the snow began and had climbed to 29.95. By the time I call her, the temperature has fallen to 27 degrees and the ground has gotten all crusty. The Charlestown gardener wonders if her newly planted shrubs can take this kind of seesaw weather. The gardeners at Memphis and Nashville are even more worried. Their temperatures have tumbled into the mid-twenties from the fifties, and the surface of the ground is turning as hard as a stone.

Where has the warm air gone? Emmaus, Baltimore, Washington, Richmond, Raleigh, Tallahassee, and New Orleans all report raw temperatures and northwesterly winds. Suddenly, there is no warm air in the south. But when I

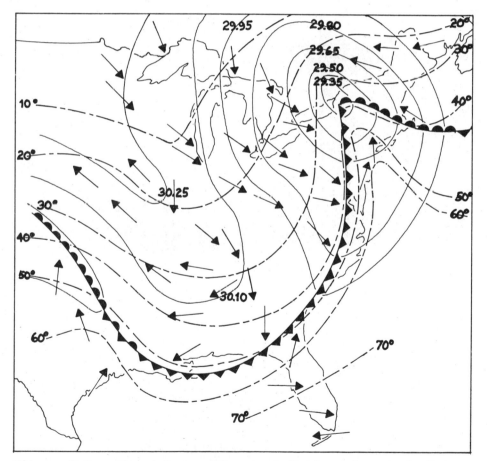

This map diagrams the weather conditions reported by the gardeners twelve hours after the first reporting. It shows how the storm system has shifted.

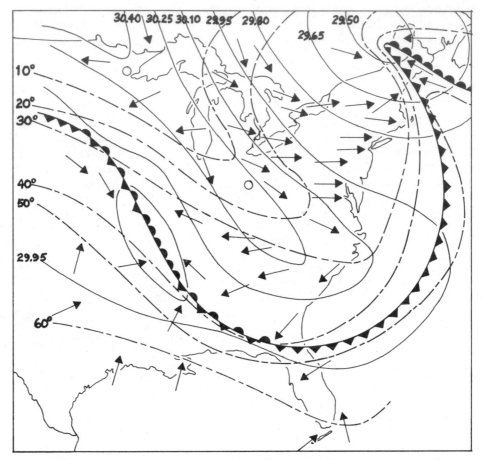

The weather conditions reported twenty-four hours after the first reporting. This map shows that the storm system has shifted still further.

call the gardeners in Philadelphia and New York, they report that a few hours ago the rain tapered off and their temperatures began to rise. The weather is sort of balmy and showery, like you might expect during a winter vacation in Bermuda. Each gardener reports a vigorous south wind and a low barometer near 29.65.

The Canadian gardeners complain that their weather is going from bad to worse. In Montreal the barometer has tumbled almost a third of an inch since morning and there is snow and a 20-mile-an-hour southeast wind. Four hundred miles to the southwest, the gardener in Toronto complains of a 25-mile-an-hour north-northwest wind, a barometer of only 29.62, a temperature of 20 degrees, and a snowshower. Across the lake in Buffalo, the wind and temperature are just as bad, and you cannot see your hand in front of your face for falling, blowing, and drifting snow. Detroit, which had the worst weather twelve hours earlier, now has broken skies, a light northwest breeze, and a barometer of 29.83.

The moment I get the reports plotted on the map, I see what has happened. The same circle of winds and pressures is there, but the whole pattern has moved. In fact, despite what the Syracuse gardener thought, the circle of the winds is centered exactly over him. Moreover, the circle of pressure has more rings than it used to. The lowest pressures on the map are much lower than they were in the morning—about 15/100 of an inch lower. Winds around the storm are brisker than they were and more places seem to have heavy rain and snow.

The S-shaped pattern of precipitation and temperature has also moved and the upper part of the S has narrowed considerably. The cold front appears to be catching up to the warm front so that only two cities, New York and Philadelphia, are in the warm air. In Massachusetts, we are just at the edge of the warm air.

By the time I have finished drawing the map and mulling it over, the warm air is upon me. The rain stops, and before I go to bed I go outside to take a walk on the squishy soil. A soft, mild southerly wind is blowing. On an impulse I turn on the spotlights that illuminate the yard. The lawn is littered with the results of winter's souvenir hunting by the dog. The snow has melted off the garden, exposing the wreckage of last summer's plants. The rain has puddled on top of the frost layer and turned the top few inches of the soil the consistency of brown bean soup. The mulch around the strawberries is thin and the ground around them has gone soft. I hack up the remains of the Christmas tree with a hatchet and spread the twigs over the plants. Better late than never. Then off to bed.

At about four A.M. I am awakened as the wind comes whistling in from the west-southwest, bringing rain, then sleet, then a vigorous snowsquall. Sleepless, I wander about the house, peering out first one window, then another. In the spotlight I can see the flakes falling; they are large and feathery. I watch them dreamily, hoping that they are catching in the branches of the Christmas tree and drifting over my strawberries. The wind pries and batters at the west windows of the house. The storm center is north-northeast of me. I wonder how the gardener in Montreal is getting on.

When I call the gardeners at nine o'clock the next morning, the storm has practically swept off the map. The center of the circle of the winds is just north of Quebec City. The circle has become even tighter than before and its ring of lowest pressure is nearly 29 inches, as low as any barometer I have ever seen at the farm. The S shape of the temperatures and precipitation has become grotesquely distorted: the lower curve is huge and distended and the upper curve has practically shriveled to nothing. Of all the gardeners in my network, only those at Caribou, Maine; Quebec City; and Portland, Maine, report south or east winds. Everywhere else in the Northeast the winds are northerly or westerly and the air is bitterly cold. Montreal reports heavy snow and a ferocious northwest wind.

After I have drawn my new map, I go out to give the dog his morning run. He cowers in the lee of the house looking at me doubtfully as I wade out into the wind and blowing snow. The ground is already frozen hard and the limbs I spread over the strawberries the night before are drifted and crusted with snow. Above I can see blue sky through the scurrying clouds. Here at the farm, the storm is about over. During the last day I have been through one complete cycle of the winds. My winds have gone from northeast to northwest, proceeding around the compass in a clockwise direction. As my winds changed, the maps which my network of gardeners helped me draw showed that a great whirlpool of air was rushing by to my north. The bad weather, the falling barometer, the dramatic wind and temperature changes all seemed to be the result of the passing of this great vortex. The mystery of the cycles of the winds appears to be solved.

Back in the house before I leave for work I give the map one last glance. My eye strays down to its left-hand corner. My gardeners in the lower Mississippi Valley reported east winds and increasing clouds! Could it be for those gardeners that the cycle of the winds is starting again?

3

THE LIFE CYCLE
OF A CYCLONE

Discovering that the cycles of the winds are caused by the movements of great whirlpools of air across the countryside opens up a whole new set of questions. Where do these whirlpools come from? What makes them? Why do they bring such vigorous weather contrasts? Are they always the same shape? Or do they change form as they move across the face of the earth?

Weatherpeople call the whirlpools which cause the cycles of the winds "cyclones." A cyclone to a meteorologist is any vortex in the atmosphere which rotates in a counterclockwise direction in the northern hemisphere, a clockwise direction in the southern hemisphere. All cyclones have low pressure at their center, and weatherpeople often refer to them as "lows." If a cyclone becomes vigorous enough to cause bad weather it gets called a "storm." On any given day, dozens of cyclones may be wandering the face of the globe bringing clouds and bad weather wherever they stray. They appear on satellite maps as great swirls of cloud, just exactly as if one had stirred a dishpan full of sudsy water in a counterclockwise direction.

Cyclones have integrity and structure: they are units, wholes, that move around. They even have appendages. Look back at the cyclone in the previous chapter. On each map, the cyclone has a sector of warm air surrounded by a precipitation pattern shaped very roughly like an inverted V. On either side of the warm sector are the two great appendages of a storm: the cold front, where cold air is replacing warm air on the west; and the warm front, where warm air is replacing cold air on the east. The whole structure moves as a unit across the country. In fact, it moves at quite a good clip. Big as they are, cyclones can move across the earth at 25 to 50 miles per hour.

Cyclones have individuality as well. Recently, I went through all the weather maps for a single calendar year looking at the different shapes of cyclones. There were cyclones with two warm fronts and storms with two cold **25** fronts and storms that were stretched out into funny shapes. There were cyclones which moved slowly and cyclones which moved rapidly and even cyclones that didn't move at all or moved backwards! Every storm was so much an individual I was hard pressed to find examples of a "typical cyclone." The maps on the next page show some of these oddball cyclones. These maps are just like the maps of our cyclone in chapter 2 except that I left out the temperature lines to make them simpler.

Cyclones develop: they are born, grow up, reach maturity, become senescent, and die. The storm in the previous chapter not only moved from southwest to northeast, it developed as it went along. Each twelve hours the storm intensified and the weather around it grew worse. The storm changed

Cyclones as seen from a satellite. You can see that two major storms are affecting the U.S., one just departing the East Coast, the other just beginning to go to work on the West.

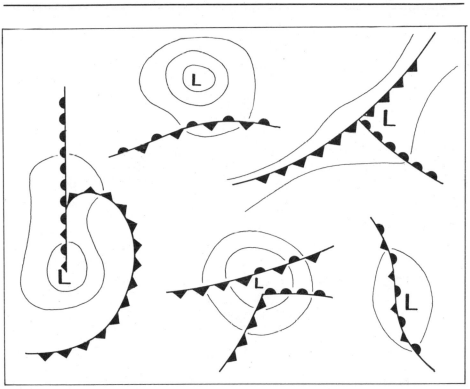

Shown here are five atypical storm systems.

shape as it developed. Each twelve hours its warm sector became a little narrower and rotated around the center of the storm in a counterclockwise direction. Cyclones, then, are not just objects that roll unchanging across the face of the earth. They are dynamic, changing things whose nature is altered in familiar ways as they move along.

In the next illustration you can see the entire life cycle of the cyclone we studied in the previous chapter. Maps 1 through 3 show the beginnings of the storm. In map 1, there is barely any sign of it. There is a large area of good weather and high pressure in the center of the map. What little raininess and low pressure exists is at the margins of the big high pressure in the middle of the map. By the second map, a cyclone has formed along the southern edge of the high-pressure area. At this point, it is just a little bump on the front between cold air from Canada and warm, tropical air from the Gulf of Mexico, and the only weather it is causing is a little showeriness over the Corn Belt. By the third map, it is beginning to look a bit like a cyclone. It has a definite warm sector and low-pressure center. Thus, in thirty-six hours a cyclone has materialized, beginning as a very diffuse area of showers over the western plains and becoming a recognizable whirlpool of air over the lower Mississippi Valley.

(continued on page 30)

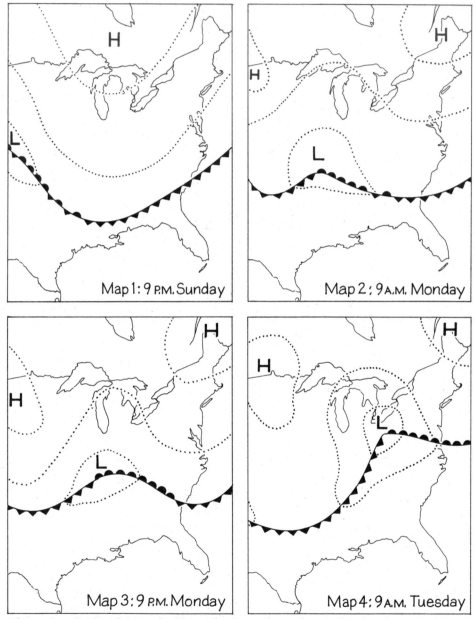

This series of maps depicts the life cycle of a cyclone, showing its development over a four-day period.

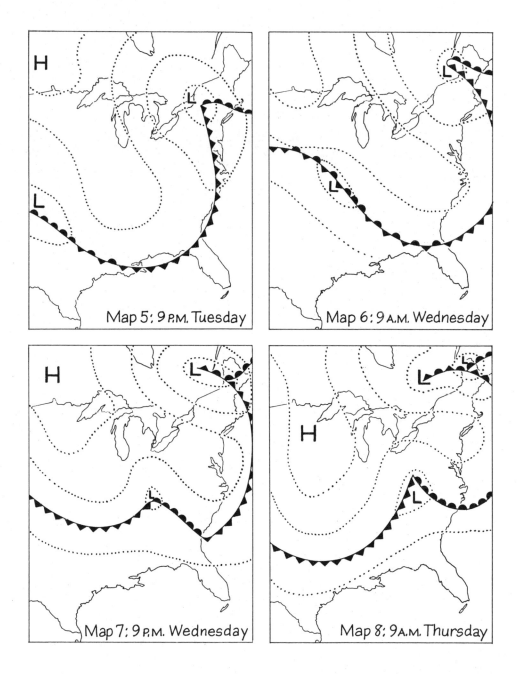

Map 5: 9 P.M. Tuesday

Map 6: 9 A.M. Wednesday

Map 7: 9 P.M. Wednesday

Map 8: 9 A.M. Thursday

Maps 4, 5, and 6 are the maps we are already familiar with. The storm moves up the St. Lawrence Valley; its lines of equal pressure tighten, and its warm sector narrows as it pulls cold air from Canada down behind it. In map 7, the cold front has caught up with the warm front and the cyclone has begun to die; by map 8, the original cyclone's low-pressure center has started to fill and the meteorological action is beginning to be transferred to other places on the map.

Map 8 also illustrates another way in which cyclones reproduce themselves. If you look closely at map 8 you can see two places where the dying cyclone is making a new one. As the cold front catches up with the warm front, the center of the old storm elongates so that the lowest pressures are now transferred to the point where the cold and warm fronts diverge. Here a new storm will form. Given the season of the year and its position over the Maritime Provinces of Canada, this new storm will probably become a scourge of the North Atlantic shipping lanes. In time, the gardeners of England may come to know of this storm.

To see the cyclone's other offspring, you have to look along the other end of the cold front. Here, in the same general area where the original cyclone developed less than a week ago, a new one is getting established. It seems to be moving more directly eastward than did its parent and may bring some snow to the Mid-Atlantic region before it's had its day.

The Birth of a Storm

To be watching the weather from a point near where a storm is being born is a strange meteorological experience. The Atlantic Ocean south of New England is a famous birthing ground for storms, and the birth often takes place near enough to shore so that New Englanders feel its effects. Typically, the birth occurs as a warm front moves up the coastline in winter. The coastline is so much colder than the warm ocean waters of the Gulf Stream that the warm front makes much more rapid progress off shore than it does over land, and a little kink forms in the front. Here the new storm is likely to develop.

When this occurs, we get a very odd sequence of winds up in New England. First the wind starts out on the clockwise cycle. As the parent storm moves up the St. Lawrence Valley to our west, the wind blows first out of the east, then the southeast, perhaps even the south. Precipitation begins: snow, rain, sleet, freezing rain, what have you. Soon, however, it turns to rain. The rain, in turn, tapers off to drizzle and the weather just seems to go limp—for a while.

But then subtly, the weather begins to change. Instead of continuing their clockwise march, the winds swing back around to the northeast. The temperature dips and the drizzle begins to freeze. The change comes so quietly that if you aren't watching you may not notice and take a tumble on the front walk as you saunter out to get the mail or climb into your car. Soon, however, there can be no doubt that the storm has a new life. The barometer begins to fall steeply, the winds begin to shift around the compass in a counterclockwise direction: northeast, north-northeast, north, and so forth. The drizzle turns to light snow, the light snow to heavy snow. What has happened, of course, is that the new storm has developed to the south of New England and is passing off to the southeast. Instead of being to the southeast of the center, as we would have been if the parent storm had continued up the St. Lawrence River Valley, we are northwest of the center. It is this capacity of the Atlantic seaboard to manufacture weather overnight that makes the eastern United States the great weather forecasting challenge it is.

Anticyclones and Their Characteristics

Cyclones, which bring foul weather, travel in the company of anticyclones, which bring fair weather. Anticyclones are clockwise circles of the winds. Anticyclones are not as noticeable as cyclones. They don't produce dramatic weather and don't really stand out on satellite photographs. But you can recognize them if you study weather maps carefully. Look at the wind arrows in the maps in chapter 2. Look particularly at the arrows in the cold air behind the cyclone in map 8, when the center of the cyclone was over southeastern Canada. These winds rotate around a center in western Minnesota and the rotation is clockwise: southward over the western Lakes Region, westward over the southern Plains, and northward over the eastern Rockies. As with the counterclockwise circle of a cyclone, the winds in an anticyclone blow roughly along lines of equal pressure, but in an anticyclone the winds "toe-out," i.e., they blow slightly away from the center of the anticyclone. As in a cyclone, the lines of equal pressure form a target shape, but in an anticyclone the pressure increases as one goes toward the center of the circle. Meteorologists therefore often refer to anticyclones as "high-pressure areas" or simply "highs."

Anticyclones are the opposite of cyclones in almost every imaginable way. In anticyclones are reversed many of the dynamic processes that go on in cyclones. Cyclones are areas of rising moist air. Anticyclones are areas of descending dry air. In anticyclones, the air that is pushed aloft in nearby cyclones is returned once again to lower levels of the atmosphere in a process called by meteorologists "subsidence." As the air subsides from higher to lower levels of the atmosphere, the increase of pressure warms it. Becoming warmer, its capacity to hold moisture increases and any condensed water that is carried along in the air is evaporated, leaving a cloudless sky. Thus, while the air in a cyclone is rising, cooling, and shedding moisture, the air in an anticyclone is descending, warming, and absorbing moisture. Anticyclones are usually composed of one homogeneous mass of air, compared to cyclones which, with the exception of hurricanes, have at least three contrasting air masses. Anticyclones are areas of divergence where air flows out from a center; cyclones are areas of convergence where air flows in toward a center.

Summing Up
Weather System Development

Perhaps now, it is time to stand back and review where we have come. We have learned that weather changes in regular cycles. The cycles consist of day-by-day changes in the amount of clouds in the sky, the temperature, the wind direction, and the barometer. When we look at weather on a nationwide scale, we see that the daily cycles of the weather at any one place are caused by the movement of great circles of wind across the earth. These circles are circulations of wind with low pressure at their centers. Typically, each of these circles has a sector of warm air surrounded on both sides by cooler air. Along the boundaries between the cool and warm air, precipitation falls. The whole system moves across the surface of the earth, generally from west to east. As it moves, it brings about particular changes in the weather at each point it passes, a different sequence of changes occurring if the system passes to the north than if it passes to the south. A northward passage is accompanied by clockwise shifting of the winds and weather which first warms, then cools again. Showers both precede and follow the warm period. A southward passage is accompanied by a progressive counterclockwise shifting of the winds, and a falling then rising barometer as the weather first deteriorates, then improves.

The system of circulating winds surrounding the low-pressure center not only moves across the surface, it changes in shape in a predictable manner. The line between the advancing cold air and the retreating warm air on the west rotates around the center of the system more rapidly than does the line between the advancing warm air and retreating cold air on the east. The result is that the warm wedge narrows as it rotates eastward around the center until ultimately the cold air on the west catches up with the cold air on the east and the warm wedge is eliminated altogether. At this time the system begins a slow decline. Such systems may spawn other systems. Two common locations for such secondary development are the point of intersection between cold and warm fronts near the center of a dying system and at the far end of the cold front.

Between these counterclockwise circulations around centers of low pressure (called lows, or cyclones) are clockwise circulations around centers of high pressure (called highs, or anticyclones). Highs are characterized by fair weather and gradual temperature changes.

This is a tremendous amount to learn about the weather in a few short chapters, but there are many things we don't yet know. We don't, for instance, know why storms develop. We don't know why the warm sector of a storm shrinks as the storm gets more and more vigorous. We don't know why a storm begins to die when its warm sector is squeezed out. We don't even know where all the warm air goes. We don't know why so much of the precipitation seems to fall around the edges of the warm sector. We don't know what makes a storm move from west to east and why storms sometimes travel some paths, sometimes others. We don't know what regulates the development of storms: why some grow up very rapidly, while others never grow up at all.

If we had ways to predict the development and movement of storms, then weather forecasting would be no more difficult than forecasting the movement of a bowling ball down a bowling alley. What makes professional forecasters better predictors of the weather than we gardeners is that they have a trade secret that allows them to predict the movement and development of storms. This same secret also allows them to understand the structure of storms. It is this trade secret that I am going to let you in on in the next chapter.

4

THE WEATHERPERSON'S TRADE SECRET

The shape of cyclones and the way they change from hour to hour suggest some intriguing questions. Why is the precipitation found where it is in the cyclone? Most of it is found in the cold air next to the warm sector. How come? Why is so little of the precipitation found in the warm air south of the center of the storm? Why does the warm air disappear as the cyclone develops? Where does it go? Why does the storm intensify as the warm sector shrinks and decline when the warm air is finally used up? It is almost as if the warm air is some kind of fuel that is being consumed to make the storm go.

What Goes On above the Ground?

To answer these questions we are going to have to look up. Reconsider the first map we made from the observations of the gardeners in chapter 2. Imagine that in addition to asking the gardeners to note down their local conditions we had asked them to release helium balloons carrying instruments to record the weather conditions as the balloons rose up into the atmosphere. With the aid of these balloons we could learn the weather conditions at 1,000 feet and 2,000 feet and so forth right up into the atmosphere.

If we asked the gardener in Charlestown to release such a balloon, we would learn nothing particularly surprising. In Charlestown, you will recall, was the gardener with the mild breezes, sunny sky, and springlike weather. The balloon would drift off with the southwest wind, the sun glinting on its

34 surface. As it climbed, its instruments would record lower pressure and lower temperatures and it would be blown along by southwest winds of increasing speed. All of these observations would be expected. The higher the balloon traveled, the less atmosphere would be above it and the lower the pressure would be. As the air pressure falls, the molecules of air are less densely packed and so the temperature falls. The wind increases because the wind aloft isn't slowed down by friction with the ground.

If, however, we asked one of the gardeners in the rain area north and east of the warm front, say Pittsburgh, to release a balloon, we would be witness to quite an extraordinary sequence of events. You will recall that the Pittsburgh gardener was the one who reported a low overcast, rain, and a vigorous south wind. That gardener's balloon would drift off toward the north and disappear immediately into the low overcast. At first the pressure would fall, the temperatures would fall and the winds would rise, as at Charlestown. But at about 2,000 feet, something curious would begin to happen. The winds would begin to slacken and the temperature would level out. At 3,000 feet we would notice that the wind had begun to pick up again, but now it would be blowing the balloon toward the northeast—a southwest wind. We would also notice that the temperature is *rising*. In the next 1,000 feet, the winds would continue to increase from the southwest and the temperature to rise, until at 4,000 feet, the temperature at Pittsburgh would be the same as the temperature at Charlestown. From here on up, the weather at these two stations would be the same.

A similar set of observations could be made at Emmaus or at New York City. At Emmaus, the balloon would rise in the cold air and rush off toward the northwest until it got to about 4,000 feet. There the wind shift would occur and the temperature rise begin. In New York, the altitude of the wind and temperature shift would be a bit higher, but it would still eventually occur. In fact, wherever a balloon was released in the precipitation area east of the warm front, eventually the balloon would pass through a boundary. Above this boundary the air would be indistinguishable from the air over Charlestown at the same altitude: air that is warm and moist for its altitude, moving from southwest to northeast.

There is only one way to interpret these observations that makes sense. It must be true that lying on top of the cold, damp air that covers Pittsburgh, Emmaus, and New York City is a layer of mild, soft, springlike air just like the air over Charlestown. To put it another way, not only is there a "front" between Pittsburgh and Charlestown, as we have drawn it in the first map in chapter 2, there is also a "front" between 2,000 feet and 3,000 feet over Pittsburgh. The same front can be found between 4,000 feet and 5,000 feet over Emmaus. The warm front is thus a long, sloping ceiling on the cold air that starts at the ground between Charlestown and Pittsburgh, and rises gently toward the north and east.

We would make a similar discovery if we asked the gardeners behind the cold front to release balloons. In Cincinnati, you will recall, the wind was blowing vigorously from the north, heavy snow was falling and the temperature was near freezing and falling swiftly. A balloon released in Cincinnati would be snatched away by the northerly winds and gone from sight in a second, obscured by the falling snow. At first, as the balloon climbed, temperatures would fall and winds would rise from the north. But a few thousand feet above the surface the wind would swing around the southwest and the temperatures would rise, until an altitude was reached where the air over Cincinnati was just as warm as the air over Charlestown. The same would be true for Little Rock, Amarillo, and Tulsa—wherever precipitation was falling behind the cold front.

Once again, there is only one reasonable way to interpret these observations. Lying on top of the cold, blustery air which is buffeting Little Rock and Wichita and Amarillo and Cincinnati is a layer of soft, mild air indistinguishable from the air over Charlestown. The cold front, like the warm front, is like a ceiling on the cold air, which begins at the surface and slopes upward and westward. The only difference is that the cold front slopes westward, rather than eastward, and that the slope of the cold front's ceiling is steeper than the slope of the warm front's.

A Cyclone in Section

Understanding these three-dimensional relationships is difficult, but they have such grandeur and beauty that the pleasure of comprehending them is well worth the necessary effort. Please bear with me. Look once again at the first map of the storm in chapter 2. Imagine the cold air over Canada, Maine, and the Great Plains as a huge glacier whose greatest heights are over the Dakotas and over northern Maine. From these centers, the two sides slope down the edge of the warm sector covering the southern states. Where they meet over the Great Lakes, they form a seam, a valley which slopes upward toward central Canada. Between the walls of this valley, and lying on the slopes of the glacier is the warm air. Wherever the warm air is suspended off the ground by the "glacier," rain is falling. Because the west wall of the glacier is steeper than the east wall, the band of rain behind the cold front is narrower.

To see how this works, we could slice through the glacier from top to bottom. Let's imagine that we could take the eastern United States, land surface, ocean, atmosphere and all, put it on a table saw, and make three slices through it: one from Boston through Chicago (we'll call this the northern slice), one from Philadelphia to Kansas City (we'll call this the center slice), and one from Richmond to Tulsa (we'll call this the southern slice). If we now looked at the edges of the slices, we would see three cross sections of the atmosphere, each one with east on the right and west on the left, the surface of the earth on the bottom, and the top of the atmosphere at the top.

If we looked at each of these slices what would we see? On the southern slice, the two lobes of the cold air "glacier" would appear as two low mounds.

On the sides of the mounds, where the warm air is being held off the ground, precipitation is falling. Otherwise, the slice would show warm air. On the center slice, the mounds would make up more of the map. The warm air is now confined to the V-shaped space between. On the northern slice, the warm air has been completely lifted off the ground; held aloft over the Great Lakes region, it pours down precipitation through the thin layer of cold air below.

These cross sections are also helpful in understanding the development of a cyclone. Recall that the cold front is moving more rapidly than the warm front. This means that the westerly lobe of the glacier is catching up to the easterly lobe and squeezing the intervening warm air. When the cold front catches up to the warm front, the warm air is lifted clear of the ground. Thus, the three cross sections, south, center, and north, could also serve as illustra-

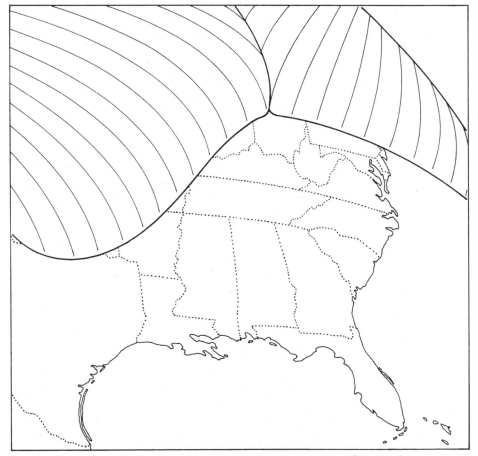

The cyclone first described by the gardeners in chapter 2 can be seen here as a "valley" in a "glacier" of cold air over the U.S. and Canada.

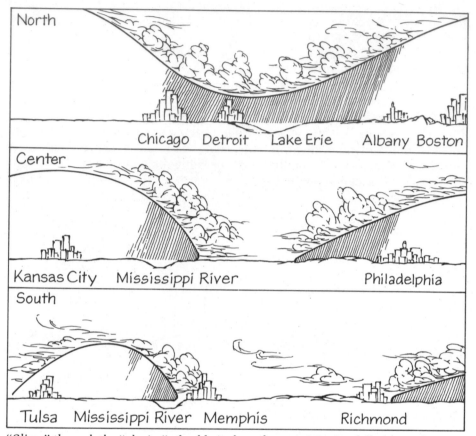

North

Chicago   Detroit   Lake Erie   Albany Boston

Center

Kansas City   Mississippi River   Philadelphia

South

Tulsa   Mississippi River Memphis   Richmond

"Slices" through the "glacier" of cold air show that precipitation falls where the warm air is held aloft by the walls of the glacier (that is, by the cold air).

tions of the development of a cyclone. The south stands for the early stages, when the warm and cold fronts are well separated and the warm sector is large. The center slice would then represent a middle stage in the cyclone's development, when the warm sector is being squeezed between the two fronts. The north slice stands for the late stage of the cyclone, when the warm air is completely suspended above the ground and the last moisture is being wrung out of it.

When the two cold air masses that form the east and west sides of a cyclone come together, the cyclone is said by weatherpeople to have "occluded." There are two types of occlusions. When the cold air behind the cold front is cooler than the cold air ahead of the warm front, the occlusion is called a "cold occlusion." When these two masses of air meet, the cold air pries itself under the milder air to form the occlusion. When the mass of cold air behind the cold front is a bit milder than the mass of air preceding the warm front, the milder air rides up on top of the cooler air to form a "warm occlusion." The common feature of all occlusions, however, is that there are two masses of air being lifted off the ground: the original warm air and one of the two masses of colder air. Since the lifting of air off the ground seems to have something to do with precipitation, small wonder it is that occluded fronts are often such bearers of rain.

The occlusion process partly answers the second question we had when we began this chapter. We now know where the warm air has gone. A cyclone starts as a little valley in the side of one of the great "glaciers" of cold air. At first the valley deepens, separating the glacier into two lobes with the valley of warm air between. But then, the valley begins to close. The westward lobe of the glacier advances faster than the eastward lobe, pushing warm air up onto the glacier surfaces. Relentlessly, this process continues until the westward glacier crunches into the eastward glacier. Soon all that is left of the warm air is a puddle lying in a shallow depression at the top of the glaciers.

What Controls a Cyclone's Movement and Development?

The one last question we have to answer is why cyclones develop where and when they do and what determines where they move, how rapidly they move, and how rapidly they develop. This question encompasses one of the great puzzles of American meteorology. All winter, along the thousands of miles of coastline from the Rio Grande to Eastport, Maine, ideal conditions are present for the formation of severe storms: warm, moist air over the ocean, juxtaposed with cold, dry air over land. But storms are not forming all the time. Several days will go by without a storm forming, and then two or three will form in a matter of days at nearly the same point of coastline. Then they won't form again at that point on the coast for a few days or even weeks. Since the conditions for the formation of storms are excellent during all the winter, something else must be determining when and where storms form.

A similar mystery surrounds the movements of storms. Once a storm forms in winter along the Gulf Coast, it can take myriad different tracks and courses of development. It may move slowly and develop rapidly over the Gulf States, bringing southerly gales to the Gulf Coast and horrendous ice storms to the southern Appalachians. It may move rapidly and directly northward, bringing blizzard conditions to Chicago and startling thaws to the eastern states. Or it can do a variety of things in between, each of which brings characteristically bad weather to some region of the country.

Weatherpeople have a trade secret which makes the predictions of a storm's movements as easy as predicting the path of a bit of flotsam careening down a stream. The trade secret was discovered by pilots during World War II, who were startled to find their high-altitude bombing runs being helped or hindered by an extraordinary eastward-moving river of air high above the ground. As planes flew higher and higher, the pilots encountered more and more concentrated currents within this atmospheric river until around seven miles up in the atmosphere they encountered the jet streams. Jet streams are intense currents of air moving at speeds as high as 100 to 200 miles per hour.

Mapping the Upper Air Stream

Just as we made a surface map of one day's weather from the observations from our network of gardeners, meteorologists now make weather maps of the upper atmosphere. All over the country, weathermen release balloons whose instruments send back observations as they climb. To make the measurements comparable, the observations from the balloons are taken at predetermined barometric pressures. For instance, when the barometers attached to the balloons read around 15 inches (500 millibars in the metric scale), a set of measurements are taken, including the wind direction and velocity, temperature, and the altitude of the balloon at that pressure. The 15-inch or 500-millibar level is a particularly interesting level of the atmosphere to know about because it marks the halfway point in the atmosphere: about half the weight of the atmosphere is above 15 inches, and about half below. From these observations a map can be drawn of the weather as it exists halfway up in the atmosphere.

Weatherpeople call such maps the "500-millibar surface." This name sounds fancy, but is really very simple. The term "surface" is used because, in a curious way, we really are dealing with the top surface of the bottom half of the atmosphere. The 500-millibar map tells you where that surface is. It's like a topographic map of the surface of the earth. The earth's surface in the United States varies from zero to several thousand feet from sea level. A topographic map tells you at what altitude above sea level that surface occurs. In the same way, the halfway point in the atmosphere varies in altitude from about 16,000 to about 19,000 feet above sea level. The 500-millibar map tells you how high that halfway point is over each observation station in the United States, and also tells you what kind of weather is going on up there.

When weatherpeople began to draw maps of these upper air surfaces, they began to make the most astounding discoveries. They found that a great river of air (the upper air westerlies) flowed in a sinuous path across the surface. The "bed" of this river changed from week to week. Sometimes the river flowed in over the northern Rockies and straight across the country to New England.

Sometimes the river wound in a great meander across the country, surging up into Canada over the Rockies and plunging down into the Gulf States, only to rush northward off the east coast headed toward northern Europe.

Moreover, the surface had tall peaks and deep valleys. On these maps the weatherpeople saw a fascinating relationship between the path of the river and the mounds and hollows in the 500-millibar surface. The real rivers that we see on the ground always flow in the centers of their valleys. But not the river of air in the 500-millibar surface. This river not only flows around the humps on the surface, it also flows around the hollows. Where the surface is low, the river flows around the hollow in a counterclockwise direction forming a U shape; where the surface is high, the river flows around the mounds in a clockwise direction forming an inverted U. The U-shaped patterns weatherpeople call "troughs," because they look like troughs on a standard 500-millibar surface weather map, and because the surface is actually not as far above sea level in troughs. The inverted U-shaped patterns the weatherpeople call "ridges," both because they look like ridges on a standard 500-millibar surface map and because the surface is actually higher above sea level in a ridge.

The most remarkable discovery of all was the relationship between the ground-level highs and lows and the upper air ridges and troughs. The relationship was by no means the obvious one. The highs were not always under the ridges nor were the lows reliably found beneath the troughs. In fact, if there was any general rule, it was that weather features on the ground tended to flow in the streams which eddied around the troughs and ridges on the upper air maps. Cyclones and anticyclones floated like great rafts in the upper air river, following the meanders as the river swept across the country from west to east.

The map on the next page depicts the 500-millibar map as it might have been prepared by weatherpeople on the first morning our network of gardeners was making observations of the cycles of the winds. You can see that there is a trough over the central part of the United States and a ridge over the west. The cyclone is located just east of the lowest portion of the trough and the center of high pressure is located just east of the center of the ridge. An experienced weatherperson looking at this chart would know immediately that the low-pressure cyclone will move northeastward and that the high-pressure anticyclone will move southeastward. Knowing what we know about the kind of weather that anticyclones and cyclones bring, we can make some very intelligent guesses about the weather that will occur in each place as the cyclone and the anticyclone sweep along in the stream.

Knowing what is happening on the 500-millibar surface can also help weatherpeople predict the development of cyclones. The part of the westerlies from just west of a trough to just west of the next ridge encourages the development of cyclones. Here the air is given a cyclonelike twist as it comes around the trough. Here also, the upper-air winds spread out and lift a bit as they depart the trough. As they do, they exercise a gentle upward pulling

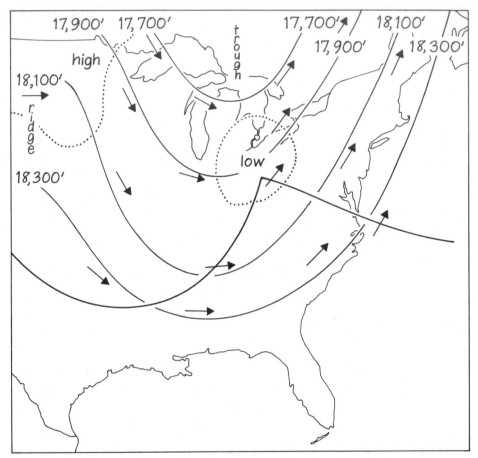

This 500-millibar map shows what the top half of the atmosphere looked like on the day the gardeners first described the cyclone in chapter 2. Compare it with the map on page 19.

motion on the lower atmosphere that encourages the development of ground-level low-pressure systems. If we see a cyclone at the bottom of a trough, we would expect it not only to move northeastward but also to develop and become stronger as it moves.

The next illustration shows that the cyclone has moved along the contours of the 500-millibar surface just as predicted. So has the anticyclone. The map also illustrates another interesting relationship between the upper-air surface and the ground-level weather. The cyclone at the ground level is starting to put a bit of a kink in the stream of winds at the higher level. The ground-level center of low pressure is making a trough in the upper atmosphere. In meteorologists' slang the cyclone is "going vertical." Strong cyclones have the

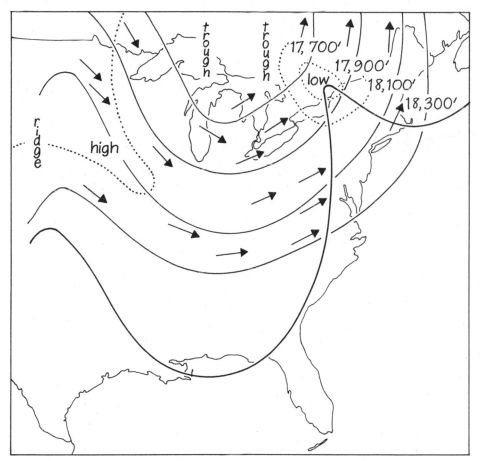

This map shows what the top half of the atmosphere looked like twelve hours later. Compare it with the first map on page 21.

capacity to rearrange the humps and valleys in the 500-millibar surface, and the cyclone charted by our network of gardeners is doing just that. If our storm keeps on getting bigger, it will in time build a ridge over the Great Lakes where before there was a trough, and a trough over eastern Canada where before there was a ridge. A cyclone that starts out as a creation of the upper-air flow patterns can rapidly become the creator of those patterns.

The sequence of 500-millibar maps on the following pages shows how this can occur. Each small map is the 500-millibar map made at the same time as the eight surface maps in the last chapter. At the beginning, before a surface low forms, there is a small kink in a northwesterly flow of winds high over the Rockies. When this kink comes over the east face of the Rockies, it begins to

(continued on page 46)

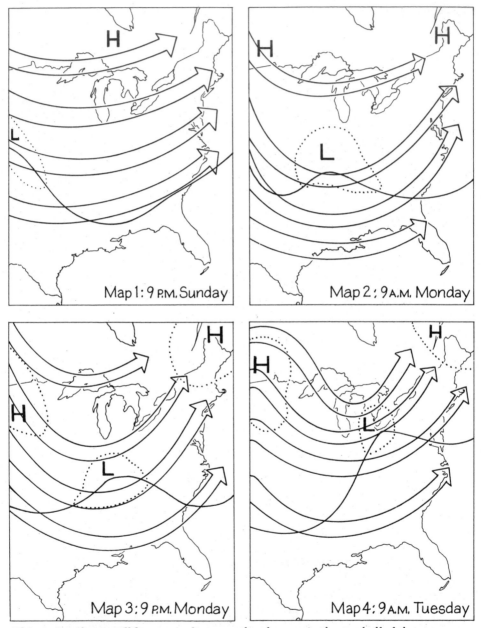

Map 1: 9 P.M. Sunday

Map 2: 9 A.M. Monday

Map 3: 9 P.M. Monday

Map 4: 9 A.M. Tuesday

This series of 500-millibar maps diagrams the changes in the top half of the atmosphere corresponding to the development of the cyclone in chapter 3. Compare it with the maps on pages 28 and 29.

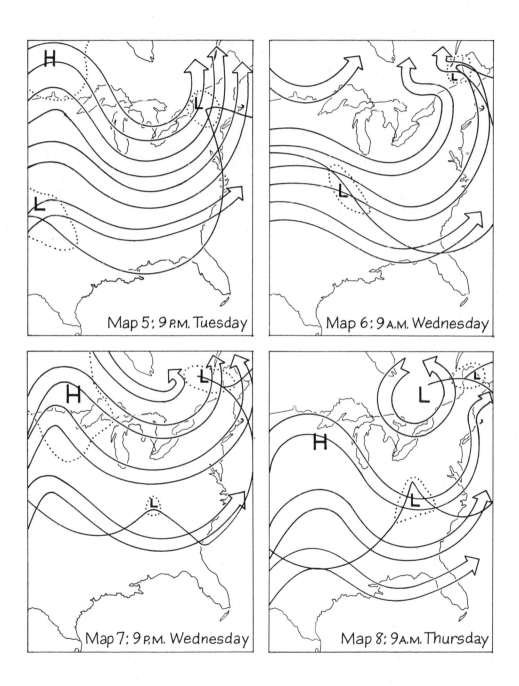

Map 5: 9 P.M. Tuesday

Map 6: 9 A.M. Wednesday

Map 7: 9 P.M. Wednesday

Map 8: 9 A.M. Thursday

organize a storm beneath it (map 2). As the storm deepens (maps 3, 4, and 5), it deepens the trough in the westerlies until by map 8, the center of the trough has become an isolated counterclockwise circulation, an upper-air "low." Although this configuration is originally the creation of a surface low, it will remain for many days to steer other surface systems.

Changes in upper-air patterns are usually gradual. Therefore, for forecasts of a few days, the weatherperson's trade secret is as good as gold and you can use it to make your own forecast. Here's what you'd do: (1) Look at the 500-millibar map. (2) Look upstream in the river of air from your location. (3) See what weather features are upstream of you. (4) Take note of how far they moved in the last twenty-four hours. (5) Now project downstream twenty-four hours. That's where you can expect those same weather features to be twenty-four hours from now. If you can know what kind of weather those sorts of weather features bring with them, then you can write your own forecast.

Of course, sometimes you need to be a little imaginative. For instance, let's say you live in Memphis and you're concerned about tomorrow's weather. A look at today's 500-millibar map shows you that there's a very weak low-pressure area floating down the stream on the east face of the Rockies. Behind that low is a big, frigid high in the Canadian Rockies. At present, the low is just causing a few snow flurries over the northern Plains. You look downstream and find that in twenty-four hours the low will be in the pit of a trough just over Louisiana with the cold high tagging along behind. Now, for reasons we will get to in chapter 8, Louisiana in winter is just a wonderful place to make a storm. So, instead of predicting a little light rain for the South tomorrow, you might predict a ferocious winter storm for the whole lower end of the Mississippi Valley.

Knowing about the upper-air westerlies so simplifies understanding the weather, I wonder why so few TV weathermen give upper-air information on their broadcasts. Upper-air maps come in over the wire in the TV station and newspaper editorial offices just like the surface maps. Personally, I'd sooner have a 500-millibar chart than almost any other weather information. Forecasts, particularly newspaper forecasts, are so often dead by the time you need to put them to use. But if I have the 500-millibar chart in my mind, I can make my own forecasts and interpret events as they develop. I suppose, though, deep down I understand why broadcast and newspaper weather information usually excludes the upper-air charts. Who wants to give away a trade secret?

5

WEATHER ENGINES–
GREAT AND SMALL

We have come a long way from the garden. The puzzle of the winds has led us first to the puzzles of cyclones and so to the puzzles of the upper air. Each time we get a puzzle solved, it spawns a few more. If you suspect that this process could continue indefinitely, you suspect correctly. It is the capacity of solutions to breed more puzzles that makes science the infinitely intriguing profession it is. But be comforted. This meandering stream of thought will ultimately carry us back to the foot of the garden. Like characters in children's adventure stories we will find ourselves back in our beds—our flower and strawberry beds—before this long and mysterious night of meteorological science is done.

The Seven Rules
for Weather Events

But before we go back to the garden, we have two more formidable puzzles to solve. One puzzle has to do with the formation of precipitation. Precipitation always seems to have something to do with the lifting of air. Why? The second puzzle has to do with the upper-air winds. Why do we find, high above the surface of the earth, this great river of air moving along at 50 to 200 miles per hour? Surprisingly, the answers to these two puzzles have to do with one another. In fact, there are seven rules which explain these two puzzles, and the same seven rules can explain almost any phenomenon of meteorology you care to name. After I have showed them to you and explained how they **47** work, I will drop you off at the end of your garden where I found you—watching and wondering about tomorrow's weather.

Rule #1: The lower you are in the atmosphere, the greater is the air pressure.

Everybody knows this rule, right? Why else do your ears pop when you go up in an elevator? It's the high-pressure air behind your eardrums trying to get out and mingle with the low-pressure air outside. This rule also explains why barometers have to be adjusted to give accurate readings above sea level and why cake mixes don't work in Denver. The rule also explains why people like to live in the mountains in the summer. Other things being equal, air under greater pressure is a bit warmer than air under lesser pressure. For each 200 feet you travel up a mountainside, you can expect to lose a degree or so of temperature just from the expansion of the air around you.

Rule #2: Warm air is lighter than cold air.

When warm and cold air from different sources are mixed, the warmer air tends to float on top of the cold, and the cold air tends to push under the warm air. You already knew this rule, too, right? Everybody knows that drafts blow along floors and that the upstairs apartment in the building is always the hottest. In a slightly different form, this rule might be called the Tomato Canner's Law. The warmer air is, the more excited are its molecules and the less of it can be held in a given space. That's why it's lighter. When you heat your mason jars, you make the air inside them thinner, and some of it spills out of the jars. When you later seal the jars and cool them, the air remaining within the jars cools and shrinks, leaving a partial vacuum.

Rule #3: Warm air can hold more water vapor than cold air.

Water vapor is water in the form of a gas. The warmer air is, the more such water gas it can hold. Conversely, the colder it is, the less it can hold. When air of a particular temperature is holding all the water vapor it can hold, it is said to be "saturated." This saturation temperature is called its "dew point" because if air is cooled below that point the water will change from vapor to droplets or to ice crystals. Another way of saying this is that the water will condense, or precipitate out of the air, hence rain and snow are called precipitation by weatherpeople. You already knew this rule, too. When you step outside your door on a cold morning, you can see your breath. It's the same breath you were breathing a moment ago in the kitchen. So how come it did not show then? The reason is that the cold outdoor air does not have the same capacity to sop up the concentrated water vapor in your breath. The vapor precipitates into water droplets and you see it.

Rule #4: Moist air is lighter than dry air of the same temperature.

This principle is very hard to believe, but physicists and chemists assure us that it is so. It is difficult to grasp because intuitively we think of air as "nothing" and water as "something." But air is "something." In fact, air is mostly nitrogen, a relatively heavy gas, whereas water vapor is mostly hydrogen, the lightest of gases. In a sense, therefore, we should think of air with water vapor in it as "diluted" air.

Rule #5: When water vapor condenses, heat is released.

For every molecule of water gas that becomes a droplet of water, a tiny jolt of heat is released into the atmosphere; and for every droplet of water that becomes an ice crystal, another, smaller, jolt of heat is released. If water vapor precipitates directly into ice crystals, a double jolt is released. The reverse is also true. Water that evaporates and ice that melts absorb heat. If you think for a moment, you will realize that you already knew this rule as well. Why else would you put ice in your lemonade? Why not just cold water? The answer is that melting ice sops up about five times as much heat as the same amount of near-freezing water. The same rule explains why the watched pot never boils. The fact is that the energy required to vaporize water is nearly six times the energy required to heat it all the way from freezing to boiling. The potential heat contained in gaseous water or unfrozen water is called "latent heat." The heat is latent because you get it back only when you condense the water vapor or freeze the water.

Rule #6: Air tries to move from high pressure to low pressure.

If you have ever popped a balloon or gotten a nail in a tire you know the effects of this rule. But sometimes the obvious requires restatement, particularly in light of the following rule.

Rule #7: The wind is left-footed.

A left-footed person who takes a walk in the woods will always end up to the right of his or her destination, because the left foot takes stronger steps than the right. When the wind tries to move on the surface of the Northern

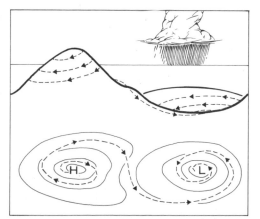

The wind is a left-footed hiker. The upper illustration shows the path of a left-footed hiker traveling from the top of a mountain to the bottom of a valley. Below, we trace the path of a breeze traveling from the center of a high-pressure area to the center of a low-pressure area.

Hemisphere, it always gets deflected to the right. This effect is called the coriolus force. Because of the coriolus force, air which tries to move from a region of high pressure to a region of low pressure can never get there directly. Imagine if you were left-footed and you started to walk down the side of a round, bowl-shaped valley. Your left-footedness would tend to make your steps fall to the right but gravity would tend to pull them back to the left. If the two influences just about balanced each other out, you would end up walking in counterclockwise circles around the valley. The same thing would happen if you tried to walk down the slopes of a mound-shaped mountain. As the left-footed person descended from the heights of the mound, his left-footedness would pull him to the right but gravity would pull him to the left so that he would descend the mound in a clockwise spiral. A left-footed person making the entire trip from the top of the mound to the bottom of the valley would first spiral around the mound in a clockwise direction and then spiral around the valley in a counter-clockwise direction until reaching the bottom of the valley.

Air moving from high pressure to low pressure must follow this same circuitous route. Such air spirals out of high-pressure areas in a clockwise direction and into low-pressure areas in a counterclockwise circulation.

The Atmosphere as an Engine

If you look at these seven principles from a physicist's point of view, they mean that the atmosphere has the capacity to be an engine. An engine, to a physicist, is a system that turns energy into work. The atmospheric engine uses the heat of the sun to move air and water around. The movements of air and water we gardeners know as wind and rain. When these movements inconvenience us we call them storms. The basic process that makes the atmospheric engine go is the vertical movement of warm, moist air. If warm, moist air can be made to move upward far enough, it will eventually cool to its dew point. At the dew point, clouds and precipitation form and additional heat is released by the condensation process. Thus, above altitudes at which it reaches its dew point, rising warm, moist air actually heats itself. The more it heats itself, the lighter it becomes and the more it rises. The more rain falls from it, the more heat is released and the more it rises. The rising air must be replaced from somewhere, and air rushes in from below. On the ground we experience the rising, warm air as low pressure and the inrushing air that replaces it as wind. As long as the inrushing air is warm and moist air, then it supplies additional energy to the atmospheric engine, so that the engine can run almost indefinitely, sort of like a self-stoking furnace.

From the ends of our gardens, we experience the atmospheric engine at work at three different scales of magnitude: the cumulus cloud, the cyclone, and the global weather circulation.

The Cumulus Cloud

Imagine a warm summer morning, the kind of day when everybody wakes up and says, "It's going to be a real scorcher today!" Looking up the valley from my house at six o'clock on such a morning, the whole bottom of the valley will be filled with mist. As the sun gets up above the walls of the valley, the mist will begin to "burn off." What is happening, of course, has nothing to do with burning. The mist has formed because during the cool, still night, the cool air puddled in the bottom of the valley. Here, its temperature eventually fell below its dew point. The moisture precipitated out in the form of mist. Now the sun is reversing the process. It is heating the moist air near the surface. As the sun gets the temperature of this air above the dew point, the moisture starts reevaporating into the air. It is often a slow process, because evaporation, like boiling, uses up a lot of energy. Until all the mist has been evaporated and the grass and leaves are dried out, the temperature near the surface of the ground will not begin to rise much above the dew point.

But by ten o'clock, the sun has usually done its work, and the valleys are clear of mist and the ground is drying out. Only now can the sun really go to work heating the air. Bear in mind, however, what has been happening. All morning long, the sun has been pumping water vapor into the atmosphere near the ground, making the air more and more buoyant. It does not go anywhere at first because it is cool, but once the lower atmosphere has absorbed all the moisture and begins to warm up, then it becomes doubly buoyant: it is lighter because it is wet and it is lighter because it is warm. By eleven o'clock or noon, the lower atmosphere has become substantially lighter than the air above it, and it begins to want to poke its way through the "ceiling" of cooler, drier air.

The process will begin over some particular "hot spot" on the landscape, like a cornfield that has been recently ploughed and seeded. The field is dark compared to the unploughed fields around it, so it soaks up more heat. Soon, a bubble of hot air forms near the earth, the way bubbles of steam form on the bottom of a pan of water that is about to boil. As soon as the bubble is warm enough to be lighter than the air above it, it lifts off the surface of the cornfield like a hot air balloon and rises upward. As it rises, the air in the bubble expands and cools, but the air around it is correspondingly cooler. Consequently, as long as the bubble can remain intact, it retains its heat advantage and continues to rise through the atmosphere.

There is one important difference between these bubbles of warm air and hot air balloons. The hot air in a balloon is contained within the balloon's sack. Bubbles of air, like bubbles of water, have a little skin around them, but it is ever so thin and ever so tenuous. Mixing occurs at the edges of the bubble, and unless the bubble is reinforced with more heat, it eventually loses its extra heat to the surrounding atmosphere and stops rising. But if the sun continues to shine on the cornfield below, and if the crosswind is not too strong, the balloon of air can rise indefinitely as more warm air is pumped in under it by the

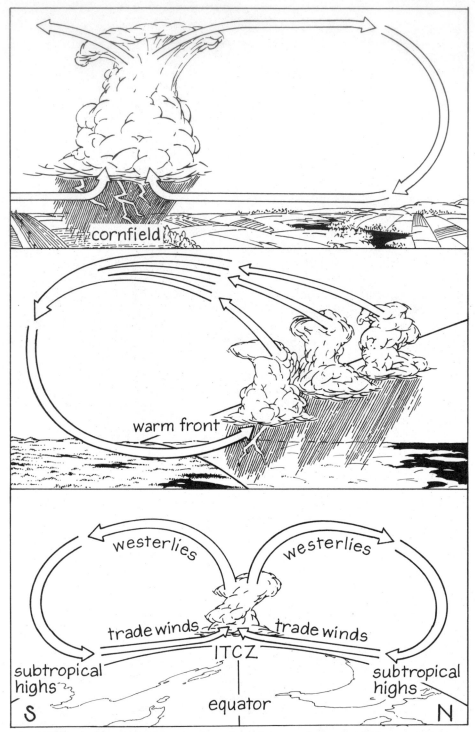

Three different sizes of weather engines at work; top, a thermal, which operates on a local scale; center, a cyclone, which operates on an intermediate scale; and **52** bottom, the Intertropical Convergence Zone, which works on a global scale.

heating of the cornfield. Such columns of rising warm air generated by hot spots on the landscape are called "thermals." Thermals are used by sailplanes, hawks, and buzzards to gain altitude on summer days.

As the column of air rises, it is eventually cooled to the point where the moisture precipitates out as a cumulus cloud. A cumulus cloud is one of those puffy, white clouds that looks like a cauliflower or a piece of popped corn. Remember that the precipitation process that forms the cloud releases an immense amount of heat. So, as the cloud is formed at the top of a thermal, the thermal is given a tremendous boost. Now the atmospheric heat engine gets down to work in earnest, converting the latent heat stored up in the water vapor first into vertical winds and then into horizontal winds as air rushes in at the surface to replace the air that is being evacuated by the thermal.

How big the cumulus cloud gets depends on the properties of the atmosphere above it. If the atmosphere aloft is right, the cumulus cloud will tend to shoot up and it may become a shower. If conditions aloft are really right, the cloud may shoot up several miles into the atmosphere, puncturing right through the upper-air westerlies and even into the lower stratosphere. When this happens, our cumulus cloud has become a "cumulonimbus" cloud or thunderstorm. I'll have a lot more to say about cumulonimbus clouds in the chapter on thunderstorms.

The Cyclonic Heat Engine

If a cumulus cloud is a "small" heat engine, then a cyclone is a middle-sized one. The warm air supply for most well-developed American cyclones comes from the tropical Atlantic Ocean. The air which gave our Charlestown gardener her false hopes of spring (see page 13 if you've forgotten them) was near the end of a very long journey. If you trace that air current backwards you will find that it originates far out over the waters of the tropics. Here, traveling over 70- to 80-degree water under direct sunshine, the air sops up heat and water like a sponge. As it crosses the Gulf of Mexico it gets caught up in the cyclone over Toledo and is drawn northward at increasing velocity. Because the wind is left-footed, the onrushing warm, moist air takes a spiral course carrying it northeastward rather than due north. Swishing northward, it eventually encounters, stuck to the ground like glue, a cold air mass entrenched over the northern states. Drawn inexorably onward by the lower pressure at the center of the cyclone, the warm, moist air rushes up the surface of the cold air and is cooled by expansion as it rises. Warm as it is and wet as it is, it does not have to be cooled much to reach its dew point. With each gram of moisture wrung from it, several hundred calories of heat are released, increasing the buoyancy of the air. As the air is drawn around in a great spiral, it becomes warmer and warmer, relative to its surroundings, and lighter. This warm, light air further diminishes the pressure at the center of the cyclone and increases the tendency of the surrounding air to spiral inward.

For a while, the cyclonic engine works at a furious pace, but more than just warm air is sucked into the vortex of the cyclone as the pressure falls. The great glacier of cold air to the west also makes a move to fill the void. Again, because of the coriolus force, its approach is devious. The cold air moves first southward around the west of the center, then eastward around its south, finally northward around its eastern margin, forcing itself under the lighter, warm, moist air. At this point the supply of warm and moist air begins to be throttled. First the supply is cut off only at the surface. But as the two cold air masses crunch together, the stream of warm air is restricted to a trickle at high altitude and finally is cut altogether. Deprived of an energy source, the cyclone dies.

The Tropical Heat Engine

The grandest heat engine of all is the tropical atmosphere. Tropical weather is strikingly different from the weather of temperate latitudes. We North American gardeners live in a world where the winds blow mostly from the west, where the upper-air river rushes overhead, where warm and cold fronts vie for the control of our weather, and where frontal cyclones churn the atmosphere under the influence of powerful coriolus forces. In the tropics, winds blow softly and steadily from the east for weeks at a time, frontal cyclones never intrude, the upper-air westerlies are unheard of, and coriolus forces are weak or absent.

The meteorological tropics are an extensive and important part of the globe. They include roughly the area from 30 degrees north to 30 degrees south latitude, from New Orleans almost to Buenos Aires, and from Cairo to Johannesburg. They embrace more than a third of the world's population and approximately half of its surface area. They include a high proportion of the world's food problems, and its areas of most rapidly expanding population.

Meteorologically speaking, the tropics are a crucial energy exportation region of the globe. Not only does most of the sun's heat fall on the tropical atmosphere, that atmosphere is more receptive to solar heat than the atmosphere of higher latitudes. Because of snow and ice surfaces on the ground and frequent cloudiness in the air, the higher latitudes waste a higher proportion of the heat they receive. Were it not for the "energy exports" we get from the tropical oceans and tropical atmosphere, our winters would be infinitely more ferocious than they are and our summers drier.

For a part of the world that receives so much solar energy, the weather of the tropics is remarkably lethargic. Except for hurricanes (which are discussed in chapter 15), only one kind of disturbance mars the serenity and monotony of day-to-day tropical weather: a band of showery weather that rings the globe near and more or less parallel to the equator. This band of weather is known as the Intertropical Convergence Zone (ITCZ) and roughly corresponds to the part of the surface of the earth where the sun's heating has recently been most intense. It migrates constantly, tagging along behind as the sun moves north-ward in the winter and spring and southward in the summer and fall. In this region where the earth's surface is warmest, the air over the surface is most buoyant, surface pressures tend to be low, and the air rises readily toward the top of the atmosphere. In the course of rising, much of the energy and moisture are wrung out of the air in the form of the showers and thundershowers that constitute the ITCZ.

The convergence zone is responsible for the monsoon, a phenomenon of crucial importance to farmers and gardeners in Asia and Africa. Where the ITCZ crosses a continent, the air rushing into the zone from the north is different from the air rushing in from the south. The air from the north is a hot, dry wind from the Sahara in Africa or from the deserts of northern India. The air from south of the zone comes mostly over the tropical oceans and is mild and moist. Where the two flows converge there are violent thunderstorms that announce the onset of the monsoon. Until the coming of the monsoon, the weather is harsh and dry. Day by day, the farmers watch the southern sky for signs of cloud buildup. Each day, the clouds come a little farther north, only to recede again at night. If the African or Asian gardener is to be lucky, the clouds must continue their advance until one day they sweep overhead and the land is deluged with water.

Farming in much of Africa and Asia is entirely at the mercy of the movements of the ITCZ. If the zone moves north early and departs southward late, then crops and grasses flourish, cattle are healthy, and people well-fed and happy. If the zone moves north late and departs early, then crops and grasses wither, cattle die, and people starve. The Sahelian droughts of the 1970s are a horrifying example of a failed monsoon. Year after year, during the 1970s, the northward movement of the rains was weak or late. The Sahel is the northernmost extent of the monsoon region in Africa. In the Sahel, a late rainy season may mean no rainy season at all: the monsoon begins its southward return journey before it has completed its normal northward movement. The misery brought on by such failures of the monsoon is difficult for temperate farmers and gardeners to conceive of. Thousands of people starved and a massive international relief effort was mounted to save the rest of the population.

The activities of the tropical heat engine are not only important to the people who live in the tropics, they are crucially important to those of us who live in temperate latitudes. The Intertropical Convergence Zone is the source of energy which powers the upper-air westerlies. The upper-air westerlies, you will recall, are the river of air which flows over the United States from west to east, carrying the surface weather systems in its flow.

The upper-air westerlies and the Intertropical Convergence Zone form one gigantic heat engine. The heated air rises over the tropics and pushes outward aloft. Wrenched by the coriolus force, it moves first northward, then northeastward, and finally eastward, becoming a river of air, winding its way around the globe from west to east. But what goes up, eventually must come down. Eventually the air cools from radiation and "subsides," i.e., it presses down from aloft to form the two gigantic subtropical high-pressure areas, one over the Atlantic Ocean, the other over the Pacific. It is these semipermanent high-pressure areas which bring such good weather to the oceans off southern California and the southeastern United States. As the air descends it turns southward and westward, making its return trip toward the convergence zone as the northeast trade winds.

Large as the global circulation is, it contains all the same elements that the thermal contains and the cyclone contains: an inrushing supply of warm, moist air that is induced to rise and thereby to release its supply of latent heat and moisture. Whether at the scale of a cornfield, or a region, or the entire tropical atmosphere, the principles are the same ones that guide the operation of the atmospheric heat engine.

And So, Back to the Garden

I promised when I got to the end of this chapter I would return us to the garden. So, here we go! I am standing on the end of my garden in Massachusetts, watching a featureless mass of clouds rise in the west. The wind is a mild southerly one and I can feel the rain coming. Looking westward, I see the lower cloud go all fuzzy and indistinct, and then I notice that distant points on the horizon are beginning to be obscured. I feel the soft wind on my skin and I think about the history of these particular molecules of air that are just now brushing my forehead. Months ago these very same molecules may have been swept up in a monsoon thunderstorm over India and hurled aloft. Wrung of their moisture, they were spewed into the upper atmosphere where, in the company of other molecules, they wandered northward. Wrenched to the right by the coriolus force, they found themselves hurtling eastward over northern China, up over the Aleutian Islands, and then pushed southward and downward around the Pacific high-pressure area until they joined another group of molecules plodding around the high. First westward toward the Philippines, now northward toward Japan, and now eastward north of Hawaii, the molecules continued their journey, picking up moisture from the ocean day after day after day. Finally, they came ashore in California with a group of molecules forming a warm front. Rushing up the slope of a cold air mass stubbornly entrenched over the Rockies, the molecules hurtled aloft again, shedding all their water over a grateful Sacramento Valley and rejoining the upper-air westerlies. The molecules now rushed northward over the Canadian Rockies and then came plunging southward and eastward out over the Atlantic. There they descended into the Bermuda High. Joining other molecules on the returning easterly flow on the south side of the Bermuda High, they came ashore, warm, wet, and weary in Florida and were dragged northward in the southerly winds of a big cyclone over the central United States. Having traveled all this distance, they now arrive to lend a little bit of softness to the oncoming rain. My corn will grow a bit better tomorrow as a consequence of their visit.

Part Two
THE
AMERICAN CLIMATE

6

THE FORCES THAT MAKE
THE AMERICAN CLIMATE

Climate is average weather. Like all averages, average weather is a funny sort of concept. Where I live, the average date of the last frost is in early May. But I've had last frosts as early as the first week of April and as late as the second week of June. In an average year, no snow falls in May and no 90-degree temperatures are recorded in April. But in 1977 we had a foot of snow the first week of May and in 1976 we had a string of 90-degree days in the third week of April. What good do average weather observations do if you cannot count on them?

The fact is that climate is a statistical concept. Like all statistical concepts, notions of climate are subject to certain paradoxes. One of these paradoxes is: the more precise a statement is, the less likely it is to be true. For instance, the statement that substantial May snows fall on my garden less than two years in ten, or that May frost strikes in forty to sixty years out of a hundred is almost certainly true for my garden, but it's not very useful. I need to know when the last frost is going to come this year, and next year, and the year after that, not when it comes in average years.

Yet, insubstantial as climatological statements sometimes seem, climates do have reality. No one would deny that the weather is different in the different regions of the country. Each region seems to have its own characteristic weather: the Gulf and Atlantic coast states are damp—warm to the south, cooler to the north. The northern states from the Great Lakes to the Cascades are cool and dry. The Southwest is hot and dry, and the extreme Northwest, cool and very damp. Likewise, no one would deny that the seasons are different. Summers are warmer than springs, winters cooler than falls. Across the Great Plains, summers are wetter than winters; on the California coast, winters are wetter than summers. Decade after decade, these differences can be observed in the average temperature and average precipitation of the different parts of the country and of the different seasons of the year.

These seasonal and regional differences in the weather have everything to do with what kind of gardening and farming can be done in different parts of the country at different times of the year. The farmers of the High Plains of Oklahoma and Nebraska rely on the combination of snow melt and spring rains to bring in a wheat crop before the heat of the summer sun begins to bake their soil. The citrus growers of Florida rely on their long, moist summers and their mild, frost-free winters to bring in their fruit crop. The corn growers of the Ohio River and Mississippi River valleys rely on the hot, humid summers to bring in bountiful crops of their slow-maturing feed corns. All over the country, careers are made, lifetimes are planned around the particular characteristics of particular regions at particular times of the year.

Believing in climate takes a certain philosophic frame of mind. If you're the sort of person who can look down on a frost-blasted bean plant and say, "Three years in ten I must expect this to happen," then climatology is the field for you. If, however, you are like me and you rail against the cold, still dawn that robbed you of your extra-early bean crop, then I fear the chapters on climate may seem just a bit unrealistic. The fact is that Earth's weather is incomprehensibly complex. While much can be said about future weather in general, or future weather on the average, little can be said about future weather at a particular place at a particular time.

Why Is Climate So Complex?

If only the earth did not rotate and if only its axis were not tilted with respect to the plane of its orbit around the sun and if only land and water were more evenly scattered about its surface, then Earth's climates would be much simpler than they are.

The sun would shine constantly at the equator and never at the poles. An immense circulation would be set up. Warm air would rise over the equator and travel aloft toward the poles; cool air would sink over the Arctic and Antarctic, and travel on the surface toward the equator. One giant area of high pressure would be formed over each pole. One giant region of low pressure would be formed at the equator. Depending on what weather you wanted, you could pick out a latitude and go live there. Each particular distance from the equator would have its characteristic patterns of precipitation and cloudiness, and these would be the same all the way around the world all year long.

But, of course, the earth *is* tilted with respect to its plane of rotation about the sun, and the earth *does* rotate around its axis, and the earth's surface *is* composed of large and irregular surfaces of water and land. Each of these facts imposes a different set of complexities on the world's weather.

Effects of the Earth's Tilt

Because the earth is tilted with respect to its orbit around the sun, the sun's apparent altitude changes constantly from month to month. For the same reason, the latitude where the sun stands directly overhead at noon is constantly changing as the earth makes its annual journey around the sun. The sun is at its farthest south in December, and travels northward during the winter and spring months. It crosses the equator on March 21 and reaches its northernmost position on June 21. In summer and fall, the sun makes its return journey, recrossing the equator in September headed south. This apparent motion of the noontime sun is most rapid when the sun is near the equator and slows to a barely perceptible drift as the sun approaches the northern Tropic of Cancer in June and the southern Tropic of Capricorn in December.

The pattern of apparent motion of the noontime sun on the earth's surface has two important consequences. The first of these is that the hottest place on the earth always lags behind the place where the daily heating is greatest. As the sun approaches a point, the heat builds up in the soil and water. After the sun passes, that stored heat is radiated back. The point where the combination of stored-up heat and daily heat coming from the sun is greatest occurs not where the sun *is* but where it has most recently been. (That's why afternoon is warmer than morning.) Over the whole year, the equator receives more heat than any part of the globe. But the places to receive the most heating in a three-month period are the extremes of the tropics because it is here that the sun moves slowly and it is here that the sun doubles back on itself as it begins its return trip.

Because of these factors, in August some of the warmest open ocean water in the world can be found in the Gulf of Mexico and Gulf of California, right against our own shores.

The Effects of the Earth's Rotation

The fact that the earth rotates around its axis imposes another set of complexities on the earth's weather. Because the earth is rotating, air moving on its surface is left-footed. It cannot move in straight lines but must bend to the right as it travels. Thus, instead of a simple northward flow of warm air high up in the atmosphere and a simple southward return flow of cold air near the earth's surface, the circulation is more complex. As we saw in the last chapter, the winds aloft bend eastward as they move away from the equator, becoming the upper-air westerlies typical of temperate latitudes. Similarly, the returning surface winds turn westward as they approach the equator, becoming the easterly trade winds that typically blow across the tropical oceans.

The contrast between these two currents, the westerlies aloft at middle latitudes and easterlies at low latitudes, tends to establish huge clockwise circulations in the atmosphere between them. Because these circulations are anticyclonic, wherever they become established they bring high pressure, minimum cloud development, and stable weather. Such atmospheric circulations are known as "subtropical highs": "highs" because they are persistent pockets of high pressure, and "subtropical" because they tend to form just outside the tropics.

Two subtropical highs affect the weather of the United States. One off the eastern coast of the United States is called the Bermuda High; the other, off the California coast, is called the Pacific High. These two anticyclones are so large and immovable that they stand as formidable obstacles to the passage of weather systems. Each dominates its ocean basin in just about the same latitudes as the United States lies. Sometimes in winter they will merge over the southern United States and Mexico to form a gigantic system of high pressure that extends from the Philippines to the Azores. Sometimes, particularly in summer, the two are separated by a substantial area of low pressure over the southwestern United States.

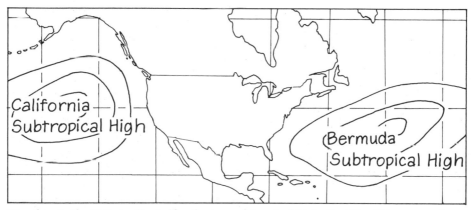

Weather in the U.S. is affected by the two subtropical highs that lie off its coasts: the California Subtropical High off the West Coast, and the Bermuda Subtropical High off the East Coast.

These high-pressure areas have important effects on the oceans beneath them. Because they are so stable and their winds so reliable and steady, they impart anticyclonic circulation to the water below them. On the eastern edge of the highs, the anticyclonic circulation brings cold ocean water southward. For example, on the east edge of the Pacific Ocean, the California current brings frigid water down the coast of California as far as Santa Barbara. On the west side of the Bermuda Subtropical High, the anticyclonic water circulation pumps huge quantities of warm water toward the North Atlantic. The result is an extraordinary stream of warm water—the Gulf Stream—flowing by the icy shores of Labrador and Greenland.

The Effects of the Earth's Irregular Surfaces of Land and Water

Finally, the fact that the earth's surface is broken up into large blocks of land and large blocks of water contributes greatly to the storminess and complexity of American weather. Land and water behave in very different ways when heated and cooled. Land masses are quick to heat and quick to cool, whereas oceans are slow to heat and slow to cool. As the sun moves north in the spring, the heat rushes ahead eagerly over the land, and lags behind over the oceans, and the continents quickly become warmer than the oceans around them. In the winter, conversely, the continents cool more rapidly, and cold air rushes southward over land while the warmth lingers over the northern oceans. The rapid heating and cooling of the continents is most dramatic in high-latitude places like Canada and Siberia, where summer days and winter nights are very long.

The difference in responsiveness of land and water to heating has two important consequences. First, the patterns of atmospheric pressure over the land and water tend to shift from summer to winter. In summer, the warm continents tend to be places of low pressure, the milder oceans places of high pressure. In winter, the northern oceans tend to be places of low pressure and the frigid continents nearby, centers of high pressure.

Second, the differential heating of oceans and land masses encourages the development of tremendous east-west temperature differences, particularly in the spring and fall. For instance, as the continental cold rushes south in the fall a situation is created where an area of great cold (the American continent) is between two areas of warmth (the Atlantic and Pacific oceans). Since the general motion of weather systems in the middle latitudes is west to east, warm, moist maritime air masses are constantly being dragged onto a cold continent and cold, continental air masses are being dragged onto warm, moist oceans. Such encounters between differing air masses supply the energy for the vigorous spring and fall gales we often experience along our coastlines.

The Air Masses That Affect American Weather

Seasonal and regional differences in American weather arise out of the interaction of various kinds of air that enter the country. Each of these different kinds of air, or "air masses," as meteorologists refer to them, has its own special character depending upon its source and recent history.

For instance, most of the moisture which falls over the United States comes directly or indirectly from "maritime tropical" air. Maritime tropical air is created over tropical ocean waters. Because it has been in long contact with warm water, it is warm and moist. The high moisture content means that maritime tropical air is very light and carries a tremendous quantity of latent heat. Latent heat, you will recall, is the heat that is released when the water vapor in moist air is condensed to water. Maritime tropical air which visits the United States most often comes from the Caribbean and western Atlantic. Just occasionally, maritime tropical air from the Gulf of California and the extreme eastern Pacific visits the American southwest.

"Continental polar" air, on the other hand, arises over the dry, cool interior region of central Canada. It is always a cool and dry air mass when it comes to visit, particularly in the winter. To reach central Canada, air must traverse the Canadian Rockies. Forced to rise, it is cooled and stripped of its moisture. By the time it reaches central Canada it is dry, and being dry, it permits radiated heat to escape readily from the ground beneath it. In the winter, central Canada receives little radiation from the sun, with the result that the air mass and the land beneath it get colder and colder. By the time such a winter continental polar air mass arrives in the United States its temperatures and dew points may be substantially below zero. Such air is the meteorological opposite of maritime tropical air. It is very dry and very heavy and contains no latent heat.

Both continental polar air and maritime tropical air are fair weather air masses when they are kept apart. Maritime tropical air can produce afternoon showers when it is subjected to afternoon heating, particularly over land. Continental polar air can produce showery weather if lower layers get warmed or pick up moisture from passing over warm, wet surfaces, such as lakes or oceans, or parts of the country that have been recently and heavily rained on. Such weather disturbances are relatively localized and relatively weak.

But when continental polar and maritime tropical air are brought together, powerful meteorological forces are unleashed. The polar air pushes under the maritime tropical air and lifts it. The lifting process cools the tropical air to its dew point and makes available its moisture for rain and its latent heat for further lifting. As we have seen in the previous chapter, this process won't stop until a lot of rain has fallen and a lot of air has been moved around.

"Maritime polar" air masses also have an important part to play in American weather. Maritime polar air develops over cold ocean waters. It is cooler than maritime tropical air and wetter than continental polar air. Because of its intermediate character maritime polar air behaves like a warm or cold air mass, depending on which of the other two kinds of air mass it is interacting with. With respect to continental polar air, it behaves like a warm air mass, overriding the colder, drier air and yielding up its own considerable quantities of moisture and latent heat. When it meets up with a maritime tropical air mass, on the other hand, it behaves like a cold air mass, forcing itself under the warmer and damper air and lifting it up.

Maritime polar air which affects the United States comes from two sources. The western slopes of the Rockies are almost constantly awash in maritime polar air which arises over the 50- to 60-degree waters of the eastern Pacific. When the westerlies are blowing vigorously across the United States, maritime air may cross the Rockies and, in a modified form, affect the weather of the central United States. During its trip over the mountains some of its water vapor is lost as precipitation and some of its latent heat is converted to heat. Under these circumstances it arrives on the Plains a drier and warmer air mass for its journey across the Rockies. Maritime polar air also approaches the United States from the east. These air masses develop over the frigid inshore waters around Labrador during the spring months and sometimes become so dense and heavy that they press westward, against the general eastward flow of things, to invade the Eastern Seaboard with dank, wintery air, even in the months of May and June.

The one other kind of air that affects American weather is "continental tropical" air. Continental tropical air arises over the deserts of Mexico and the American southwest and may spill westward into the Los Angeles basin as the "Santa Ana Wind" or intrude eastward into the western Plains as a nasty, hot wind that shrivels the crops and dries the ground to dust. The behavior of continental tropical air in interaction with other air masses is often difficult to predict. To the extent that continental tropical air is drier than maritime tropical air, it tends to be heavier; to the extent that it is warmer than maritime tropical air, it tends to be lighter. Which tendency wins out in any particular instance depends upon the history of the two particular air masses that are interacting. Meteorologists call the lines of interaction between these two air masses "dry fronts" or "moisture fronts." On such seams between the two kinds of tropical air sometimes form the most spectacular and devastating thunderstorms. It was, for instance, a moisture front that set off the great Lubbock, Texas, tornado outbreak of 1970.

The Influence of the Land

The interactions of the air masses is influenced by the geometry and regional features of the land over which they move. The North American continent has a variety of striking geographic features that dramatically affect the way weather unfolds. The most important of these features is the shape of the continent. If you compare North America with other continents you will see that it is the only continent that is shaped like a triangle and widens toward the poles. This configuration provides that a source of maritime tropical air lies directly south of a source of continental polar air. In the only other parts of the world in which this configuration is nearly reproduced—India and Southeast Asia—very large east-west mountain ranges prevent the continental and tropical air masses from getting together. On the North American continent no such barrier exists.

In fact, American mountains actually encourage the interaction of con-trasting air masses. An important feature of the North American continent is the "Cordillera," the chain of high mountains running north and south from Alaska to Central America. In the United States, this chain includes the Rockies, the Sierra, and the Cascades. Since about a quarter to a third of the weight of the atmosphere lies below the tops of these mountains, the Cordillera forms a substantial barrier to the penetration of Pacific air masses into the North American continent. Eastward-moving Pacific air masses are forced either to cross the mountains and yield up much of their moisture in the process, or to detour along the face of the Cordillera. The mountain ranges tend to constrain weather systems into three routes by which to enter the heartland of North America. Each route corresponds to a break in the height of the Cordillera. The Columbia River route brings weather systems through Washington, Oregon, and Idaho. This is the most direct route. Two other routes are less direct, but entail lower crossing altitudes. A crossing weather system can loop northward into British Columbia, scaling the mountains in the Peace River region and approaching the United States from the north over the high plains of Saskatchewan or Manitoba. Much less frequently, they can make the crossing near the southern boundary of the United States, detouring down the west coast of California and crossing the southern Rockies. Because the mountains tend to block the eastward movement of moderate Pacific air masses, the region east of the Rockies tends to be visited frequently by such immoderate and contrasting air masses as maritime tropical and continental polar, giving the region its characteristic volatile weather.

The other important feature of the North American continent for the production of weather is the presence of large inland seas. These include Hudson's Bay which divides western and eastern Canada, several large lakes in Manitoba, and most important of all, the Great Lakes system. These inland bodies of water are large enough to have a substantial modifying effect on the weather systems that traverse them. In spring and early summer, they are substantially cooler than the land around them. They tend to make the air above them cooler and denser than the air over surrounding parts of the country. They promote the development of high-pressure areas and discourage the development of low-pressure areas. In fall and early winter, the reverse occurs. The lakes are warm and moist relative to the land surfaces. They warm and humidify the air overhead, making it lighter. Thus, in the fall and early winter, the lakes promote the development of low-pressure systems and discourage the development of high-pressure systems that pass over their surface.

The Westerlies

The interaction of the air masses on the American continent is choreographed by the stream of the westerlies. Storms tend to be carried along in the westerlies like objects floating in a stream and the storms pull air masses along with them. When the westerlies are moving directly across the northern United

States, Pacific maritime polar air masses are drawn deeply into the continent. Weather systems move swiftly in from the west to east and there is little opportunity for storm development. Under these circumstances, maritime tropical and continental polar air masses are kept at bay. On the other hand, when the westerlies form a trough and plunge deeply toward the Gulf of Mexico, cold air masses are carried southward on the west side of the trough and warm air masses are carried northward on the east side of the trough. Under these conditions, continental polar and maritime tropical air are brought together and the conditions are ripe for heavy weather.

The position of the westerlies is influenced largely by the movement of the zone of maximum heating in the tropics. The westerlies are the consequence of heated tropical air trying to escape to northern latitudes. By the time this air reaches temperate latitudes it is confined to a rapidly moving eastbound stream of air. The *average* position of that stream depends on the position of the zone of maximum heating. When that zone is far north as in June, July, and August, then the westerlies are comparatively far north and the subtropical highs are placed further north on their oceans. Weather systems are deflected northward and commonly travel across Canada or the northern tier of the United States. When the zone of maximum heating is far south of the equator in December, January, and February, then storm systems may intrude more deeply into the southern part of the United States, sometimes coming as far south as the Gulf States and Florida.

Not only is the position of the westerlies important, but so also is the shape of their stream. Wherever the westerlies form a ridge, high-pressure areas will be enhanced and storm development discouraged. Wherever they form a trough, storm development will be encouraged and high-pressure areas will be weakened.

The Dynamics of Seasonal and Regional Weather

What makes weather—as opposed to climate—so maddeningly unpredictable is that the weather is produced by all three factors in interaction, not by any one of the factors alone. For example, Alabama usually has a mild and rainy December. This pattern routinely occurs because in December the geography of the Southeast, the air masses nearby, and the most common position of the upper-air westerlies are all conducive to rainfall in Alabama. The Gulf Stream is warm and moist, the Midwest is cold and dry; maritime tropical and continental polar air masses are ready for combat, and the westerlies are often found looping down in a trough across the Gulf States. But if one or more of these components should fail, if, say, the westerlies should form a trough further eastward off the Atlantic coast, then Alabama will have a cold, dry December.

Similarly, northern California usually has a mild maritime climate. In the winter, the westerlies bring ashore maritime air mass after maritime air mass and keep at bay any frigid continental polar air that may be lurking in the nearby mountains. But every so often in winter the westerlies loop down from the northeast and suddenly Californians may get a dose of continental polar air. The East Bay hills get a snowcover and northern Californians barely know what to make of it.

In the next few chapters I will be trying to say something useful about the weather typical of the seasons and regions of the United States. But while I can say a lot about what usually happens in the different parts of the country and in the different parts of the year, each gardener will know, at least when I speak of his section of the country or his favorite season, that the weather that usually happens, doesn't always happen. In fact, some years it doesn't seem like the usual weather ever happens.

7

SEASONS

The four named seasons of the year—spring, summer, fall, and winter—are astronomical seasons. They are based on the movements of the sun. Spring and summer are the seasons when the sun is in the northern hemisphere. In spring, the sun moves north, in summer it moves south. Fall and winter are the seasons when the sun is in the southern hemisphere. In fall, the sun moves south and in winter it moves north. Designating the seasons after the movements of the sun makes a lot of sense because the sun, ultimately, is the source of all the energy that makes weather possible.

But the four astronomical seasons just do not seem to represent very well the different kinds of weather we get from month to month. Astronomical summer and winter are pretty good meteorological seasons. Where I garden, anyway, summery and wintery weather pretty much begin and end when summer and winter begin and end. The correspondence could perhaps be improved a bit if summer began on June 1 and winter on December 1. But astronomical spring and fall make very bad meteorological seasons. The weather at the two ends of spring and the two ends of fall is about as different as weather can be. It is hard to think of late September's weather as being in the same season as early December's, or late March's weather being in the same season as early June's.

The lack of correspondence between meteorological and solar seasons comes about because even though the sun is the ultimate source of all the energy that makes the air warm, nevertheless the sun does not heat the air directly itself. It must act through intermediaries. Its intermediaries are the bodies of water and masses of land that make up the surface of the earth. In the surface layers of the earth and oceans, light energy of the sun is converted to heat which can then be transferred to the air. What determines the weather at various seasons of the year is the relative temperature of the earth's land and water surfaces, not the amount of heating directly received from the sun.

The best arrangement of seasons to represent the weather would perhaps be six miniseasons, each about two months long. Each miniseason is characterized by a different combination of land and water surface temperatures (see illustration). The most sensible idea would be to eliminate spring and fall altogether and just talk about early, middle, and late summer, and early, middle, and late winter. But I suspect that most readers would object to the obliteration of spring and fall. So, I have named my six miniseasons midwinter, early spring, late spring, midsummer, early fall, and late fall.

We will consider each of the miniseasons in turn, beginning with midwinter.

Midwinter
(December 21 to February 20)

On December 21 the sun stands vertical over the southern Tropic of Capricorn, 4,000 to 6,000 miles away from the United States. At noontime in places like Fargo, North Dakota, Seattle, Washington, and Caribou, Maine, the sun stands barely 20 degrees above the horizon at noon, which is lower than it stands at five o'clock on a summer afternoon. Nor is the sun above the horizon for very long in these northern places. In Key West, Florida, the day is ten and a half hours long, but in Fargo it is only eight and a half. North of Fargo, the sun's angle at noon and the daylength decrease precipitously until, at the Arctic Circle, less than 2,000 miles away, the sun never rises at all. North of the circle is an area, larger than the entire United States, which by the beginning of midwinter has not seen the sun for days, perhaps even for weeks.

Late in January, the land masses reach their coldest temperatures. The days are not only short in January, the sunlight is weak, having traced a much longer path through the layers of the atmosphere before reaching the ground. During these short days of weak sunlight, the land receives less heat from the sun than it radiates back into space and it cools steadily. The difference between radiation received and radiation lost is more dramatic the further north one lives. In January, the southern portions of the U.S. receive about half the radiant energy they receive in June; the northern portions receive only a quarter to a third of the solar heat they get in June. As a consequence, northern regions of the country are receiving from the sun only about half the heat that southern regions receive. Since the land in all parts of the country, both north and south, radiates about the same amount of energy out into space, the northernmost parts of the country are losing heat about twice as fast as the southern parts.

The land masses of North America have been quick to respond to these differences in radiation. Average daytime temperatures range from 0 degrees

(continued on page 74)

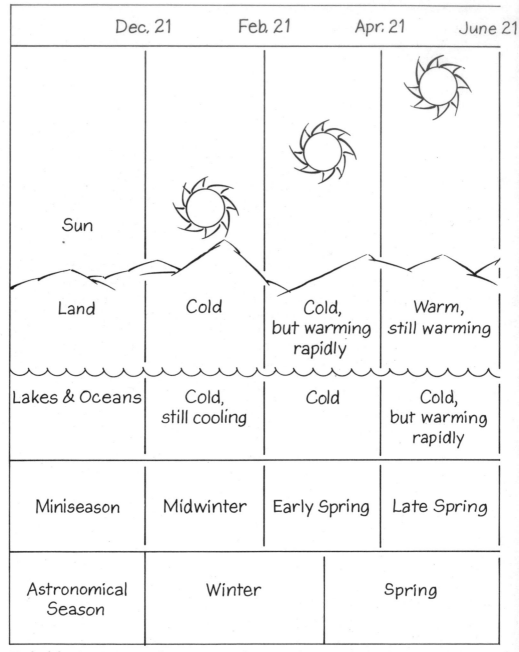

	Dec. 21	Feb. 21	Apr. 21	June 21
Sun				
Land		Cold	Cold, but warming rapidly	Warm, still warming
Lakes & Oceans		Cold, still cooling	Cold	Cold, but warming rapidly
Miniseason		Midwinter	Early Spring	Late Spring
Astronomical Season		Winter		Spring

Each of the six miniseasons has its own combination of sun height, land temperature, and water temperature.

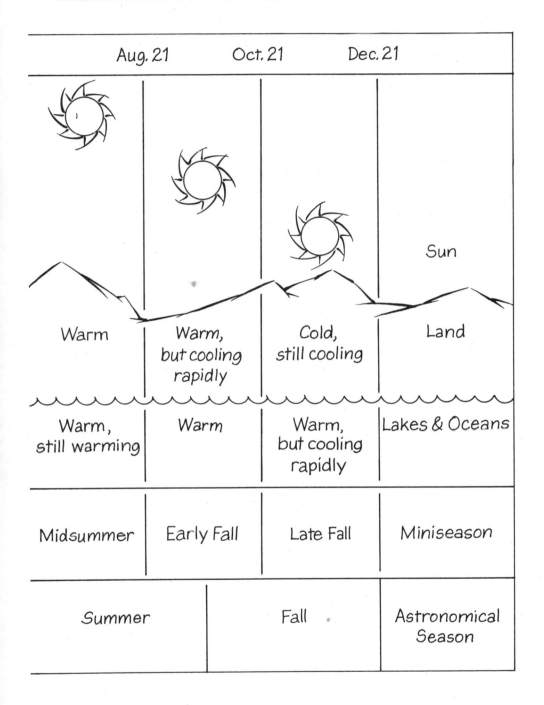

	Aug. 21	Oct. 21	Dec. 21	
				Sun
	Warm	Warm, but cooling rapidly	Cold, still cooling	Land
	Warm, still warming	Warm	Warm, but cooling rapidly	Lakes & Oceans
	Midsummer	Early Fall	Late Fall	Miniseason
	Summer		Fall	Astronomical Season

in the extreme North to 60 degrees in southern Texas and Florida, an average temperature contrast of 60 degrees over 2,000 miles. Bodies of water have been slower to respond. The Gulf of Mexico is cooler but by no means cool. Water temperatures are in the high sixties and will continue to fall slowly throughout midwinter. By comparison with the land masses around them, the Great Lakes and northern oceans are even warmer. No matter how cold the winter, open water surfaces exist on parts of the lakes, making for surface temperature contrasts of 20 to 30 degrees across their shorelines during cold outbreaks. Along the East Coast the chilly waters of the Atlantic Ocean now seem positively balmy compared with temperatures of 0 to 20 degrees which frequently occur on the nearby continent.

Areas of sharp temperature contrast encourage storm development. At this time of year the temperature contrasts are greatest between the waters of the Gulf and Gulf Stream and the continent to the north and west. A strong contrast also exists between unfrozen portions of the Great Lakes and the surrounding continent. These conditions encourage storm development over the Great Lakes and over the coastal waters of the Gulf and Atlantic seaboards. Which of these tracks a storm takes is of tremendous importance to the people who live in the eastern United States. The coastal track brings cool or wintery weather to the seaboard cities, because cold air is drawn in on the north and west sides of the storm, as it marches up the coast. The Great Lakes track brings mild weather and thaws to most of the East as Gulf air is drawn up ahead of the storm, and then stinging cold snaps as air from the Canadian plains is drawn in behind the storm.

Since storms travel in the upper-air westerlies, the position of the westerlies and the subtropical highs determines which of the storm-breeding areas will most often be in use. In midwinter, the subtropical highs have returned to their most southern position and the westerlies often cross the western coast as far south as California and depart the eastern coast as far south as the Carolinas. Consequently, January is the time when California gets its heaviest rainfall. January is also the time for Gulf and Eastern Seaboard storms to develop. The states of the interior are likely to have persistent cold, clear weather with occasional snows from storms traversing the Ohio River Valley from the lower Mississippi Valley, and occasional thaws from storms that traverse the Great Lakes and pass down the Ohio River Valley. The Gulf States are likely to have rainy drab weather and the Eastern Seaboard states to have wintery weather from storms which form in the Gulf, pass eastward to the Carolina coast, and then head northeastward over the Gulf Stream toward the Maritime Provinces in Canada and Labrador. These storms, if they pass close enough to the coast, bring the great winter blizzards of the Eastern Seaboard.

Midwinter is the low point of the gardening season. By January, the frost zone has conquered all of the United States except a narrow band a few miles wide extending along the coasts southward from the Olympic Peninsula in the

West, and southward and westward from the Carolina coast in the East. In the extreme South, midwinter is the time to harvest the late citrus fruit and early vegetables that fetch good prices in snowbound northern markets. Along the Gulf Coast, only a few cool-season crops such as small grains can be grown in midwinter, but by late in this period the fields are being prepared for early spring plantings of vegetables for the northern markets.

For northern gardeners, there is precious little cheer in midwinter. The ground is frozen hard across the North except near the West Coast. Those northern gardeners who must look for signs of spring should look to the sun. January 22 may be the coldest day of the year, but it is by no means the shortest. Daylength has increased ten to twenty minutes since the shortest day (December 21). Most of that change has occurred in the afternoon. On western windowsills house plants are already beginning to respond to the lengthening days.

Early Spring
(February 21 to April 20)

In the two months from February 21 to April 20, the sun is moving northward at its fastest rate. During this time it travels about 24 degrees, from 12 degrees south to 12 degrees north of the equator. This distance represents more than half of the total distance that the sun will travel in its six-month passage from the Tropic of Capricorn to the Tropic of Cancer. During the same period, daylengths increase by two to three hours, and sun angles by 24 degrees. The increases in solar radiation are most dramatic in the northern parts of the country. Across the northern tier of states, the amount of solar radiation nearly doubles. Further south, where radiation levels have not fallen so low, the increases are proportionally smaller. By the end of the early spring period, the difference in radiation received in the North and in the South is rapidly being equalized.

The earth is slow to respond to these increases in solar radiation. By the spring equinox, which occurs right in the middle of early spring, mean daily temperatures still average below freezing in most of the northern tier of states, and nighttime temperatures may still be close to 0. Still, this represents a moderating from mid-January of as much as 30 degrees. Increases in temperature in the South are less dramatic, bringing mean temperatures in the Gulf States only into the sixties. Temperature contrasts from north to south across the United States remain sharp during early spring, amounting to more than 40 degrees.

While the land surfaces have reached their coolest temperatures in the middle of January and have been warming since then, water surfaces continue to cool until the early part of March. By the equinox on March 21 they have only just begun to warm again. In the Great Lakes Region and in the Gulf Region, the progressive cooling of the water and the beginning warming of the land have brought the land and water surfaces approximately to the same temperature. Temperature contrasts in the Great Lakes Region and the Gulf States now amount to barely 10 degrees, one way or the other. The one place where dramatic differences in temperature still exist is off the coast of New England. Here, cold inshore waters of the Labrador current still contrast with Gulf Stream waters which are at their coolest for the year, but still very warm compared to New England coastal waters.

By mid-March, the subtropical highs and the mean position of the westerlies have begun to slip northward again. The California wet season has begun to peter out and storms more frequently cross the United States at the latitude of the Ohio River Valley and the Middle Atlantic States. Storms moving in this track bring rain or snow to the upper Ohio Valley, and showery and thundery weather to the Gulf States and Florida. When they cross out into the Atlantic, such storms can take advantage of the temperature contrasts between the Gulf Stream and the New England coastline to become powerful ocean-going storms. These spring gales help to make the New England spring one of the windiest in the country.

Early spring is a time of dramatic contrasts in gardening activities across the country. Across the northwestern and north central states, the soil is slow to thaw. But the winter wheat has begun to green on the Great Plains and by the end of the period small grains of all sorts are growing in Colorado, Kansas, and across the Ohio Valley to the Middle Atlantic states. Corn planting is in progress in the South and the planting of tender crops like tomatoes and watermelons soon follows.

Late Spring (April 21 to June 20)

Between March 22 and May 22, the days lengthen two to three hours in most parts of the country. By May 22 they are very nearly as long as they are going to get. In late spring (as in summer), the sun delivers its most direct radiation to the northern hemisphere. In the extreme southern United States, the sun stands just a few degrees off the vertical at noon. As one proceeds northward across the country, the angle becomes progressively less direct so that in North Dakota, for instance, the noontime sun stands only at 60 degrees. However, the less direct sunlight in North Dakota is compensated by the greater length of North Dakota's day, so that as the sun approaches the summer solstice at the end of late spring, all parts of the United States, north and south, begin to receive about the same amount of solar radiation per day. The change is most dramatic in the northern United States, where the earth is now receiving three times the radiation it received in January.

Across the North, particularly, the land has at last begun to respond to this onslaught of radiation. Average temperatures in the northern tier of states increase more than 30 degrees from mid-March to mid-May. In May, northern gardeners can generally expect high temperatures above 60 degrees, low temperatures above 40 degrees, and daily averages above 50 degrees. Land temperatures in southern areas continue to increase, but more slowly, so that daily mean temperatures across the South are in the seventies. The slower heating of the South and the more dramatic heating of the North have now brought the North/South contrast across the country to a mere 25 degrees.

As always, the bodies of water are much slower to respond. In late spring the temperature of large lakes and oceans begins to increase. The Gulf and Gulf Stream temperatures are in the seventies; the temperatures of the deep lakes struggle into the forties.

The late-spring temperature changes have obliterated most of the temperature contrasts across the country with one important exception. The contrast between the lake surface temperatures in the Great Lakes and surface temperatures of the surrounding landscape may exceed 20 degrees. As late spring wears on, the temperature contrast between the lakes to the north and the warm Ohio Valley to the south should make possible vigorous storm development. Sometimes such storms occur. But more often than not, storms do not get to take advantage of this strong temperature contrast. At this season of the year, the westerlies have pushed far northward and storms are most commonly carried across the northern United States or southern Canada. The result is that storms traveling in the westerlies are most often carried to the *north* of the Great Lakes. In this case, the lakes have the effect of diminishing the strength of the storms. Their cold surface chills the supply of Gulf air moving northward to feed the storm, and the storm is thus deprived of the heat necessary for development. The worst weather these storms can manage is a succession of warm and cold fronts that sweep across the northern United States, bringing the characteristically showery weather of the late spring season.

By mid-May, summer growing conditions can be found across most of the southern half of the United States; soils are warm enough to permit planting of tender vegetables in most of the area south of the Mason-Dixon line. The further northward push of warm soil temperatures is delayed by the cool weather around the Great Lakes. In the High Plains, well away from the influence of the lakes, soils heat rapidly to corn-growing temperatures. But in Minnesota, Wisconsin, Michigan, New York, and New England, the soils are still chilly. Here only cool-weather crops can be planted with assurance.

May 30, near the peak of late spring, is an important day to all American gardeners. On May 30, on the average, the frost zone is finally banished from the United States. Except in the most grudging of mountain valleys, the gardening season has finally begun in earnest for all of us.

Midsummer
(June 21 to August 20)

On June 21, the sun stands directly over the northern Tropic of Cancer. For the last two months it has been within 10 degrees of the Tropic and it will stay within the same 10 degrees for the next two months. In Key West, Florida, the sun is just a bit south of the zenith at noon. Even in Fargo, North Dakota, it is nearly two-thirds of the way up in the sky. The days are more than thirteen and a half hours long at Key West; in Fargo they are nearly sixteen hours long. These conditions will remain pretty much unchanged throughout the period of midsummer. So precisely does the daylength compensate for the height of the sun in the sky that the energy received by different parts of the country in July depends much more on the amount of cloudiness than it does on latitude. The drier mountainous regions of the West receive the most energy. Less is received as one moves eastward toward the moist Eastern Seaboard states. In July, Fargo, North Dakota, and Houston, Texas, receive almost precisely the same amount of energy from the sun. As a matter of fact, Portland, Maine, receives more solar radiation than Miami, Florida.

In July, even when the land is universally warm, the oceans and deep lakes are just beginning to catch up. Temperatures in the Gulf of Mexico and Great Lakes will not reach their maximum until early fall. In the South, the Gulf of Mexico and the Gulf Stream are in the seventies, contrasting little with the warm inshore waters or with the land surface. In the North, the Great Lakes' temperatures have reached the sixties. But their comparative coolness continues to have a storm-suppressing effect on any weather systems that pass over or to the north of them.

Midsummer weather throughout North America is characterized by the poverty and weakness of its storms. Ordinarily, the westerlies are found at the most northern position. Storms which are carried along in their current are confined to southern Canada, where they have little thermal contrast to work with in generating wind and rain. In this languid season, even the westerlies themselves are torpid. The energy that powers the westerlies comes from the temperature contrast between the light tropical air trying to escape aloft and the dense Arctic air that is trying to penetrate southward at the surface. With the weak north/south temperature contrasts of summer, the westerlies must inevitably be weak.

The subtropical highs have also moved to their northernmost position during this season. They are centered well up on the Carolina and California coasts. The Bermuda High, in particular, often expands well into the eastern United States at this time, bringing maritime tropical air to the land surface. Between the eastern and western subtropical highs, a surprising new feature has appeared. Over the very hot desert regions of the Southwest, a thermal low has developed. Like a cyclonic low, it is an area of low pressure, but unlike a cyclonic low it is stationary and is located well outside the westerlies. It does, however, affect the weather in the region. The low pressure aloft encourages convection and the influx of moisture from the Gulf of California, and the showery weather that gives some parts of Arizona a mini-monsoon at this time of year.

With heat so evenly distributed and storms shunted so far north, the gardener's anxieties in midsummer shift to the distribution of water. With warm, moist, maritime tropical air from the Gulf of Mexico spreading deep into the continent, there is no lack of moisture in the air over the eastern half of the country. The problem is the absence of a mechanism to wring that moisture out of the air. The usual mechanism is a cold front dangling down from a low-pressure area that sweeps along in the westerlies through southern Canada. But if the westerlies move too far north or become too weak, then parts of the United States can go for weeks or even months without substantial rainfall. Such a drought is a calamity at any time of the year, but it is particularly distressing in midsummer because the high temperatures and rapid growth rates demand so much more moisture for the plants.

July 22 marks the middle of midsummer. It is also the day on which I expect to pick my first corn, my first tomato, and my first green pepper. My neighbors, who spend less time cloud-gazing and more time hoeing and fertilizing, generally beat me by a week or more. No matter. July 22 is for me the apex of the gardening year, the day toward which all my gardening efforts have been directed for months.

Early Fall
(August 21 to October 20)

Early fall is the mirror image of early spring. During the two-month period from August 21 to October 20 the sun will descend 24 degrees in the sky and days will shorten by two to three hours. The effects will be most dramatic in the North, which will lose half its July radiation by the end of the period. On September 21, halfway through the period, the days and nights are of equal length everywhere in the world. From that date on, the days will be shorter the further north you live. Added to the lower angle of the sun in the Northern Hemisphere, the shorter days will result in a precipitous decline in the amount of radiation received by the land. On September 21 the sun sets at the North Pole and does not rise again there for six months. As the early fall wears on, more and more of the North will be altogether deprived of solar radiation.

Considering the dramatic changes in the distribution of solar radiation that have started to take place by the middle of early fall, the weather is remarkably unchanged. Across the South, gardeners have lost barely 5 degrees in daytime temperatures. Northern gardeners, however, are living on the edge of gardening disaster. Because of the rapidly increasing length of nights in the North, northern gardeners have lost since July nearly 15 degrees in *average* minimum nighttime temperature. By the end of September many of these gardeners will have had their first killing frost. Even if frost does not strike, the long, cool nights will bring to an end the growing season for such heat-loving crops as tomatoes, melons, squash, and corn.

In early fall, temperature contrasts are minimized between the land and bodies of water. Both along the shores of the Great Lakes and along the shores of the Gulf of Mexico and the Atlantic, the slight retreat of land temperatures from their midsummer highs and the slight additional heating of the bodies of water have finally brought the temperatures of land and water very near to one another.

The weak temperature contrasts make early fall's weather the most tranquil of the year. But there are two flaws that mar this serenity. First of all, the westerlies are back. The westerlies are more influenced by the retreat of the sun than is local weather, and by late August they have begun their southward movements. The average path of the westerlies during early fall once again crosses the northern United States. The twists and turns of the westerlies now more frequently dip down into the southern parts of the country, encouraging the development of low-pressure systems, even where local factors are not particularly conducive.

Similarly, the subtropical highs begin their southward retreat in early fall. In the west, the Pacific Subtropical High is once again permitting ocean storms to come ashore in the Pacific Northwest. In the East, the Bermuda High has retreated far enough to permit coastal storms to form off the Eastern Seaboard. By New England tradition, the first such storm is said to form on the twenty-first of September, when the sun is crossing the "line." Hence, September coastal storms are known to many coastal zone residents as "line" storms.

But the most significant aspect of the weather in early fall is the hurricanes. Hurricanes develop only over waters exceeding 80 degrees in temperature. In late August and early September, the waters off the Atlantic and Gulf coasts reach their annual peak temperatures of 80 to 85 degrees and are more than warm enough to support hurricane development. The movements of the hurricanes are governed by the Bermuda Subtropical High. In August the High is at its furthest north and west, and hurricanes are usually carried westward through the Caribbean to come ashore on the east-facing coasts of Texas and Mexico. As the summer wanes and the subtropical high retreats southward and eastward, the hurricanes begin to recurve more frequently; that is, they turn northward toward the Gulf Coast. By September, the recurving occurs in the open Atlantic and the hurricanes more frequently thrust up the Gulf Stream to strike the Eastern Seaboard. Only by late October have the tropical waters cooled sufficiently to prevent further hurricane development.

All over the United States, the harvest is in full swing during early fall. Corn, apples, spring wheat, peanuts, and hay are all being gathered. In some places, however, planting is under way. Winter wheat is being sown on the High Plains, and in parts of Florida, Texas, and California, fields are being prepared for winter vegetables.

Late Fall
(October 21 to December 20)

Compared to the mildness of early fall's weather, late fall is a period of vigorous climatic contrasts. In northern Canada temperatures average below zero. In the Gulf of Mexico, they average 65 to 70 degrees, resulting in a temperature contrast in the U.S. of nearly 60 to 70 degrees from north to south across the continent and 40 degrees across the country. These contrasts are concentrated in the northeastern part of the country where the rapidly cooling land is in contact with slower-cooling bodies of water. Temperatures in the Great Lakes of 50 degrees and in the northern Gulf Stream of 60 degrees contrast sharply with land surface temperatures, which are in the thirties, and air mass temperatures, which may drop down to zero during severe polar outbreaks.

This new distribution of temperatures across the country offers new opportunities for storm development. The Gulf and Carolina coasts provide sufficient contrasts to encourage some storm development, and late fall storminess does often occur in these areas. But the average position of the westerlies is still too far north to encourage much storm development in the South. In fact, the westerlies are so located at this time of the year that they frequently bring storms into position to take advantage of the sharp temperature contrasts in the Great Lakes Region and in the waters east of New England.

Late fall is thus often the season for vigorous storms to develop over the Lakes and move down the St. Lawrence Valley—the so-called "Great Lakes Lows." When this pattern develops, the eastern United States is on the south side of the storm track and is subjected to alternations of unseasonably warm weather followed by unseasonably cold weather.

Late fall is also a season when lows develop over the waters south of Labrador. When this pattern occurs, frigid polar air pours into the United States from central Canada, crossing the Great Lakes as it comes. When the cold, dry air crosses the warm lakes, the effect is explosive. There are showers, thunderstorms, squalls, and snow flurries.

With the further retreat of the westerlies, storms regularly traverse the West Coast. Rainfall of an inch a week now extends down the coast as far as northern California.

By mid-November, the increasingly deep and frequent penetrations of continental polar air have terminated the growing season in all but the most southern parts of the country. By the end of November, only places within 100 miles of the ocean still have not had their first frost. In fact, in portions of the East, north of Cape Hatteras, the frost zone extends right out to the barrier beaches.

Between September and November, most gardeners east of the Rockies lose 25 degrees of average temperature. Even where frost has not intruded, the shorter days and the chilly nights discourage the growth of all but the hardiest plants across all of the nation except parts of California, Texas, and extreme southern Florida. Commercial farmers have completed the harvest of corn, soybeans, and sorghum. Seeding of winter wheat is complete. In the extreme South, the winter vegetable season and citrus harvests begin in earnest.

On December 8, only two weeks before midwinter begins, the first sign of spring may be observed all over the United States. On the previous day, the seventh, the afternoon is the shortest of the year. For reasons known only to astronomers, the shortest morning occurs a whole month later in early January. By the shortest day, December 21, the afternoons have actually lengthened three or four minutes, and by the time the shortest morning is reached, the afternoons are lengthening quite rapidly, almost a minute a day. Before I learned this interesting astronomical fact, I used to think that the first sign of spring was the appearance of the seed catalogs in my mailbox. I now know the first sign of spring occurs on December 8, when the afternoon is just a little . . . ever so slightly . . . longer than the afternoon the day before.

8

EASTERN WEATHER

Because the circulation of the earth's atmosphere is so very complex, how far north or how far south you live has only an indirect effect on your weather. The weather in a region is determined by the air masses that reach it; the nature of the air masses is determined by the temperature of the earth's surface in the areas where the air masses arise; the temperatures of these surfaces are in turn determined by the sun. Where you live on the surface of the earth is important mostly because it determines which sorts of air masses get to you how often, and how modifed they are by the time they get there.

Local geographic features also have an important effect on what sort of weather you get. Mountain ranges, lakes, rivers, and coastal zones all modify the weather. Lakes and oceans put moisture into the air and mountain ranges wring moisture out. Mountains give a lot of resistance to the flow of air and slow up winds. Oceans, large lakes, and flat plains offer almost no resistance at all and the winds are barely slowed as they sweep across these surfaces.

Where you live is important, finally, because it determines how close you live to a storm track and which side of the track you live on. A storm track is a pathway along which storms frequently form and move. For a storm track to exist in your neighborhood, upper-air westerlies and local factors have to combine frequently to encourage storm development. The upper-air westerlies are necessary because the little kinks and eddies that form in them help to get storms started at the surface. Local factors are necessary because, without temperature contrasts and moisture differences at the surface, a storm, once begun, does not have the energy sources necessary for it to grow. Because local factors and the average positions of the westerlies change with the seasons, storm tracks change as well, so that where you live in relation to an important storm track may depend as much on the season as it does on your geography.

When you keep all these factors in mind, the United States divides up into six meteorological regions. The weather in each of these regions is the result of **83** a different set of local geographic features, air masses, and storm tracks. Since the regions don't correspond to state boundaries I've included a map of each. Each map illustrates the particular package of geographic and meteorological features that give that region its character. The regions themselves divide into two groupings. The western regions (the Mountain Region, the Pacific Coast Region, and the Great Plains Region) go together because mountains are the dominant features determining their weather. The eastern regions go together because their weather is largely determined by temperature contrasts between bodies of water and land masses. They include the Eastern Seaboard (the area abutting the Atlantic Ocean), the Gulf Region (the area abutting the Gulf of Mexico), and the Great Lakes Region (the area abutting the great fresh-water seas of the North American continent).

The Eastern Seaboard

The Eastern Seaboard is defined as the part of the country between the crest of the Appalachians and the Atlantic coastline. There are five air masses which annually affect the weather of the Eastern Seaboard. Maritime tropical air develops over the waters of the Caribbean and the western Atlantic and approaches the Eastern Seaboard either from the southeast or southwest. When it approaches from the east, it is often the cause of some of the rainiest or snowiest weather that the Atlantic coastal states receive. Under these circumstances, it usually rides up over cooler air at the surface and unloads its moisture. When it approaches from the southwest in summer it often brings the sustained spells of hot, humid weather that characterize much of this region during the summer months.

Continental polar air develops over the dry, cold heartlands of central Canada and approaches the region by two routes. How it approaches the region determines its properties. If it comes directly out of Quebec on a north-to-south path, then the air is excessively cold and dry. Such air is very stable and brings clear skies. If, on the other hand, it arrives on a more indirect route, passing over the waters of the Great Lakes, then its lower levels may be a little bit warmer and more moist. When continental polar air is so modified, it is unstable in the lower levels and a slate-grey overcast develops as soon as the sun gets to work on the moisture in the lower atmosphere.

Atlantic maritime polar air is similar to continental polar air that has been modified. Atlantic maritime polar air is manufactured over the cold water and ice floes of the extreme North Atlantic. Like continental polar air, it is cold; but like modified continental polar air it is damp, particularly at lower levels. Most of the year maritime polar air is an unwelcome visitor to the Eastern Seaboard. It usually brings grey skies and drizzle. Often maritime polar air helps to make the great northeast storms that batter the Eastern Seaboard, particularly in winter.

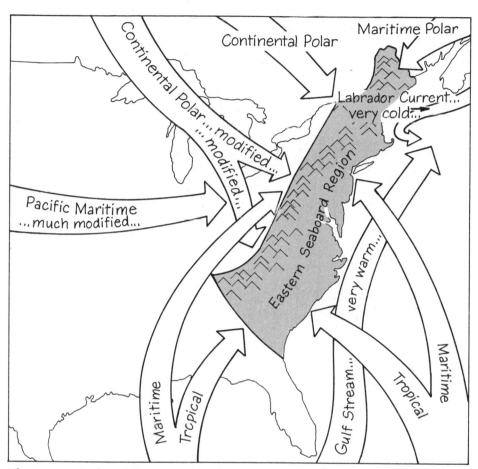

The Eastern Seaboard Region and the factors that make its weather.

If you live on the Eastern Seaboard you know that the way in which the various air masses affect your local weather depends a lot on how close you live to the ocean. In winter, when maritime tropical air is drawn in over frigid land, its moisture is instantly condensed into fog, sometimes freezing fog. These clammy fogs and drizzles are carried onto the shore by the easterly winds that precede low-pressure systems. In early summer, southwest winds drag maritime tropical air across the chilly water of the Gulf of Maine. The effect is to pack fog into the crevices of Maine's irregular coast, giving that state its famous fogbound summers.

The ocean has a spectacular modifying effect even on the coldest of winter continental polar outbreaks. As the cold northwest winds which carry this air blow out over the Atlantic, the surface of the water goes instantly to work moisturizing the lower layer of the air, warming it slightly and making it unstable. A few miles offshore, fair-weather clouds form. A few miles beyond that, the clouds thicken and begin to look grey. A few dozen miles farther out, snowsqualls form on the open ocean. The modifying effect of the ocean on the air is so immediate that during vigorous winter polar outbreaks satellite pictures show the coastline of the Eastern Seaboard outlined in its minutest detail by white clouds. So effective is the Atlantic in modifying continental polar air that by the time it reaches Bermuda, barely 500 miles offshore, air that was at 0 to 10 degrees is barely even cool.

Mountains also make a significant contribution to the weather of this region. Varying in height from 2,000 to 6,000 feet, the Appalachian Range defines the western boundary of the region. Not only do the mountains possess a cooler and damper climate themselves, but they contribute in very important ways to the climate of the lowlands to the south and east of them. Although they are not very high, the mountains form a considerable barrier to the intrusion of continental polar air into the coastal plains because such air is so dense it "hugs" the ground as it moves. The barrier is greatest where the mountains are highest in relation to the land west of them. Thus, the greatest effect is seen downstream of the southern Appalachians and the northern mountains of New England. These mountains not only slow the passage of cold, they modify it. If the air has picked up moisture in its passage over the Great Lakes, then the lifting action of the mountains wrings that moisture right back out and causes snow flurries. Thus, often for a couple of days after the passage of a continental polar cold front through New England, the coastal plains will be sunny and dry while the Appalachians are draped in low clouds and snowsqualls.

The mountains can also have an effect on maritime air which is blown ashore by the easterly winds in advance of low-pressure areas. Even the small coastal foothills of the Appalachians can put enough lift on this air to wring it out. The higher mountains inland can have an even greater effect. The southern Appalachians often record dangerous amounts of rainfall when hurricanes come ashore in the Carolinas. Similarly, the White and Green mountains of New England often get the heaviest snowfalls when northeast storms strike the New England coastline.

In serving as a partial barrier to the intrusion of cold air masses, the Appalachians spare the Eastern Seaboard states some of the worst of winter's weather. Winter is just a bit slower to come and just a bit less harsh in the seaboard states than it is in the corresponding states west of the Appalachians. Albany's winters are colder than Boston's, Nashville's are colder than Norfolk's. Hardiness zones, which are based on the coldest temperatures a winter has to offer a region, drift southward as one traverses the Appalachians. But the same mountains that help to make the winters a bit milder along the coast contribute to the delay of spring in the region. The mountains hold back warm air masses from the Midwest and leave the New England spring to be influenced by the cold Atlantic Ocean. Once warmed to the temperature of the ocean, the land is slow to warm further because each additional degree of temperature on the land encourages the onset of cooling sea breezes.

Storm Tracks and Typical Weather Patterns

The two storm tracks which have the most effect on Atlantic seaboard weather are the St. Lawrence Valley storm track and the coastal storm track. The St. Lawrence track is followed in all seasons of the year but most commonly in summer and fall. In summer, a storm passing in this track brings rain, followed by a spell of muggy weather, followed by thundershowers and cooler weather. The further north you live in the region, the longer will be the periods of cool, dry weather, and the shorter the periods of warm, muggy weather. In winter, the storms in the St. Lawrence track bring thaws to the region. Because of the relative warmth of the Great Lakes in winter, the storms pass to the north of the Eastern Seaboard region well developed and often thoroughly occluded. Their warm-air supply is well established and as they pass by, they haul quantities of warm, moist air up the coast in advance of them. Then as they pass, they haul down huge quantities of continental polar air behind them.

Winters in which storms in the St. Lawrence track predominate can be terribly hard on plant life in the region. The alternation of maritime tropical air in the fifties and sixties with continental polar air in the 0- to 30-degree range prevents any snowcover from developing and results in the alternate freezing and thawing of the ground, heaving out the roots of strawberries and deceiving ornamental trees and shrubs into premature blooming. Winters in which the storms pass in the coastal track are colder, but easier on the vegetation. First of all, the weather stays cold, moderating from time to time but without unseasonable thaws. Secondly, every so often, one of the storms comes close enough to the coast to lay down some snow. The snow insulates the ground both from unseasonable thaws and from the harshest cold.

A common and distressing pattern for the winter weather of this region is for St. Lawrence storms and Atlantic coastal storms to alternate. First, an Atlantic storm comes along and dumps a lot of snow on the land. Then a St. Lawrence storm comes along and melts it all to slush. When this alternation occurs, dismal fogs form where the warm maritime tropical air is drawn in over the cool, moist snowcover. When the inevitable cold snap comes and the continental polar air pours out of Canada, then ice floes form on the fields and pastures. As a child, I used to love this weather because it turned the haymow into one gigantic rink for skating. I could travel practically to the neighbor's farm and never take my skates off.

Although all parts of the region are subject to the same meteorological influences, they are subject to them in vastly different degrees. At the southern end of the region, in Georgia and the Carolinas, maritime tropical air dominates for months at a time and comes relatively undiluted. Polar air comes less frequently, and usually in an attenuated form. In New England these relationships are reversed. Polar air is a frequent visitor and tropical air rarely gets entrenched.

Gardening in the Eastern Seaboard Region

The length of the growing season varies dramatically from the extreme north to the extreme south of this region. The frost-free period in parts of Georgia exceeds 240 days; in parts of New Hampshire it is less than 90. Altitude also plays an important role in determining the length of the frost-free period: Boston, Massachusetts, has a longer frost-free period than portions of mountainous West Virginia. A gardener who moves from a coastal location west to the mountains will lose one to two months of growing season in the move. Since the cities are concentrated in the lowlands, people trying to escape the cities to find cheaper land and a more rural life style also are likely to find a shorter growing season. Many Eastern Seaboard residents are living on land that was formerly the best agricultural land of the region. The urban backyard garden may be the last way to make use of this precious regional resource.

Eastern Seaboard gardens are normally blessed with copious summer rainfall. In fact, in a normal summer, where summer temperatures are coolest, many gardeners can get through the whole summer without resorting to watering.

The Gulf Region

The weather of the Gulf Region of the country is dominated by maritime tropical air. Even in the depths of winter in the coldest years, water temperatures in the Gulf of Mexico never fall below 65 degrees. The low-lying coast provides no obstacle to the movement of sultry air masses off the surface of the Gulf and in over the land. Consequently, temperatures in the nearby region can never deviate very far or very long from the balmy temperature of the water surface. How far and how long depends entirely on the distance to the Gulf shore and whether the wind is blowing onshore or off.

Aside from the ever-present maritime tropical air, three other air masses contribute to the weather of the Gulf Region. Occasionally, Pacific maritime and continental tropical air penetrate this far east. When they do, they can destabilize the atmosphere and cause severe thunderstorms and even tornadoes. This sort of weather occurs in the Gulf Region in late winter and early spring, when the westerlies are frequently found crossing the region. A much more frequent contributor to Gulf weather is continental polar air. Continental polar air arrives in the region directly off the plains. No major topographical features restrict its flow from Canada to the Gulf. Only the Ozark Mountains on the west provide a minimum defense. Consequently, when upper air conditions are right, continental polar air masses can make the trip from the tundra to the bayous in just a few days.

The intrusion of continental polar air into the Gulf Region in winter creates a dramatically unstable situation. As the heavy, dry, cold air pours out over the warm moist sea surface, surface-to-air mass temperature contrasts of 30 degrees or more are created. Within hours, the lower levels of the polar air mass become warmed and moisturized, making them lighter than the layers above them. Before very long, this warm surface layer is trying to poke its way up through the cold air mass, producing showery and squally weather on the Gulf.

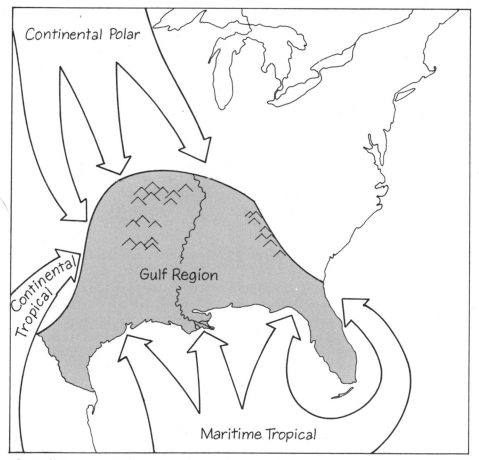

The Gulf Region and the factors that make its weather.

As soon as the polar air drifts eastward in the westerlies, warm Gulf air begins its counterattack. Encouraged by the southerly winds on the west side of the cold high-pressure area, the mild, moistened air tries to push inland over a landscape which has been kept at frigid temperatures three or four days. The cold air over this surface is slow to retreat and slow to warm, so the return flow of mild air off the Gulf is forced to overrun the air at the surface. Thus, in winter, a stationary front is often found draped over the Gulf States. South of the front is mild, showery weather and temperatures in the upper fifties or even sixties. Just north of the front is every manner of dreary winter weather: fog, drizzle, freezing fog, freezing drizzle, rain, freezing rain, ice pellets, sleet, and even occasionally, snow. This uneasy warfare between continental polar air and the powerful modifying effects of the Gulf will continue—often for days—until the westerlies turn northward and sweep the intruding polar air mass out of the area.

Continental polar air is the only encumbrance to the complete occupation of the region by maritime tropical air. During the summer, the continental polar air is restrained in Canada and maritime tropical air takes over the Gulf Region for most of the summer. The summer atmosphere of the Gulf Region becomes part of the Bermuda Subtropical High. The center of the High is displaced westward at this season, and steamy tropical air moving in a clockwise direction around the high is drawn out of the Caribbean through the Gulf of Mexico, and northward across the Gulf Region. This air flow is not torrid—remember that the Gulf water temperatures never do exceed the eighties—but the air is enormously moist. Average dew points in the seventies and relative humidity above 80 percent are commonplace in summer in the Gulf Region. Since the human body cools itself by evaporating moisture from its surface, the presence of all that water in the air means that human beings cannot get cool.

Storm Tracks
and Typical Weather Patterns

For much of the year, the westerlies flow to the north of the region. Under these circumstances, the only effect of storms moving in the westerlies is first to set a flow of Gulf air over the region and then eventually to interrupt it with an outbreak of continental polar air. Except for the most severe outbreaks in the depths of winter, this air is welcome as a clear and refreshing break to the torpid sultriness of Gulf weather.

In late fall and midwinter, however, the upper-air westerlies are often blowing strongly across the South and a storm track is established along the coastline. Storms form over the Gulf Coast and move eastward to the Atlantic coast or northward to the Great Lakes region. Usually, the development of storms traveling in these tracks is reserved for the time when they reach the Atlantic Coast or the Great Lakes. Strong winds from frontal cyclones are relatively infrequent in the Gulf states. In fact, in contrast to Eastern Seaboard weather, Gulf weather is comparatively tranquil and windfree.

Hurricanes are the major exception to the general tranquility of Gulf weather. Every year, the Gulf Coast can expect to have at least one formidable hurricane and several lesser tropical disturbances. Since hurricanes thrive on warm water and since the Gulf of Mexico is, if anything, warmer than the open Atlantic or Caribbean, hurricanes often come ashore on the Gulf Coast at the peak of their development. Peak gusts over 150 miles per hour have been recorded at several shoreline points along the Gulf. The effects on humans of Gulf Coast hurricanes are all the greater because Gulf weather is normally so benign. Housing in the South is often lightly constructed. Most of the time, heavier construction just is not necessary. Consequently, damage and loss of life from windstorms in the South is greater than the frequency of these events would lead one to expect.

Gardening in the Gulf Region

But for its excessive humidity, the Gulf Coast would probably be America's most enviable garden spot. Except in the extreme west of the region, rainfall is abundant and evenly distributed over the year. East of Texas, rainfall amounts average more than an inch a week. Few places have a single month in which the average rainfall is less than two inches and many have months in which the rainfall exceeds five inches.

Temperatures are nearly ideal in the Gulf Region for growing things. In winter, the influence of the tropical water in the Gulf keeps temperatures from falling very low and in the summer, it keeps them from going too terribly high. These effects are particularly dramatic within sight of the Gulf, where temperatures above 90 degrees and below freezing are unusual. Further away from the coast the effects diminish rapidly so that inland points, like Birmingham, Alabama, and Little Rock, Arkansas, have more than thirty days with temperatures below freezing and more than ninety days with temperatures above 90 degrees.

Overall, the climate of the Gulf States resembles nothing quite so much as it does a northern greenhouse. Cool and dank in the winter, hot and dank in the summer, the climate is ideal for all the heat-loving crops that are such a challenge to grow in the North. There is no doubt in my mind that if I were a garden I would want to live in the Gulf Region. Since I am a gardener, I am happy enough to live in a drier climate.

The Great Lakes Region

The Great Lakes Region is the part of the country where continental polar air and maritime tropical air do battle for control over the surface of a huge

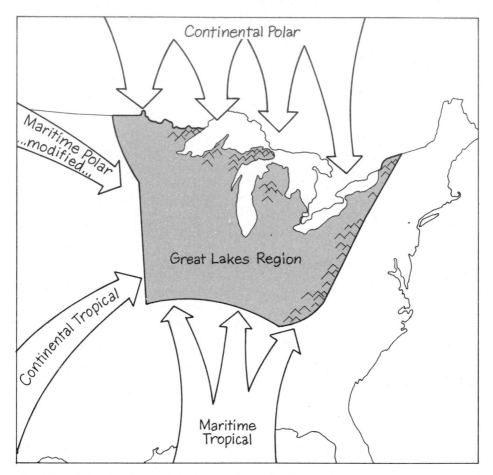

The Great Lakes Region and the factors that make its weather.

system of freshwater inland seas. This geographic situation is absolutely unique in the world. Not only are the Great Lakes the largest freshwater bodies in the world, they are uniquely positioned for inland seas of any type. Nowhere else in the world are inland seas situated where there is ready and direct access both to continental polar and to maritime tropical air. It is the interaction of these contrasting air masses over its unique topography that gives the Great Lakes Region its varied weather.

The only moderating factor in Great Lakes weather is the intrusion from time to time of mild maritime polar air from the distant Pacific Ocean. Its route of travel is long and it loses much of its moisture in the trip, so that it arrives in the Lakes Region as a moderate air mass: not warm, not cold, and not particularly dry or wet. It makes its appearance this far east only when the westerlies are blowing directly west to east so that Pacific air masses move swiftly across the Rockies and down over the Plains. Under these circumstances, the Pacific maritime air intrudes between the maritime tropical and the continental polar air and establishes a temporary buffer zone between them.

The lakes contribute enormously to the complexity of the interaction between maritime tropical and continental polar air in the region. The lakes have a longer "memory" for temperature than the land surfaces that surround them. In winter, when the area is dominated by continental polar air, the land surface quickly takes on the characteristics of the cold air over it. The lakes on the other hand, "remember" the long, warm summer days. Long after the land has gotten as cold as it is going to get, the lakes are still giving back to the atmosphere the heat they accumulated over the summer. Similarly, in summer the lakes "remember" the winter cold even when tropical air masses push across them. For weeks after the high sun of summer has warmed the fickle ground to temperatures in the eighties, the lake surfaces are still in the lower fifties. At this season of the year, the lakes become little islands of polar cold in a sea of maritime tropical air.

Although the lakes remember both cold and warmth, their memory for warmth is particularly good. Water that is cooled from 70 to 60 degrees becomes slightly heavier. Thus, if there is 70-degree water and 60-degree water in the same column of lake water, then the 70-degree water will be found floating on top of the 60-degree water. The same will be true with 60-degree water and 50-degree water and so forth down to about 40 degrees: the cooler the water, the heavier it is and the lower down in the lake you may expect to find it.

What this means is that no part of the surface of the lake will stay at 40 degrees until all the water beneath that part has been chilled to at least 40 degrees. Until that time, the warmer water below will just float up to the surface and replace the cold water, returning the surface to the warmer temperature. How quickly a lake cools at a particular location depends entirely on the depth of the column of water underneath that location. The fact is that four of the five Great Lakes are very deep, indeed. With the exception of Lake Erie, which is only a little more than 200 feet at its deepest, all the lakes have parts that are at least 700 feet deep, and Lake Superior, the northernmost of the group, is more than 1,300 feet at its deepest. Lake Superior is a particularly spectacular weather modifier because it has few shoal areas. Most of the lake bottom is at least 500 feet deep. To freeze Lake Superior, the atmosphere would have to cool a volume of water about the size of the state of New Jersey and more than 500 feet deep.

The fact is that there simply is not enough time in a winter to get all that water frozen. Long and severe as the midwestern winter is, it is not long or severe enough to cool any of the deeper lake waters to freezing. Of the five lakes, only Lake Erie regularly freezes over completely in the winter. The others remain 20 to 60 percent open no matter how cold the winter. This means that when temperatures are 20 degrees below zero and the air is dry at Sault Sainte Marie, only a few miles away out in the middle of Lake Superior is an area where the water temperatures are near forty and the air near the surface is steaming like a hot bath. The "steam" which forms over open bodies of water in frigid weather is called Arctic Sea Smoke.

When the lake surfaces are warmer or colder than the land surfaces, then a variety of localized meteorological phenomena occur. In early fall, late fall, and midwinter, the lakes contribute heat and moisture to the atmosphere. The heat and moisture make the air over the lakes more buoyant and volatile than the air over the surrounding land. During the early fall, the buoyancy helps to form strong thunderstorms, sometimes with waterspouts on the lake surface.

Later in the season, the warm surface waters of the lakes make possible the lake effect snowstorms for which the region is famous. Continental polar air rushing across the lakes receives an injection of moisture in its lowest layers. When this shallow layer of moistened, warmed, unstable air hits the opposite shore it is kicked upward by the hills and immediately releases its moisture as snowsqualls. The severity of these lake effect snowstorms depends on the length of the fetch. "Fetch" refers to the distance traveled over the water by the winds before they hit the leeward coast. The severity also depends on the topography of the coast. Some parts of the Great Lakes coastline have more texture than others and these are called "snowbelts." Snowbelts with annual accumulations of greater than six feet occur along parts of the coastlines of all the lakes. Accumulations in some hilly areas adjacent to the lakes regularly exceed ten feet!

Ironically, even though it is cold Canadian air that causes the lake effect snow, Canadians don't experience these effects as often as Americans. When the people in Rochester are experiencing a blinding lake effect snowstorm, the people of Toronto will be experiencing a sunny, cold day with a strong offshore breeze. If they go to the top of the observation tower in downtown Toronto, they may be able to see clouds on the southern horizon. Those are the clouds that are giving Rochester such a beating.

The lake effects which occur in late spring and summer are the reverse of the winter lake effects. During this season of the year, the lakes actually extract heat and moisture from the air above them. Spring and summer are the seasons for Great Lakes fogs. Maritime tropical air crossing the lakes is cooled in its lower layers. Since maritime tropical air typically has dew points in the upper sixties and since the lakes' surfaces are typically in the fifties and low sixties, the effect of the cooling is to condense the moisture in the air into fog. Unlike the warmed and moistened continental polar air, which is unstable, the cooled maritime tropical air is excessively stable. The colder, denser layer clings to the surface of the lake like cold molasses. Such fogs can make spring weather a misery in coastline cities, while only a mile away from the shore or a few hundred feet straight up the weather is sunny and warm. Since maritime tropical air comes on southerly winds, these fogs are most characteristic of the northern or Canadian shores of the lakes.

Storm Tracks
and Typical Weather Patterns

The Great Lakes Region is one of the great crossroads of stormy weather in the world. Storm tracks converge on the lakes from all the western points of the compass. "Alberta lows" blow down on the lakes from the northwest, North Pacific lows approach through the Dakotas, and Colorado lows approach through Wisconsin and Illinois. In fact, all the major storm tracks of the United States pass through the Great Lakes Region *except* the Gulf Coast-Eastern Seaboard track. During the fall and winter months the effect of the lakes on storms traveling through the area is to encourage them. In the summer months, on the other hand, the lakes appear to suppress the development of storms and encourage the development of high-pressure areas.

Gardening in the Great Lakes Region

The Great Lakes Region has a rigorous climate for gardening. Because the lakes are cold, springs are later and cooler near the lake shores than they are a few miles inland. Summer rainfall isn't abundant along the lake shores, particularly in the coastal and northernmost parts of the region. During the growing season, the cool lakes discourage showers from forming. Few places in the Lakes Region get as much as an inch a week of rainfall during the growing season months.

On the other hand, living near the lakes has some advantages to gardeners. The hottest days of summer are moderated. Daily maximum temperatures above 90 degrees are rare along the lake shore and less common in the whole region than they are in many places much farther north. The late growing season characteristic of the area has some important side benefits. Fruit trees and vines which should not begin to grow too early in the spring are retarded by the cloudy and chilly lake shore weather. In the fall, the warm water of the lakes retards the first frost and prolongs the fall growing season, protecting the same fruit plants from early frostkill. These effects make the shores of the Great Lakes one of the country's great fruit-growing areas.

In short, the Great Lakes Region is the place for gardeners who do not mind their summers a little cool, a little cloudy, and a little dry, and who like their weather vigorous and exciting in the winter.

9

WESTERN WEATHER

In the western regions I have included all those areas to which the western mountains make a significant meteorological contribution: the Pacific Coast Region, the Mountain Region, and the Great Plains Region. The weather in all of these regions is, more or less, mountain weather. Mountain weather differs in important ways from lowland weather. In lowland regions, most rainfall occurs when warm, moist air is lifted by contrasting cool, dry air. In mountainous regions, moist air can produce precipitation without the assistance of cold, dry air, because the mountains themselves provide all the lifting that is necessary to condense the moisture out of the air. We have already seen these effects on a small scale in the Appalachians and in the small hills along the Great Lakes. But the effects of the Rocky Mountains and the Sierra are incomparably greater. These mountain ranges poke up almost a third of the way into the atmosphere. Mountains this tall so alter the weather they deserve a chapter all of their own.

How the Mountains Affect Western Weather

The effects of mountain ranges on air masses are called "orographic" effects. When air is forced up the side of a mountain, it expands and cools, about 5½ degrees for each 1,000 feet of altitude. The cooling air eventually reaches its dew point and begins to release its moisture as rain or snow. As the precipitation is released, a great deal of heat is released also, so that when the air arrives at the top of the mountain range it is both warmer and drier than air 96 at the same altitude that has not recently climbed a mountain.

When the same air comes down the other side of the mountain, it is recompressed. Compressed, it is heated at a rate of 5½ degrees per 1,000 feet. When it arrives back at sea level, its temperature is much higher than it was before its trip, and its dew point is much lower. Consequently, the relative humidity of the air is much, much reduced.

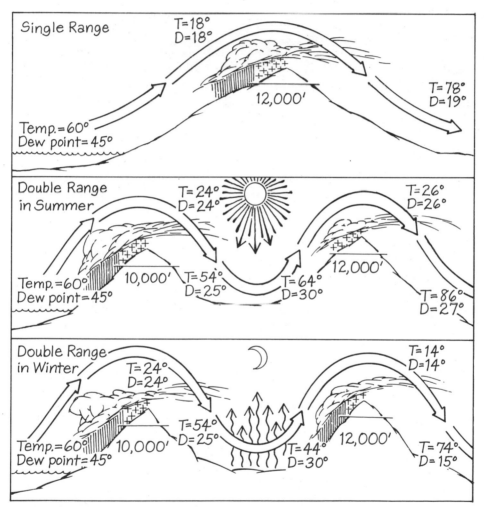

Orographic effects on weather. When moist air crosses over a mountain range or two, it usually comes back to sea level warmer and drier for its trip. How much warmer depends on how wet it was to begin with, how long it stayed up in the mountains, and what the conditions in the mountains were while it was up there. The top illustration shows the moist air crossing a single mountain range. At center the moist air crosses a double range in summer. The bottom illustration shows the moist air crossing a double range in winter.

This example presupposes that the air just goes up one side of the mountain and down the other. Of course, not all mountain ranges are like garden walls. Some mountain ranges have extensive plateaus at their tops, so that the air can linger at high altitudes for several days. For instance, between Sacramento and Denver there are three major mountain ranges: the Sierra, the Washach, and the Rockies. Between these are two high plateaus, the Great Basin and the highlands of central Colorado. Air traversing this route not only has to go up and down three times, it also has to stay at altitudes greater than 5,000 feet for much of its trip.

How air changes when it crosses such a plateau depends partly on the conditions existing on the plateau. Orographically dried air permits radiation to pass readily in either direction, either from sun to earth in summer or from earth out into space in winter. In this manner, such air facilitates its own cooling or heating. If the season is winter, the nights are long, the sun is low, and the land is snow covered and cold; then, with each passing day, the air will become colder. Then when it descends to sea level, it will come as a mild, dry air mass. If, on the other hand, the season is summer, days are long, the sun is high, and the land is hot; then, with each passing day, the air will become heated further. When it returns, it will be a much hotter air mass for the period it has spent in the Great Basin.

During summertime, the intense heating of orographically dried and warmed air masses contributes to the formation of the Arizona Thermal Low. In the southwest mountains, the sun's heating is so intense that the ground becomes hot and the air above becomes very light and buoyant. Such air is so much warmer than the air in the two subtropical highs that it is lighter. Consequently, a low-pressure area is created over the southern mountains, separating the Bermuda and Pacific Subtropical Highs. Unlike temperate cyclones, this low is stationary, and provokes only showery weather. But its counterclockwise air circulation does influence the weather of the western part of the country in two important ways. First, the northwest flow around the west side of the low pulls cold maritime polar air into the California coast. Second, the southeast wind flow around the east side of the low pulls moist air out of the Gulf of California and brings it ashore in the desert regions of the Southwest.

Large mountain ranges not only have the power to change the air masses that cross them, they also have the power to alter the organization of weather systems. Imagine a well-developed low-pressure system approaching the coast of California. The low is thoroughly occluded and its front approaches the California coast a little ahead of the storm. In the upper air behind the low center, at 18,000 to 30,000 feet, is a kink in the upper-air westerlies—a moving trough that corresponds to the surface low-pressure system below. When the storm hits the coast, two things happen.

First, as the occluded front is thrust up the sides of the Sierra Range, the air-mass contrasts represented by the front become inconsequential compared with the effects of the lifting. All three air masses in the occlusion—the two cooler air masses at the surface and the warmer air mass above—are mixed, warmed, and dried by their crossing of the mountains and arrive in the Great Basin as a single, very ill-defined cold front.

Compared to the continental polar fronts that eastern gardeners are used to, these mountain cold fronts are very difficult to find. They often amount to little more than a band of showers, a slight wind shift, and a barely noticeable dip in temperature.

The second thing that happens when storms encounter the West Coast is that the lower-level counterclockwise circulation of the storm gets blocked by the mountains. Instead of crossing over the mountains this circulation often slides northward along their western face, weakening gradually. The upper-air circulation above the storm, however, is not blocked. The kink in the westerlies continues across the mountains in the upper-air flow and arrives over the eastern face of the Rockies as a small, moving upper-air trough without any corresponding lower-level circulation. If, as often happens, there is a stationary front lying near the east face of the Rockies when one of these upper-air troughs comes along, the upper-air circulation will immediately go to work on the lower-level front and produce a storm. These "disembodied" troughs help to give the Great Plains their unpredictable and volatile weather.

The Pacific Coast Region

The Pacific Coast Region is the province of maritime polar air. All year long, maritime polar air masses rush across the Pacific and bash themselves against the western mountains. So persistent and powerful is this west-to-east ocean flow that other air masses seldom penetrate the Pacific Coast Region. Rarely, continental polar air sweeps westward out of the mountain region and spills over into the Sacramento Valley, or pours through the Columbia River Gap, bringing snow to cities like Portland, Oregon, or even to the hills around San Francisco Bay. A few times a year, continental tropical air will spill into the Los Angeles Basin from the desert to the east, bringing a hot wind to places accustomed only to gentle ocean breezes. But such intrusions are uncommon. Day after day, week after week, the climate of the Pacific Coast Region consists of cool ocean breezes off the Pacific.

Most of the factors that cause Pacific Coast weather are constant. The mountains stay in the same place and are always of the same height. The ocean stays put and changes its temperature only a few degrees from month to month. These stable features help to give California one of the most equable climates in the world.

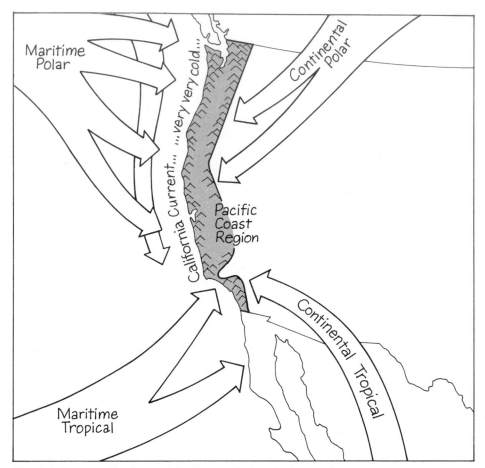

The Pacific Coast Region and the factors that make its weather.

Storm Tracks and Typical Weather Patterns

To the extent that West Coast weather is seasonal, it varies in response to the seasonal movements of the westerlies and of the Pacific Subtropical High. The average position of the subtropical high shifts northward in the spring and southward in the fall. In July the high is intense and occupies a position off the coast of Oregon. The westerlies that travel clockwise across the top of the subtropical high must detour far north in the Pacific to reach the west coast of North America. Storms which travel in the westerlies rarely penetrate as far south as Oregon, let alone to California. In January, however, the Pacific Subtropical High is located abreast of the southern California coastline. Now the westerlies frequently flow southeastward over the region and storms regularly come ashore on the northern California coast. The frontal systems of these storms dangle southward from their centers, bringing rain as far south as the Los Angeles Basin. Los Angeles gardeners can set aside their watering hoses for a few weeks and begin to fret about mudslides.

How much rainfall Pacific Coast gardeners get from winter storms depends entirely on how far from the coast, how far north, and how far up the mountain they live. Higher gardens, more northerly gardens, and gardens closest to the shoreline catch the most raininess and the most storminess.

Summer weather along the Pacific coast is controlled by a whole set of mechanisms that are unique to the Pacific Coast Region. Between the Pacific Subtropical High and the Arizona Thermal Low, a pressure gradient develops in the summer months. Throughout the summer this gradient supports a steady flow of mild, moist air blowing onto the coastline from far out in the Pacific. For complicated physical reasons, these onshore winds cause a flow of ocean water *away* from the coastline. This offshore ocean current must be replaced by water from somewhere, so water wells upward from the deep ocean canyons just off the West Coast. This upwelling water is very cold, barely 50 degrees. As the mild ocean wind crosses the cold inshore waters it is cooled below its dew point and heavy fog forms along the coastline.

This atmosphere-ocean system is tremendously important to the West Coast environment. It makes possible the growth of redwood trees in the fog zone along the coastline. The coast redwood relies on fog drip to supply some of its moisture for growth. The system also makes possible the California fishing industry. The cold upwelling water is rich in oxygen and nutrients, and fish and other sea organisms thrive in it. The cool winds off the ocean give to places like San Francisco, Pacific Grove, and Eureka, California, a summer climate that is very moderate indeed. In fact, summers on the northern California coast are cooler than winters in most parts of Florida.

Regrettably, the ocean winds are also partly responsible for the poor air quality of some California coastal cities. San Francisco and Los Angeles both sit in mountain basins open to the west. When the cool air flows into the basin from the coast it gets trapped. The layer of cold air is very shallow, less than a few thousand feet. Above this layer the air is warm, dry, and cloudless. The presence of cold ocean air capped by warm air creates an inversion situation which keeps pollutants from the cities from escaping upward. This situation makes possible the terrible smogs which unfortunately are characteristic of these California cities.

Gardening in the Pacific Coast Region

What gardening is like in the Pacific Coast Region depends on where your garden is. Examples of every conceivable climate—from tundra to rainforest to desert—can be found here. Want to garden where summer temperatures struggle to reach 60 degrees, where growing seasons are long but growing degree-days are in short supply, where the sky is mostly cloudy and where rainfall is copious in winter? Pick a garden spot within sight of the Pacific Ocean. For a bit more summer rain, move north. For a bit more summer warmth, move south. Want to garden where July temperatures are hot, where the sky is mostly clear, where winter rains are less copious and summer rains nonexistent? Pick your garden spot in one of the interior valleys. For a bit more rainfall, move north. For a longer growing season, move south. Finally, do you want to do your gardening in a land of deep winter snows and short growing seasons? Move up into the mountains. For more snow, move higher, or farther north, or both. For a longer growing season, move lower, farther south, or both.

California weather is almost totally a matter of place. A drive of a few miles, closer to the water or farther from it, higher up the mountain or down, a bit farther north or a bit farther south, can radically alter such crucial gardening statistics as the date of first frost, the length of the growing season, the amount of rainfall, the percentage of possible sunshine, and the average number of growing degree-days. In describing the variability of their climate, New Englanders say, if you don't like the weather, wait a few minutes. Californians who don't like their weather, drive a few miles.

The Mountain Region

The high mountain ranges of North America form a natural fortress against weather. On the west is the crest of the Sierra Nevadas and the Cascades. The peaks in this range tower as high as 14,000 feet, but the ridge line itself varies between 5,000 and 10,000 feet. On the east lie the Rockies, a mass of mountains with peaks above 12,000 feet and with many ridgelines substantially above 10,000 feet along most of their length. These mountain peaks are so high that more than a quarter of the atmosphere lies below them. Consequently, air masses do not get into the Mountain Region without a powerful push from upper-air forces.

The air mass most frequently found in the Mountain Region is maritime polar air. This air supply arrives from the West Coast Region much dried and somewhat warmed from the orographic effects of its journey over the Sierra Nevadas. In addition, continental polar air masses sometimes push into the Mountain Region from the Great Plains, and continental tropical air intrudes from the hot, dry regions of central Mexico. The least common air mass in the Mountain Region is maritime tropical air, which occasionally makes its way into the extreme southern end of the region from the waters of the Gulf of California.

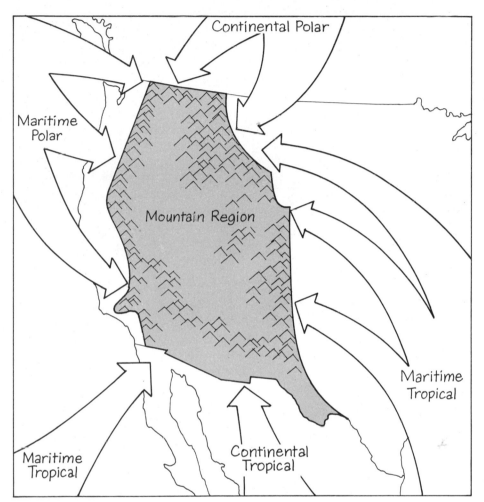

The Mountain Region and the factors that make its weather.

Storm Tracks
and Typical Weather Patterns

Two storm tracks are found in this region. Normally, storm systems traverse the mountains intact only when the stream of the upper-air westerlies happens to fall along one of the weak points in the mountain fortress. When this occurs, a storm system is guided through the mountain along a comparatively easy path and is more likely to retain its surface cyclonic properties to some degree. Two such low passages exist. One is across the extreme southern

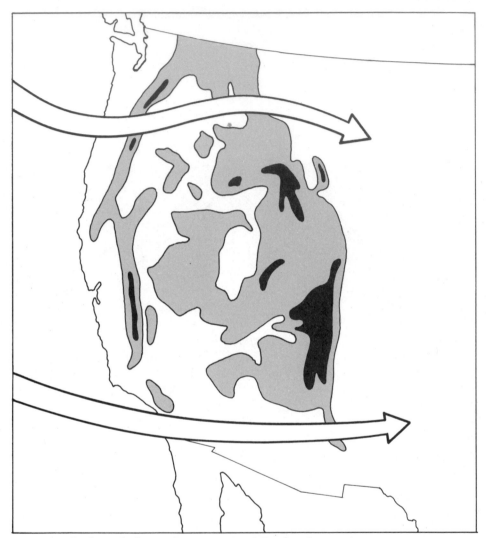

Storm tracks through the Rocky Mountains. Like the pioneers in reverse, storms traversing the Rockies tend to be channeled by the mountains into a northern or a southern route. Lighter shaded areas are below 5,000 feet, darkest areas are above 10,000 feet.

end of the region; it carries storms through southern California, Arizona, and New Mexico to a point on the Texas-Oklahoma Panhandle area. This storm track is not often traveled because the westerlies are seldom found this far south. Far more common is a track which carries storms through the Pacific Northwest, crossing the Rockies along the Idaho-Montana border. Since the westerlies are often found in this position, this track is by far the more frequently taken of the two.

Mountain weather has its own special winds and its own special clouds. Mountain ranges put bumps in the streams of air that cross them. The air traversing these bumps is forced to rise a little bit and, in rising, is cooled. If such a bumpy airstream is near its dew point, the air will be condensed in the upward parts of the bumps and reevaporated in the lower parts, making remarkable clouds that look like flying saucers. Because of their shape, the clouds are called lens clouds. If the condensation altitude of the atmosphere is lower than the top of the mountain, the clouds will actually sit on the top of the mountain or just upwind of its crest. Such clouds are called cap or banner clouds.

The Mountain Region also has its special winds. Warm, dry winds blow down the lee side of mountain ranges when moist air is being lifted up the windward side. These are the fierce Chinook winds that can wreak havoc in cities like Boulder, Colorado. Other kinds of mountain winds are the cold winds that blow down from high mountain valleys on still nights, the morning winds that blow across the floor of a valley from east to west when the rising sun shines on its western wall, and the evening winds that blow from west to east across the same valley when the setting sun shines on its eastern wall.

Gardening in the Mountain Region

As a general rule, the weather in the Mountain Region is dry, sunny, and mild. But this is a region where generalities are not very informative. Most of the crucial gardening parameters depend strictly on how high the garden is. Annual rainfall in the high country around the perimeter of the Mountain Region ranges from around twenty-five inches in the southeast to around eighty inches in the northwest. Rainfall in the lowlands averages less than twelve inches a year.

Altitude dictates not only rainfall but temperature as well. As a rough rule of thumb you should expect to lose 5 degrees of temperature for every 1,000 feet of altitude and every 200 to 300 miles of northward travel. These effects should add to each other, so that if you move up 1,000 feet *and* northward 250 miles you would expect to lose 10 degrees in average temperature. Such a move could trim several weeks off your growing season. Growing season varies from more than ten months in the southern lowlands to less than two months in the high country.

In consequence, people planning to do gardening in the mountain states should pick their locations with care. A trip to the local agricultural agent should be helpful. If he can't give you precise details about the growing season in your local area, he surely can give you the name of somebody who can.

The Great Plains Region

The Great Plains may have the most complex weather in the world. Modified maritime polar air frequently enters the area from the Mountain

Region. In addition, three highly contrasting types of air masses regularly visit the Plains Region: continental polar air from Canada, maritime tropical air from the Gulf Region, and continental tropical air from the mountain states. These air masses not only come from diverse sources, but they typically arrive in the region in a completely unmitigated form. Thus, the air mass contrasts which occur across the Plains Region are often highly extreme.

In addition to all the complexities arising from the interaction of contrasting air masses, the Plains Region experiences many phenomena imposed on its weather by its geography. The Plains are not a flat tablelike area, but in fact a gigantic inclined plane, rising from 1,000 feet on the east to over 5,000 feet on the west. This may not sound like much of a rise for a distance of more than a thousand miles, but it is enough to change the nature of the air moving over the Plains. For instance, winds blowing out of the east in advance of cyclones must

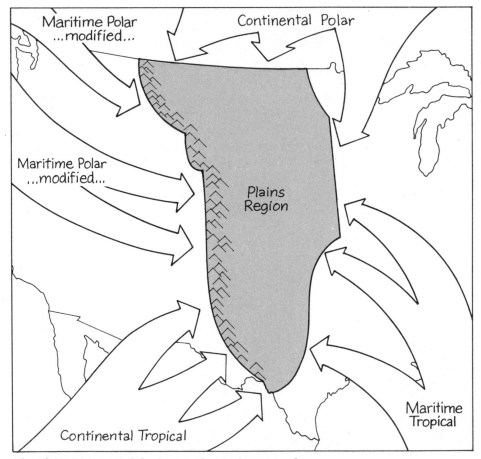

The Plains Region and the factors that make its weather.

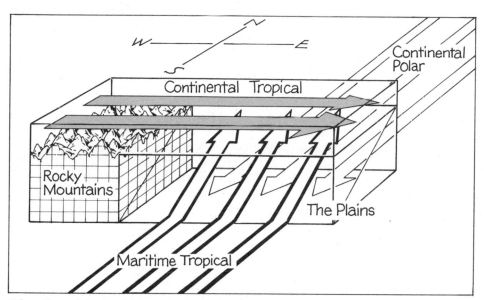

The effect of the Rockies upon Plains weather is to produce very complex laminated atmospheres. Here, a maritime tropical air mass is lifted by a continental polar air mass, while overhead, a continental tropical air mass from the Great Basin overrides all.

ride uphill just as if they were riding up the slope of a warm front. The lifting causes moisture condensation, but because the lifting is done by the earth itself, the cloudbanks sit right on the ground. The result is periods of drizzly, dank weather which Plains meteorologists call "upslope" weather.

The mountains just to the west of the Plains also have marked effects on Plains weather. These mountains make possible some extraordinarily complex laminated atmospheres above the Plains Region. In the late spring and summer, the intense heating of the sun in the Mountain Region makes air masses that are extremely warm and buoyant—either continental tropical air masses or highly modified Pacific maritime air masses. When these air masses move eastward off the Rockies they may float out on top of the air masses already occupying the Plains Region. For instance, it sometimes occurs that there is a stationary front running through the Plains Region when one of these hot, dry air masses intrudes at upper levels. When this occurs, the atmosphere can then have three distinct layers, each moving in a different direction.

The possibilities for meteorological mischief in this situation are almost limitless. The contrasting movements of the different layers can stimulate vigorous turbulence. If the upper-air westerlies further complicate the situation, by providing overhead one of those little disembodied cyclonic kinks, wild thunderstorms can result. The Great Plains has more severe local storms than any other place in the world. Oklahoma has more tornadoes than any equivalent area in the world and eastern Wyoming has more hailstorms.

Storm Tracks
and Typical Weather Patterns

The storm tracks that pass through the region are the extensions of the northern and southern tracks of the Mountain Region. Storms often intensify dramatically as they emerge from the mountains and make contact with the contrasting air masses that so often inhabit the Plains.

The area just east of the Rockies is a great breeding ground for new cyclones. As Great Plains storms form and press on eastward, they pull Gulf air up ahead of them, and polar air down behind them. These conditions bring terrible blizzards to the northern Plains and equally terrifying dry winds to the southern Plains. If weather has been dry and if fields are in a fallow condition, these cold, dry winds can bring the duststorms that earned the region the name, "Dustbowl."

Gardening in the Plains Region

Gardening or farming in the Great Plains requires greater-than-average agricultural fortitude. There are more ways to lose a crop to the weather in the Plains than anywhere else in the country. Flood, hail, wind, immoderate and unpredictable heat, immoderate and unpredictable cold are regular features of Plains weather. Compared with most places of the same latitude, the Plains have harsher summers and harsher winters. They have more days below freezing and more days above 90 degrees. They have shorter growing seasons and lower hardiness zones. Their rainfall is lower and less reliable. Everything about Plains weather suggests that gardeners in that region have reason to be proud of every leaf and fruit they bring to the table.

It is a bit unnerving to realize that as a nation we rely on this harshest and most unpredictable of meteorological environments to grow a high proportion of our grain supply.

A Final Word on Regions

When I set out to write these chapters on the weather in the different regions of the United States, I thought by the time I got done I would know where in the country I would most like to garden. Now that I've written them, I guess I think every section of the country has its good features and its bad ones.

If you asked the garden plants where they would want to live, most would vote for the Gulf Region. The warm summers and the mild, moist winters seem just about ideal for most plants. Although the summers are too hot to accommodate spring plantings of cool-weather crops like Brussels sprouts and spinach, these plants grow quite well if planted in the fall in the Gulf States. On the other hand, a number of cool-weather crops, like cabbage and peas, seem to respond particularly well to being grown in cool weather with an increasing daylength. For these conditions, the northern summer can't be beat.

Whatever the plants want, however, some consideration ought also to be given the gardener. As a gardener I might really like the quick, hot springs of the Plains or the lingering, mild autumns in the Lakes Region. Or I could really enjoy the stable, reliable climate of the Pacific Coast Region, or the sunny, mild weather of much of the Mountain Region. In my own region, I really enjoy the fact that rainfall is so copious. I don't like to irrigate. Water that comes from the sky just seems to do more good.

There just does not seem to be any one region that has all the advantages. In a village in central New England lives an old gentleman who inhabits a small cottage. This man has developed quite a reputation in the region not only for his skill as a musician but also for his gardening. Just outside the cottage is a tiny garden, tidy and lush, with a huge compost pile standing nearby. Just about May first of each year, the gentleman arrives in his bright yellow Volkswagen and moves into the cottage. Within hours, the garden is planted. During the summer, he plays his guitar on the front stoop of the cabin and tends that beautiful little garden. When fall rolls around, one by one, the crops are harvested and the soil tilled up until there is only a row of greens and one or two huge Brussels sprouts plants. And then suddenly they are gone. And so is the car. Local tradition has it that this same old gentleman has another cottage in south Florida. Just about November first of every year he arrives in his bright yellow Volkswagen. Within hours he has his garden planted.

Now *that's* what I call gardening with the weather.

Part Three

COPING
WITH THE WEATHER

10

HOW TO WATCH
A WEATHER FORECAST

There are two steps to coping with the weather. Knowing what to do about a particular set of weather conditions is the second of those steps. Boarding up your windows when a hurricane is coming, or covering your garden when frost is forecast, or watering your garden when a sustained heat wave threatens can make your household a safer place and your garden a more productive one. But the *first* step in coping with the weather is having early warning of what the weather is likely to be. With an accurate forecast, you can anticipate undesirable weather conditions and sometimes do something to mitigate them. The height of the gale is too late to board your windows. The time to water a dry garden is before it wilts, and the time to provide cover to a cold garden is before the temperature begins to fall. Consequently, coping with the weather means anticipating the weather and anticipating the weather means dealing with media weather forecasts.

I am sure that there are times in all of our lives when we would gladly throw a brick at the television. But the fact is that there are some jobs that television does exceedingly well. One of these jobs is the presentation of forecasts and other weather information. Mind you, television weather broadcasts can be just as exasperating as any other form of television. Traditionally, in television newsrooms, the weather forecast is viewed as a period of comic relief between the news and the sports. Each forecaster becomes either a wit or a butt in the local newsroom. Often the transitions from the news segment to the weather segment are accompanied not only by soap commercials but also by bad puns, meteorological calamity-mongering, low-caliber sage remarks, and obscure personal humor. What all this has to do with weather is beyond me, but unfortunately it must be borne if television weather forecasts are to make a contribution to your understanding of the weather.

The information that many TV weather broadcasts provide is extraordinarily complete. Professional forecasters of only a decade ago would have given their eyeteeth to have even half of the information that is broadcast

112

nightly by today's TV weatherpeople. But if you are going to get the most out of one of these broadcasts, you have to know what you are looking for. The presentations are rapid and accompanied by numerous distractions. This chapter will help you to be ready for the information, and help you to separate out the meteorological wheat from the TV chaff.

What to Look For

Conditions in the Local Region

Most broadcasts begin with a summary of conditions at or near the broadcast station. Often the report is of conditions at the nearest airport. Sometimes it may come from a city observatory or from instruments actually located at the broadcasting site. These reports will include, generally, the high and low temperature for the last twenty-four hours, the current temperature, the relative humidity and/or the dew point, the wind direction and velocity, the barometric pressure and trend, and sometimes the number of degree-days. Most of this information you can duplicate at your own home, so unless you're interested for some reason in the difference between your own weather and the weather at the station I would advise you to ignore most of this information. One type of information, however, is crucial. The dew point and relative humidity are difficult to get at home. These numbers give you invaluable information about how much water there is in the air. The dew point is the more useful of the two because it also tells you the temperature at which water will start to condense out of the air. Since the condensation and evaporation of water vapor is what makes weather go, it is a terribly important number. From it you can guess how likely a thunderstorm is on a summer evening and how likely a frost is on a winter one. If you are curious about how this one measurement can make such a difference, look ahead to the chapters on frost and thunderstorms.

Many stations give the temperature and the relative humidity but *not* the dew point. If that's what you're dealing with, don't panic. The dew point can be calculated from the temperature and the relative humidity with the help of a chart, such as the one on page 118.

The list of current conditions at the reporting station is usually followed by a map showing the temperature, wind condition, sky condition, and precipitation, if any. To fit all the information on the map the forecaster will often use symbols borrowed from United States Government weather maps. As the forecaster verbally summarizes the conditions in the region, look for sharp differences between the numbers on the map. Notice particularly differences in wind direction and temperature. Observe carefully the weather that is upwind of your position on the map. Very often the weather a hundred miles

(continued on page 116)

Understanding Weather Codes

Most newspaper and television weather maps make use of simplified versions of the symbols used by the National Oceanic and Atmospheric Administration (NOAA) to plot weather observations on their official weather maps. Using these codes, the information relevant to a particular locality is plotted directly on the map at that location. The cluster of numbers and codes for a particular weather station is called its station report. The illustration below shows a sample of a station report which NOAA prints with all its weather maps.

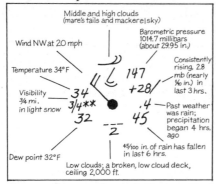

A sample weather station report. Source: Daily Weather Maps, U.S. Department of Commerce (Washington, D.C.: Government Printing Office, May 24–30, 1982).

At first glance the sample station report looks pretty complicated. But many of the symbols are designed to look like the thing they represent, so that more often than not, your intuitions about what a symbol means will probably be more or less correct.

Each station plotted on the map is represented by a circle. The proportion of the circle that is blackened in represents the sky condition, that is, the proportion of the sky that is covered with cloud. So ◐ is a sky with a few clouds, ◑ is a sky half covered with clouds, and ● is a sky almost completely covered. Wind direction is shown by a funny sort of arrow. It is funny because it is missing half of its feathers and has no head. The "arrow" is drawn with its head plunged into the sky-condition circle and with its feathers pointing toward the wind direction, as if the arrow had been flying in the same direction as the wind, just before it struck. The more feathers on the shaft the stronger the wind. Thus, ⌐○ is a 10-mile-an-hour northwest wind and ○⌐ is a 30-mile-an-hour southeast wind and ○⌐ is a 25-mile-an-hour northeast wind.

To indicate the kind of clouds covering the sky, the NOAA has thirty symbols that look more or less like the cloud represented. For instance ⌒ and ⌒⟋ represent different kinds of cirrus clouds, the wispy high clouds which we sometimes call "mare's tails." The symbol ⌣⌣ represents the puffy middle clouds we call a "mackerel sky," and ∠ is the thin veil of cloud that often obscures the sun just a few hours before a storm. The puffy "heap clouds" so common in the summer sky are represented by ⌒ . If the puffy cloud is heaped up high, the symbol is ⌒ . If it has a cirrus cap or "anvil" on it, as do most well-developed thunder-clouds, the symbol becomes ⌂ . A low, flat cloud deck is represented by ── ; if the deck has breaks in it, there are breaks in the symbol representing it, thus ─ ─ ─ . High and middle clouds are shown above the sky-condition circle, low clouds below. Just beneath the low cloud symbol appears a number which repre-sents the "ceiling" in thousands of feet. The ceiling is the altitude at which you would hit the cloud deck if you were climbing in an airplane.

To the left of the sky condition circle are plotted the temperature, visibility (how far the observer can see), the dew point, and a symbol representing what sort or sorts of weather phenomena were taking place at the time of the observation. To represent these phenomena, the map plotter has over a hundred different symbols at his disposal. Fortunately, many of the basic symbols look exactly like what they are supposed to represent, and many of the others are combina-tions of these basic symbols.

For instance, ＊ stands for light snow and ＊＊ stands for moderate snow. ．• indicates moderate rain, and ，， stands for light drizzle. If there is an S lying on its side, tangled up in the rain or drizzle symbols, then that precipi-tation is freezing as it falls. Thus ⌇ is light freezing drizzle. If a little triangle appears below a pre-cipitation symbol, then the precipi-tation is showery. Thus ⁎⁄▽ means that a light snowshower is in prog-ress. Once you get into the spirit of this system, you can guess the meaning of many of the symbols. ≡ is fog; ⹀ is light fog, and ≡≡ is patchy fog. ⌇⌇ means visibility obscured by smoke, ∝ means haze, ⩙ means a dust devil, and ⤵ means ... want to guess? You guessed right! Thunder and light-ning.

To the right and upper right of the station's sky-condition circle is plotted information about baromet-ric pressure. On government maps, the information is usually plotted in tenths of a millibar, the metric equivalent of inches of mercury. The first number, on the upper right, is the current pressure. It appears as a three-digit number. Since observations on the millibar scale are not often below 0940 or above 1040, the observer can omit the first two digits without fear of confusing anybody. Consequently, the number 147 in this position means that the pressure is 1014.7

(continued on next page)

Understanding Weather Codes *(continued)*

millibars, or just under 30 inches of mercury. Just beneath the present pressure number is a positive or negative number and a symbol. Together these represent the change in the barometer in the last three hours. The number is the change in tenths of a millibar. For example, +28 means that the pressure has risen 2.8 millibars in the last three hours. The symbol shows how that rise has come about. ⁄ means a steady rise, and ⌐\ indicates a rise followed by a fall. Had the barometer fallen, then risen, the symbol would have been \⁄ .

Finally, on the lower right of the station report appears information about the weather over the last six hours. This consists of a symbol representing the type of weather experienced, followed by a number of hours to represent how long the weather has been in progress.

If precipitation has been in progress during that time, the total accumulation is given in hundredths of an inch.

Now at last you're ready to read a station report from a weather map. Here's the station report for Springfield, Illinois, on the morning of July 15, 1970, at seven A.M.

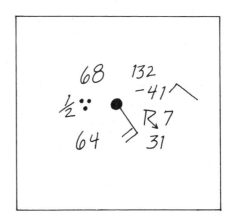

upwind will be your weather in only three or four hours. In the frost season, if you are watching a late-night broadcast, look for the lowest temperature on the map. If the temperatures anywhere on the map are near freezing, then you had better think about frost. If the map shows thunderstorms or heavy weather nearby, pay attention to what the forecaster says about its direction. If the bad weather is anywhere to the west of you, the chances are it will be yours pretty soon.

Radar Display

The regional observations will often be backed up by a radar display. Even in a large storm, heavy weather is usually quite a localized phenomenon.

What it tells you is that the temperature is 68 degrees, dew point is 64 degrees, wind is southeast at 20 miles per hour. Sky is overcast, visibility 1/2 mile in moderate rain. Barometric pressure is 1013.2 millibars, and has fallen 4.1 millibars in the last three hours, even though it began the period by making a slight rise. In the last six hours there was a thunderstorm. Precipitation has been in progress for seven hours and 31/100 of an inch of rain has fallen. (The height or type of overcast are not given on this report.)

Here is another station report, from Little Rock, Arkansas, on the same morning.

In Little Rock, the temperature is 73 degrees, the dew point 70 degrees, the wind southwest at 10 miles per hour. The sky is 1/4 overcast; visibility is 7 miles in haze. The overcast consists of both high and middle clouds. The pressure is 1020.1 millibars and has risen 1.2 millibars in the last three hours, most of that in the first two hours. There has been no significant weather in the past six hours.

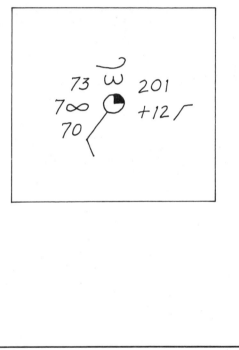

Because it is localized it can slip between the observing stations represented on the regional map. Some forms of weather, like downpours, hail, tornadoes, and snowsqualls can appear between the time that the reports are put on the map and the time the broadcast starts. The radar display gets around all these disadvantages.

The function of radar is to show the location of any severe precipitation or weather in your neighborhood. The radar image is generated by sending pulses of radio waves out into the atmosphere and then recording the echoes which bounce back from droplets of water, snowflakes, or hailstones in the atmosphere. The stronger a storm is, the larger are the droplets and crystals it can suspend aloft. The larger the droplet or crystal, the more intense the reflection. Therefore, the more intense the reflection, the more severe is the indicated weather. A bright radar image tells you that a cloud has a lot of energy in it for wind and a lot of moisture for precipitation.

In interpreting a radar display, it is crucial to be aware of the position of the antenna with respect to your own location. Some stations have their own radar systems. But most get their radar image by dialing special phone numbers which connect the station's videotape equipment to one of the radar installations maintained by the National Oceanic and Atmospheric Administration (NOAA). Since the forecaster can choose which location to dial, you may see displays from more than one antenna on the same channel. Fortunately, most

How Do I Estimate Dew Point from the Relative Humidity?

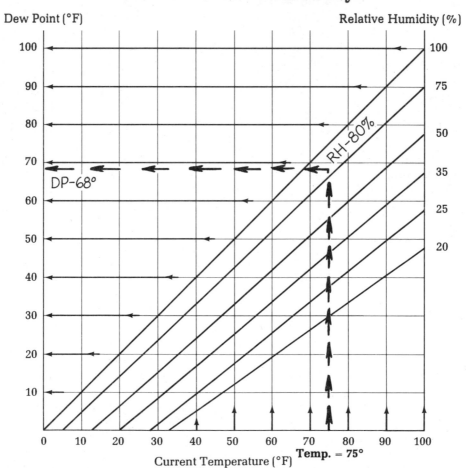

First, find your current temperature on the bottom scale. Then, move directly up until you hit the relative humidity line closest to your current relative humidity. Finally, go directly to the left-hand scale and read off your dew point. For example, if your temperature is 75° and the relative humidity is 80%, then the dew point is 68°.

radar displays include a schematic map, showing state boundaries or geographic features, so you can get your bearings. The location of the antenna is important because the images are less accurate at greater distances. Since the radar beam angles upward from the ground it can overshoot low clouds at distant locations. The further you are from the antenna, the worse the weather may be that hides beneath the beam of the radar.

The particular location is also important because every radar display has a pattern of "echoes" on it that have nothing to do with the weather. This pattern is reflection from nearby buildings, hills, and mountains, and meteorologists call it "ground clutter." Look at the radar display one day when no rain is falling so that you can learn the ground clutter pattern for your area. Knowing that pattern helps you to recognize significant echoes quickly when bad weather is in the offing.

Watch the radar display closely if you're interested in rain or snow, or if you're afraid of wind or hail. In winter, when you know the way weather systems are moving on a given evening, the radar display will often give you a good idea of how many more hours of rain or snow are left to come or how long it will be before rain or snow begins. During the thunderstorm season, the radar will often tell you if you're going to get relief from a drought or if you're going to get hail or gale winds. Where I live, we get about one tornado a year somewhere nearby. This is nothing to compare with Oklahoma, but still, on those hot summer afternoons when the air is stuffy and the thunder rumbles in the west, I sure like to know where the big storms are and which way they are moving.

Satellite Imagery

Most TV weather forecasters will make some use of satellite imagery during their broadcast. Satellite imagery consists of still or motion pictures of the clouds taken from some 20,000 miles out in space. Television stations are provided with single pictures and with animation loops, jerky motion pictures made of stills taken every fifteen minutes or so over a twelve-hour period. On most weather broadcasts, satellite pictures are the only clues you will be given to upper-air flow patterns. Inspect the stills for striations in the cloud patterns which indicate how the upper-air westerlies are blowing. Watch the animation loop for the movements of the clouds. Once you get a sense of how the clouds are flowing, look upstream of your location and see what cloud masses are bearing down on you. If the mass of cloud approaching you is compact and bright on the satellite picture, then you can expect some bad weather.

On late-evening broadcasts, the forecaster will sometimes present stills made with infrared light. Infrared imagery measures and converts to a visual image the heat radiated by the earth. Cool places show up as bright white spots. The method emphasizes high clouds, particularly in summer, because the tops of high clouds are very cool and show up as brilliant white areas. This technique is particularly effective in revealing the anvil tops of large thunder-

How a Surface Map Is Drawn

Once the meteorologist has plotted all the station reports, he can proceed to draw a surface weather map. Basically, the procedure is the same as the one we used to create a weather map from the observations of our gardeners in chapter 2. First, lines of equal pressure are drawn. These are essentially the same as the lines of equal pressure described in chapter 2, except that government meteorologists use the metric unit, millibars. A common separation between lines of equal pressure is 4 millibars, or about 12/100 of an inch. Once the lines of equal pressure are drawn, then centers of high and low pressure are identified and marked with H and L or High and Low. Now the meteorologist attempts to locate the fronts on the maps. He is looking, just as we did in chapter 2, for bands of rapidly changing weather with sharp temperature differences, wind shifts, changes in the direction of the barometer, and precipitation. Where he finds several such places arranged in a line, he draws a front. Fronts where cold air is replacing warm air are called cold fronts and are symbolized by ▼▼▼ . Fronts where warm air is replacing cold air are symbolized by ◢◣◢ . A stationary front is symbolized by ◢▼◢▼ . When a cold front has caught up to a warm front, forming a so-called occluded front, the representation is ◣▼◣▼ . Finally, the map is shaded where precipitation is falling. The result of all these steps, plotting the station reports, the isobars, finding the highs and lows and fronts, and shading in the precipitation, is a standard U.S. Weather Bureau surface chart, like the one reproduced here.

storms, which show as sharply defined white blobs on the picture. Sometimes these infrared images are computer enhanced. Computer-enhanced images are much more confusing to figure out, because the computer alters the "natural" gradation of the greys in the picture to increase its contrast. In an enhanced image, a black area is black either because it is very warm or because it is very cool. Since very warm areas and very cool areas are rarely near each other in the image, the enhancement will produce no confusion to forecasters who have a few minutes to study the picture. But in the five or ten seconds the TV station gives you to look at it, the enhanced image is harder to process. Look for the dark spots *within* lighter areas. These are your most active centers of weather.

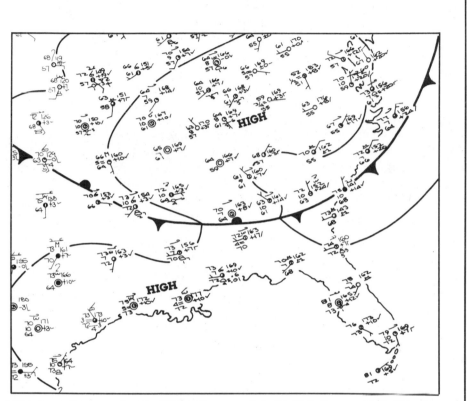

NOAA weather map for the U.S. at 7 A.M. on July 17, 1970. Source: Daily Weather Maps, U.S. Department of Commerce *(Washington, D.C.: Government Printing Office, 1970).*

The Surface Map

Next the forecaster will show you a surface map of the weather over the entire United States. The surface maps shown by forecasters vary tremendously from one forecaster to another. Some show you standard weather maps without station reports, including fronts, highs, lows, and lines of equal pressure called isobars. Others remove the isobars and shade in areas of precipitation. Still others show very schematic maps with a few fronts—highs, lows, raindrops, and snowflakes. I prefer the maps with the most information. These are usually the maps with isobars. The isobars permit me to form a visual image of the landscape of the atmosphere: not only where its high and low points are, but also where its ranges and valleys can be found. Trying to get a sense of the weather's action from a map without isobars is like trying to plan a mountain hike using a map without topographic lines.

When you are looking at the surface map, it is important to remember that you are looking at an interpretation of the weather, not a picture of the weather. The weather analyst who draws the maps puts the fronts on the map where he thinks they ought to be to provide the best interpretation of the station reports he is getting from around the country. On some days, all forecasters would agree on those placements; other days they would not.

Forecasters differ in the rules of thumb they use in placing fronts on a map. Some draw a front only where they see evidence of frontal zone activity: wind shifts, dew point changes, changes in sky conditions, etc. Other forecasters chart fronts on the assumption that there are always one or more continuous fronts that ring the globe from east to west. On such forecasters' maps, there will usually be two frontal boundaries across the map all the way from east to west. The assumption underlying maps with continuous fronts is that the surface features of the map are a manifestation of the upper-air streams. Since the streams are continuous from west to east across the country, so should fronts be continuous.

Even the simplest of these national weather maps contains a lot of useful information that must be grasped in a very short time. There are a couple of ways of thinking of these surface maps that makes them easier to comprehend. One method works particularly well for maps with continuous fronts. Think of the United States as being under the occupation of three forces: the cold forces from Canada, the warm forces from Mexico, and the moderate forces from the United States itself. When I turn on the TV weather in the evening, I prepare myself to see how the war is going between the forces of moderation on the one hand and the forces of immoderate cold and immoderate warmth on the other.

Another way to look at these maps is in terms of the movement and development of the storms on it. Looking at the weather map each evening becomes like an evening stroll in the garden, except that instead of looking to see how this little plant and that little shrub are getting on, you see about the fortunes of the various storms on the map. How is that little storm in the northern Rockies getting on? Has it traveled south to Kansas as it was expected to do? Is it growing? Is it being well nourished by warm air from the Gulf of Mexico? Is the storm giving a good account of itself? Is it bringing blizzards to Denver and tornadoes to Oklahoma City? That's my storm!

Whatever mnemonic device you use, it is fun, useful, and instructive to try to remember the weather map from day to day. As you look at the map, try to fix in your mind an image of it so that you can mull over that image after it is gone. Once you get good at remembering, you will be able to compare the image of today's map with your memory of yesterday's map and then project an image of tomorrow's map. When you start remembering such comparisons, you are doing what the professional weather forecasters are doing.

While the map is on the screen, the forecaster will be giving you his analysis of it. If you are less interested in making your own forecast and more interested in understanding what the forecaster thinks is going to happen, then you will want to expend more effort in listening to what he is saying and less effort in trying to memorize the map. During the analysis, the forecaster will tell you how the highs and lows are expected to move on the map and what potentials for storm development exist in their present positions. For instance, if there is a low poised off the Carolina coast and a high poised in southern Canada, he will talk about the possibility that the low will move northward and—drawing on the warm air above the Gulf Stream and the cold air in Canada—produce a massive snowstorm over the northeastern states. Or if there is a low over Wisconsin, a warm, wet mass over the Ohio River Valley, and a cold, dry air mass over the Plains, he will talk about the potential for tornadoes in the Ohio River Valley. Once you have listened to such analyses for a few months, you need only look at the map yourself to know what potentials exist for a given kind of weather situation.

The Upper-Air Chart

A very few forecasters will give you a representation of the upper-air currents. Since upper-air patterns are more stable than surface patterns, and since the surface features—the lows and highs—tend to flow in the upper-air streams, you usually can make your forecast almost as well as the forecaster once you have been shown both a surface and an upper-air map. If you know where a low was yesterday and you know where it is today, then you know how fast the stream is flowing. If the forecaster shows you which *way* the stream is flowing, then you can guess where the low will be tomorrow. If you know from experience what sort of weather you have at your location when lows are in that position, then that kind of weather is your weather forecast. What's more, it's a forecast made for *your garden*, not for some airport tarmac a hundred miles away.

My favorite TV forecaster is a genial little old man who wears rumpled tweedy clothing and glasses, talks with a gravelly voice, and rarely banters with the newsroom staff. The station is too poor to have a radar rig. At first glance his surface map seems a simple, primitive sort of thing. But superimposed on the surface features is a pattern of faint white lines crossing the country from west to east which indicates the upper-air flow patterns. Better still, the forecaster tells me what the government computers are predicting for the upper-air flow patterns. Armed with this information, I can make my own forecasts for twenty-four hours without ever going back to the TV. Plain as this man's weather broadcast is, I would sooner spend a minute with him than with any other forecaster in the Northeast.

The Forecast

Last in most weather broadcasts is the daily forecast. The voice of the forecaster will tell you what the weather will be for the next two to five days while the screen presents the printed forecast, usually superimposed on alluring slides of local, seasonal weather. The printed forecast on the screen is the forecaster's "best bet." But his patter in the background conveys additional crucial information. If he is a good forecaster he will give you some idea of his confidence in his forecast. Sometimes this information is given in the form of a percentage: a 50 percent chance of rain, or something of the like. What this means is that, out of a hundred times that the meteorological elements are arranged approximately as they are at this moment, rain will occur in fifty of them. Don't let the fancy language fool you. "A 50 percent chance of rain tomorrow" amounts to a statement that the forecaster doesn't know whether it's going to rain or not. A 30 percent chance of rain means that tomorrow it's most likely to do something other than rain.

When listening to the forecaster's patter, it's terribly important to keep in mind the alternatives the forecaster is considering and the consequences to you if one of those alternatives should happen to occur. If a forecast calls for a 70 percent chance of snow and the weather is fair, then you probably won't complain much. But if the forecast calls for a 70 percent chance of fair weather and it snows, you may wish you had made preparations. Remember, the snow that falls when there was a 30 percent chance of snow is just as slippery as the snow that falls when there was a 70 percent chance of snow.

During the gardening season, I often find that these probability forecasts encourage me in wishful thinking. My garden tends to be droughty, and I need to water it faithfully if we don't get rain for a while. When a week has passed without rain, I begin to watch the weather forecasts for signs of rainfall. In the summer around here, "a chance of showers" is a very common forecast. If I defer my watering every time I hear the forecaster offer me a chance of showers, I may have a pretty dry garden before the rain actually comes. Such forecasts are actually directed toward people for whom rain is an inconvenience and who are worrying about whether they should take a topcoat or an umbrella when they leave home. They worry about unexpected rain. I worry about the unexpected lack of rain. When I'm on my toes and I hear a forecast like "20 percent chance of a shower" I go directly out and water the garden. The forecaster is telling me that there is an 80 percent chance that it won't rain at all, and that is the outcome that I most fear.

In evaluating the forecast, you must keep in mind the relationship between your location and that of the people for whom the forecaster is primarily predicting. Most of the people who buy soap and headache remedies *live in cities.* Most organic gardeners *live outside cities.* In your locality, you may get a different kind of weather, you may get the same weather before or after, or you may get more or less intense weather than the city people. However, if you are savvy about your local weather, you can easily interpret the city forecast for your country weather. If you are upwind of the weather station, prepare to get your weather sooner than forecast. If you are nearer the storm track than the weather station, prepare to get more intense weather than is forecast. If you live near moderating influences like large bodies of water, prepare to have your weather moderated by them. If the storm track is going to carry the storm between you and the forecast station, you might expect totally different weather than is forecast: snow where they have fair skies and mild breezes, a cold rain where they have tropical thunderstorms.

After the Forecast

One of the nice things about having read this book is that you are going to be able to tell when a forecast is going wrong. Long before the local radio stations catch on and stop broadcasting the stale forecast from the night before, you will know that the weather is not developing as predicted. I take the greatest pleasure in second-guessing the professionals. One rainy winter night recently, the weatherpeople told me that our rainstorm was going to move rapidly off to the east. My bedroom windows face east, so when I woke in the morning and opened an eye, I knew I should see sunlight. When I didn't, I opened the other eye and watched the motion of the clouds. It wasn't from northwest to southeast, but from east-northeast toward south-southwest! I knew immediately that the forecast had not come true.The low center was still to the south of us. More bad weather to come. What did the forecaster say would happen if the storm didn't move as fast as predicted? Greater development? More cold air sucked into the system? SNOW? Better get a move on. Heave *ho!*

11

FORECASTING FROM THE END OF YOUR GARDEN

Gardeners, of all people, are most qualified to be amateur weather forecasters. We gardeners naturally notice weather because weather really makes a difference in our lives. An untimely bit of bad weather—a spring deluge, a summer hailstorm, an early fall freeze—can nullify weeks, even months, of conscientious work in the garden. And a favorable break in the weather, a well-timed hot spell in June, a particularly soft and gentle April, can bring forth such gardening miracles as the July 4th tomato and Bastille Day sweet corn. We gardeners are destined to be good weather forecasters because the weather *matters* to us.

Observing the Weather

The key to a good, do-it-yourself forecast is careful observation. Unlike a NOAA forecaster, who has reports from all around the country to work with, we do-it-yourself forecasters have to base our forecasts on what we can manage to observe from the ends of our gardens. To pull off this trick, we must develop a keen eye for the weather. As you stroll out to the end of your garden, observe the sky and ask yourself the questions that follow.

What Types of Clouds Are Overhead?

Clouds give you a great deal of information about the state of the
atmosphere: how much moisture is up there, which way the wind is blowing,

and how rapidly it is blowing. Meteorologists classify dozens of different cloud types. Just ten of these are useful for a do-it-yourself forecaster to recognize. To identify these ten types, you have to make three kinds of decisions about each cloud:

(1) Is a cloud a heap cloud, a layer cloud, or a filament cloud?
(2) Is precipitation falling from the cloud?
(3) Is it a high cloud, a middle cloud, or a low cloud?

Heap Cloud, Layer Cloud, or Filament Cloud?

If a cloud looks like a heap of cotton balls or a cauliflower head, it is some kind of "cumulus" cloud. The puffy white clouds that appear on fair, cool summer days are cumulus clouds. So, too, are the menacing mounds with yellowish tops and black undersides that build up on hot, sticky summer afternoons. If, on the other hand, a cloud is a dull, flat layer drawn out in horizontal strands or covering the sky like a veil, then it is a type of "stratus" cloud. Stratus gives the sky a most depressing and featureless appearance. A cloud which has some of the characteristics of both stratus and cumulus is called "stratocumulus." The flattened grey rolls of clouds so often seen at the beginning and end of storms are stratocumulus clouds.

Stratus and cumulus clouds have very different implications for the state of the atmosphere. A stratus cloud suggests that the atmosphere is organized into stable horizontal layers. This kind of atmospheric structure most commonly occurs when warm, moist air overruns cooler, drier air. The presence of warmer air above cool air inhibits cloud development in the upper levels of the cool air and encourages cloud development in the lower levels of the warm air layer. Consequently, when you are looking at a bank of stratus, you are usually looking up through the cold air mass at the bottom of a warm air mass. As we saw in chapter 2, this sort of overrunning occurs in advance of cyclones where the warm front is pushing ahead against the cold air.

Cumulus clouds, on the other hand, suggest a turbulent atmosphere. As we saw in chapter 6, a cumulus cloud is made when air is lifted up and cooled below its dew point. The force that lifts the air arises from the fact that lower layers of the atmosphere are relatively warmer than higher levels, and the atmosphere is tending to roil like heated water in a pan. The cumulus clouds represent the rising currents of air, the clear air between them the falling currents of air. The taller the cloud, the greater is the extent of the turbulence and the more the cloud suggests that showery or squally weather is on the way.

If a cloud is all white and looks like thin filaments of goose down or milkweed floss, then it is called a "cirrus." Cirrus clouds are so delicate and insubstantial that they do not appreciably dim the sun or moon or blur the edges of the sun or moon's disk. A cirrus cloud which is gathered in tiny balls is called "cirrocumulus." A cirrus cloud which is drawn out in a featureless sheet or matted network of filaments is called "cirrostratus."

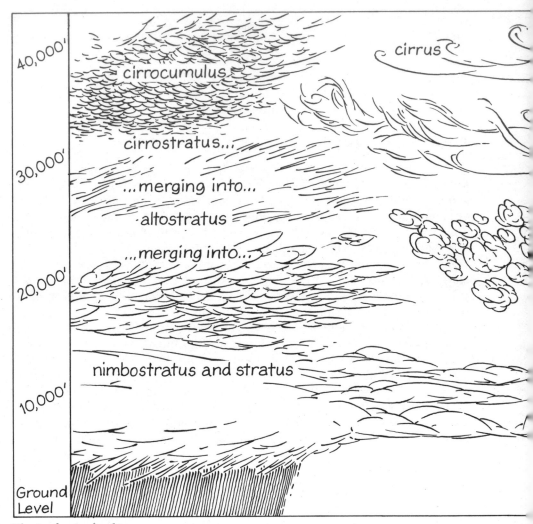

40,000'

cirrocumulus

cirrus

cirrostratus...

30,000'

...merging into...

altostratus

...merging into...

20,000'

nimbostratus and stratus

10,000'

Ground
Level

The ten basic cloud types.

Is Precipitation Falling from the Cloud?

If a cloud has substantial precipitation falling from it, it is called a "nimbus" cloud: nimbostratus if it's a stratus cloud; cumulonimbus if it's a cumulus cloud. Cumulonimbus clouds often grow to great heights in the atmosphere and are often capped by thin, flat cirrus veils called "anvils." Because cumulonimbus almost always bring thunder and lightning, most gardeners I know call them "thunderheads."

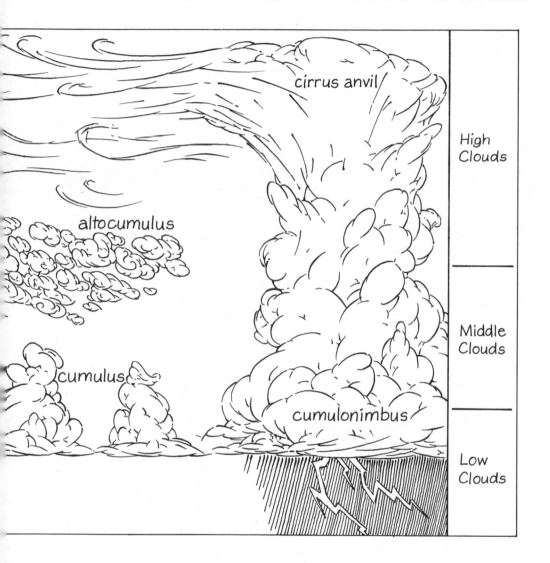

Are the Clouds High, Middle, or Low Clouds?

Guessing at the altitude of a cloud is easier to do than it is to describe: high clouds simply look further away than low clouds. In general, the lower a cloud is, the less well defined are its features, the larger its elements appear, and the taller it is likely to appear relative to its width. Lower clouds usually have dark undersides and a solid, bulky look. Higher clouds, on the other hand, appear comparatively thin. Their features are more detailed, finer, usually more distinct. Higher clouds lack dark bottoms and the sun's disk can be sharply seen through them.

Meteorologists classify clouds in three altitude groupings: high clouds (above 20,000 feet), low clouds (under 7,000 feet), and middle clouds (between 7,000 and 20,000 feet). Middle clouds are given the special prefix "alto" by weatherpeople. Consequently, a cumulus cloud at middle altitudes is called an "altocumulus." The most difficult problem in gauging the altitude of clouds from the ground is distinguishing middle clouds from the other two kinds. High clouds can be told from middle clouds generally because high clouds are always cirrus clouds. Cirrus clouds appear so wispy and insubstantial because they are wholly composed of ice crystals. Only at the highest altitudes is the atmosphere cold enough to convert all of its water droplets to ice crystals. Consequently, anytime you see a cirrus cloud, you can safely assume it is higher than 20,000 feet—definitely a high cloud. All high clouds, therefore, usually bear the prefix, "cirro."

Giving a rule of thumb to distinguish middle from low clouds is more difficult. Low clouds have dark grey undersides and usually obscure the sun completely. They often have a ragged, unkempt appearance. Middle clouds have pale grey undersides. The sun (or moon) is always visible through middle clouds, but it is substantially dimmed and its outlines are indistinct. Some middle clouds can be identified because they come in highly recognizable and familiar patterns. For instance, altocumulus gives the sky a flocked appearance with blobs of white alternating with blue spots in between. Some readers may recognize it as a "mackerel sky." Altostratus is familiar as the grey veil of cloud that often obscures the sun several hours before a storm begins. If you see either of these patterns, you can be sure that you are dealing with middle, rather than low clouds.

Particularly with stratus clouds, the altitude of the cloud tells you something about the imminence of bad weather. Clouds generally lower and thicken as bad weather approaches, so the lower a cloud deck, the sooner you can anticipate that the rain will begin.

Which Way Are the Clouds Moving?

Once you have a bit of middle or high cloud in view, figure out which way it is moving. Determining the direction of movement can sometimes be more complicated than it would seem. Let's say for the moment that a layer of high clouds, with very neat, easily observed features is moving over you from west to east. If you look at the clouds to the west of you, they will appear to be moving directly east. So far so good. But when you look at the clouds to the northwest of you, they appear to be moving off in a northeasterly direction, and clouds in the southwest sky appear to be running off toward the southeast. Could it be that the clouds are parting over your head as over some giant reef?

No, it couldn't. The clouds are all moving due east, but because of perspective they appear to spread out as they come overhead, the clouds on the north side appearing to move a bit northward, the clouds on the south side a bit south. If you turn around, you'll find the process is reversed. As the same clouds recede toward the eastern horizon, they appear to come together again. The phenomenon is related to a meteorological oddity called "Noah's ark." Sometimes, clouds arrange themselves in parallel bands with clear places in between called "streets." If a sky has very long, compact streets which stretch from horizon to horizon, they will appear to spread and converge overhead like the gunwales of a ship. The streets are of course parallel, and only appear wider overhead because they are closest to the observer. Noah's ark is an optical illusion.

The best place to judge the direction of cloud movement is directly overhead. Near the zenith, perspective effects are minimized, since all the clouds are comparatively close to the observer. If you are not blessed with any clouds at the zenith, however, or if you are too lazy to crane your neck, then I can suggest some other tricks. If you look in the general direction that the clouds are coming from, some of them will appear to be going off to the right, some to the left. The clouds which are moving neither to the right nor to the left are coming right for you.

Often, you will find yourself trying to judge the motion of clouds that are not conveniently placed in the sky upwind or at the zenith. In this case you will have to do your best to guess their actual motion from their apparent motion, being sure to take into account the effects of perspective.

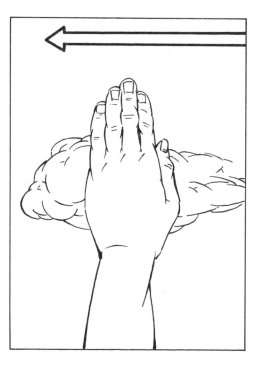

Holding your arm outstretched above your head, you can measure the speed of high clouds by timing how long it takes them to traverse the width of your hand.

How Rapidly Are the Clouds Moving?

If you have fixed a cloud in view and know what direction it is moving, you might as well take another minute to determine how rapidly it is moving. The width of your hand, held directly above your head with your arm fully extended, covers about a half mile of sky at the level of middle clouds, and about a mile of sky at the level of high clouds. Therefore, if middle clouds are moving at a hand-width a minute, they are moving about 30 miles an hour. High clouds moving about a hand-width a minute are traveling about 60 miles an hour. Two hands a minute gives you 60 miles an hour for middle clouds and 120 miles an hour for high clouds. Winds in the middle to upper atmosphere frequently blow at 60 miles per hour. Middle or high clouds moving much faster than 60 miles per hour suggest that the upper-air stream is flowing rapidly. Motions much slower than 60 miles per hour suggest that the stream is flowing slowly. In combination with other information, you can use upper-air wind speeds to predict the intensity of oncoming weather and the speed with which it will come. I'll explain how in a few pages.

Is There Any Significant Layering or Patchiness in the Clouds?

As you are rounding out your cloud observations, make a mental image of the way the clouds are organized in the sky. Pay close attention to any differences in direction or speed between the clouds at different altitudes. Such differences can be very significant. Inspect the sky for any systematic differences in cloud cover between different parts of the sky. Are the clouds lower, thicker, and denser on the one side of the sky and are they higher, thinner, and lighter on the other? Depending on the clarity of the atmosphere, the angle of the sun, and the speed at which the clouds are traveling, you often have in view several hours of cloud progress from your vantage point on the ground. If part of the sky is cloudy and part is clear, and the line between clear and cloudy weather is moving toward you, it is a simple matter to estimate how soon the sky will clear. Because of perspective, it will take clouds about the same time to climb one-third of the way up in the sky as it takes to climb from there to the zenith. If you see clouds on the horizon at nine A.M., and one-third of the way up at ten A.M., you can bet that the sky will be half cloudy by eleven, mostly cloudy by noon, and completely cloudy by one P.M.

What Is the Surface Wind Direction?

In chapter 1, I already discussed ways for judging the wind direction on the ground. Unfortunately, wind direction on the ground is not always precisely what meteorologists mean by the surface wind direction. To a meteorologist, the surface wind is the regional circulation of air, not the little puffs and eddies that swirl around local geographic features. There are some situations in which local wind direction will not give you very good evidence of the regional surface wind flow. For instance, if you live on the side of a valley, you know that night winds blow down the slope of the valley on a still night. If you live next to a large body of water, you know that sea or lake breezes blow from the body of water toward the land on still, warm afternoons. Since these local winds are not part of the general atmospheric circulation, they may be misleading.

There are a few rules which can help you decide how much you should trust a local breeze as an indication of surface wind flow. In general, a stronger wind is more trustworthy than a weaker wind. Steady winds with a constant wind direction are more trustworthy than gusty, variable breezes. Winds observed early in the morning and at dusk are more reliable than winds observed in the midafternoon when the sun's heat fosters local breezes. Finally, winds that are moving in the same direction as *low* clouds are more to be relied upon than winds that are not. These rules sound complicated, but, really, basic good common sense applies. If you use the rules for a few seasons, you will soon come to know your local breezes and learn to discount them in estimating surface winds.

How Fast Is the Surface Wind Blowing?

In judging wind speed, it is useful to bear in mind that the effects of wind increase rapidly as its speed increases. A 10-mile-an-hour wind is a gentle breeze. Leaves move, the weather vane turns, a small flag is gently unfurled. A 20-mile-an-hour wind is already an irritant. That wind that last Sunday made it impossible for you to read your newspaper on the lawn beside the garden— that was a 20-mile-an-hour breeze. Not only do Sunday supplements blow around, but small branches move in the trees, leaves dance and rush, and small trees sway. A 30-mile-an-hour wind is usually unpleasant to be out in. If you encounter a 30-mile-an-hour wind in a city street, you have to lean into it and push a bit to get through. If you find yourself confronted by the wind, in any sense, as you move about the yard, you are probably dealing with a 30-mile-an-hour wind. Winds much greater than 30 miles an hour are fairly unusual and we will save our discussion of them until the chapter on hurricanes.

How High Is Your Barometer?

The terms "high" and "low" for barometric pressure are a holdover from the days when a barometer was a tall tube of mercury, like a huge thermometer. Nowadays, a barometer is a dial with a needle, more like a speedometer. Most barometers are still calibrated in "inches of mercury" with 29 inches to

Beaufort Scale of Wind Speeds and Effects

Beaufort Number	Miles per Hour	Force	Effects
0	less than 1	Calm	Smoke rises vertically; no visible movement
1	1–3	Light air	Smoke drift shows wind direction; tree leaves barely move; wind vanes don't move
2	4–7	Light breeze	Wind can be felt on face; leaves rustle; small twigs move
3	8–12	Gentle breeze	Leaves and small twigs in constant motion; dry leaves blow up from ground; light flags extended
4	13–18	Moderate breeze	Small branches move; raises dust and loose paper
5	19–24	Fresh breeze	Large branches and small trees in leaf begin to sway; small crested waves form on inland water
6	25–31	Strong breeze	Large branches in constant motion; telephone wires whistle; umbrellas hard to handle
7	32–38	Moderate gale	Whole trees in motion; inconvenient to walk against the wind
8	39–46	Fresh gale	Twigs and small branches break off trees; walking is difficult
9	47–54	Strong gale	Bricks loosened on chimneys; roof slates or tiles blow off; ground is littered with broken branches
10	55–63	Whole gale	Trees uprooted; considerable structural damage to buildings
11	64–75	Storm	Widespread damage
12	75 and over	Hurricane	Severe and extensive, disastrous damage

the left, 30 inches to the right, and 29.50 in the center of the scale. The scale is broken down into tenths of an inch and sometimes smaller markings as well. (If you want to learn more about barometers, look in chapter 17.) Under average weather conditions, the barometer reads around 29.95 inches, or just to the left

Observing Natural Weather Indicators

According to a long tradition of weather lore among farmers and country dwellers, the natural world offers all sorts of clues to the approach of rain.

For instance, certain flowers, such as the scarlet pimpernel, dandelion, and daisy are said to close up when it's going to rain. Milkweed closing at night is also taken as a sign of rain. Various trees, among them the lilac, cottonwood, poplar, sugar maple, and sycamore, warn of bad weather by showing the lighter undersides of their leaves. The scent of flowers is particularly noticeable before a rain. It is also said that when the wind makes a hollow sighing sound as it rustles through the trees in a wood, rain is on the way.

Animal behavior is another traditional indicator of bad weather. Farmers say that their cows stay close to the barn and either lie down and chew their cud or gather in a corner of the field and turn their tails to the wind when stormy weather is approaching. Goats, too, are said to turn tail to the wind when it's going to rain. Fish splash around near the surface of the water, and spiders spin only short webs (they spin longer webs in nice

weather). It is also commonly believed that bees stay in the hive or fly only short distances when rain is coming. And it's been said that stormy weather can be expected when ants travel in lines, and fair weather is due when they scatter.

Another traditional saying is that birds fly high when the barometer is high, and stay low when the barometer is low. Robins and blackbirds, it is said, don't sing from the treetops as they do in sunny weather, but stay low in the branches when bad weather is imminent. And when the birds stop singing altogether, rain and thunder are probably on the way.

Some dogs seem to be able to sense an approaching thunderstorm long before it becomes evident to people, and grow very restless. Rabbits, too, can detect a thunderstorm when it's still far away— they tend to sit still, with only their ears twitching. And cats, it has been said, give clues of their own: when they lick their coats against the grain, the weather will be bad; but when they wash themselves normally, it's a sign of fair weather to come.

of 30 inches. A barometer above this average value is "highish," a barometer below average is "lowish." Below 29.70, I would call a barometer definitely "low" and above 30.20 I would call it "high." Readings below 29.55 and above 30.45 are very low and very high respectively.

Is the Barometer Falling or Rising?

If you regularly check your barometer for height, it is a small additional effort to check it for trend. Most barometers have a pointer needle to help you remember what the last reading was. Each time you read the barometer, set the pointer over the registering needle. The next time you go to the barometer, gently tap the glass to set the registering needle and then observe the difference between its position and the pointer needle's position. A movement of less than 1/20 of an inch per hour (half of a tenth) is slow movement. A movement of 1/20 to 1/10 of an inch per hour is a rapid change, and a movement of more than 1/10 of an inch per hour is a very rapid movement. The longer a time period over which these rates of movement are sustained, the more significant they are and the more attention you should pay to them.

What Is the Temperature?

Temperature, more than any other weather measure, is affected by the sun, so as you make your observations, try to compare them to the same time yesterday. If today's reading is colder or warmer than yesterday's reading at the same time, that fact may be significant. In addition, temperatures should rise during the forenoon hours and fall during the late-afternoon and evening hours. If you observe rising temperatures in the evenings, or falling temperatures in the morning, these trends are particularly significant.

How Humid Is the Air?

Unless you have special instruments to measure the air's humidity, you are going to have to infer it. One clue is the clarity of the atmosphere. Clear visibility over very great distances is a sign of low humidity. Haze, or blueing of distant hills, or obscuring of distant landmarks is a definite sign of high humidity. If the moon or sun are reddened in an otherwise cloudless sky, then high humidity is indicated. Another clue is the amount the temperature falls overnight. If the temperature falls 30 degrees or more from sunset to sunrise, then you know that the air has very little moisture in it. If the temperature falls only slightly overnight and mists quickly form at nightfall, then moisture levels in the atmosphere are high.

Making Your Forecast

Once you have made your observations you are ready to try your hand at forecasting. You will fit your observations together in various ways to make educated guesses about your weather situation and how it will develop. You need to figure out what sorts of weather systems are nearby, how they are likely to move and develop, and what weather they are likely to bring you.

Inferring the Weather Systems in Your Vicinity

From the information gathered about local wind direction and speed, you can determine the location of high- and low-pressure centers in your vicinity. Stand with your face toward the wind and extend your right arm straight out and a little behind the plane of your body. You are now pointing in the general direction of the center of low pressure near you. Now, extend your left arm out

You can find the nearest centers of low and high pressure by facing into the wind and extending your arms as shown here.

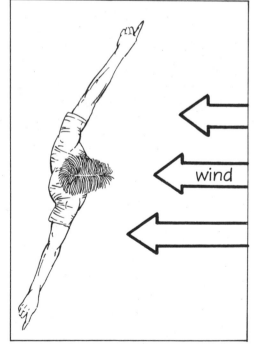

and a little in front of the plane of your body. This arm now points toward the nearest center of high pressure.

This method assumes that the pattern of winds around the low and high areas is approximately circular. This assumption is usually safe, except very near to fronts. In this case, the method will often induce you to point toward the front itself with your right arm rather than at the low center to which the front is connected. This error occurs because fronts are themselves local centers of low pressure. If you have reasons to believe that you are in a frontal zone—rapid changes in the temperature are taking place, the barometer is changing direction, and/or the winds are shifting very sharply—then you might delay for a few hours your attempt to locate the highs and lows.

Your judgments about highs and lows in your vicinity can often be confirmed by looking at low and middle clouds. If the arm-pointing procedure tells you that you have a high to the east and a low to the west, usually the clouds will confirm this fact by being thicker, lower, and/or more continuous to the west than they are to the east. On the other hand, if the arm-pointing procedure tells you that you have a high to the west and a low to the east, then usually the clouds will confirm this fact by being thicker, lower, and/or more continuous to the east.

Determining the Likely Future Movement of the Weather Systems in Your Vicinity

Weather prediction is helped enormously by visualizing the weather systems as rafts floating along in the upper-air westerlies. Let us imagine that the wind in your face tells you that you have high pressure to the northeast of you and low pressure to the southwest. If the stream were moving from the southwest to the northeast, then the low-pressure system would be "upstream" of you and you would have every reason to expect some bad weather.

How different would be your expectations if the upper-air stream were moving from northwest to southwest! In that case you would have every reason to expect that the low would be swept off to the south of you and never come any closer than it is now.

Notice that the position of the low with respect to your location is the same in both examples. What differs is the direction of flow of the upper-air stream.

If you have some way of determining which way the upper-air stream is flowing at a given moment, then you are in a much better position to gauge how the weather systems in your vicinity are likely to move. Cirrus clouds are the best indicators of the movement of upper-air winds. Next best are middle clouds, but remember to compensate for their lower altitude when you estimate their speed of movement. All cirrus clouds and most middle clouds flow along in the upper-air stream. Therefore, the direction of the movement of

Here's an example of how you can use your knowledge of the upper-air stream to predict movements of cyclones in your vicinity. Left, the system is moving from southwest to northeast, with the observer upstream from it. In this case, the low-pressure area is moving toward you. Right, the system is moving from northwest to southeast. In this case, the low is moving away from you.

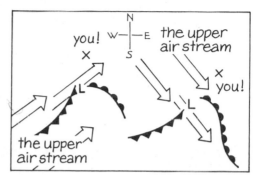

these clouds is the direction of flow of the stream. Since weather systems float along in the upper-air stream, the movement of high clouds tells you which way the weather systems in your vicinity are likely to move. By using the clouds to infer the direction of the stream, you can tell which weather systems are coming at you, which are going away from you, and which are sliding by you on one side or the other.

You can also use your high cloud observations to make inferences about the likely development of the weather systems bearing down on you. You will recall that the shape of the upper-air stream sometimes affects the weather systems that float along in it. If the upper-air stream flows directly from west to east, then the weather systems simply travel along in the flow and are relatively unaffected by it. Meteorologists call this sort of pattern a "zonal flow." Storms zip across the country from west to east with little development. Each geographic zone tends to have changeable weather, but weather that is more or less appropriate to its location and season. But if the stream is distorted into great meanders, then these meanders slow the progress of the weather systems and intensify them in systematic ways. The part of a meander from the peak of a ridge eastward to the bottom of the next trough strengthens the high-pressure systems that flow through it and weakens the low-pressure systems. Contrariwise, the part of the meander from the depths of a trough eastward to the peak of the next ridge tends to strengthen low-pressure centers and weaken high-pressure centers.

The extent of these effects depends on the speed of the winds in the upper-air flow. Faster winds move surface systems along rapidly if the winds are straight west-to-east winds. When the upper-air stream meanders, however, then faster upper-air winds have a different effect. They convey more energy to the surface weather systems but do not necessarily move them more rapidly. Consequently, evidence of high wind speeds overhead is an ambiguous sign. Depending on the shape of the flow, rapid speed may mean that weather systems are moving especially rapidly or it may mean that they are likely to be especially intense.

Fortunately, the direction of upper-air winds over your location often gives clues to the shape of that flow upstream of you. Upper-air winds blow from southerly directions on the east side of a trough, from northerly directions on the east side of a ridge. The more from the south the cirrus clouds originate, the more likely it is that you have a trough to the west of you. You would therefore expect that any low-pressure systems that floated down the stream would be intensified and high-pressure systems would be weakened. On the other hand, the more from the north the cirrus clouds are moving, the more likely it is that you have a ridge to the west of you. In this case, you would expect any low-pressure areas which came along in the stream to be weakened and high-pressure areas to be strengthened.

Cirrus cloud movements directly from the west or thereabouts are more ambiguous. They could mean that you are in a general west-to-east wind flow or that you are at the peak or the depth of one of the ridges or troughs in a meandering flow. The clue to resolving the ambiguity is in your barometer's behavior.

Upper-air ridges tend to capture high-pressure areas beneath them. Consequently, if the barometer is steady and high, and cirrus clouds are flowing west to east, then you are probably under the peak of a ridge. The weather should remain fair for at least a day, perhaps several. If the barometer is steady and low and the cirrus is moving west to east, then you are probably under the bottom of an upper-air trough. Your weather will remain unsettled for a while. Expect only slow improvement of your weather at best. Finally, a variable barometer with the same high cloud movement would suggest a zonal or straight west-to-east flow of weather systems. Expect rapid changes in your weather.

These upper-air indications are most useful if cirrus cloud movements suggest that the upper-air flow is steady from a single direction. Upper-air flows usually change very slowly. But sometimes, upper-air patterns aren't so slow to change. Small troughs can flow in the upper-air westerlies, just like eddies can flow in a stream or ripples can travel down a length of clothesline. These ripples in the westerlies show up from the ground as hourly changes in the direction of movement of the cirrus clouds overhead. When these changes occur, you will want to revise your forecast to account for them. Clockwise changes in the direction of cirrus cloud movements suggest that a ridge is moving toward you in the stream. Under these circumstances, you might want to make a more optimistic forecast than the present indication could usually warrant. On the other hand, counterclockwise changes in the movements of cirrus clouds suggest that a trough is moving toward you. You might, in this case, want to make a more pessimistic forecast than you usually would under your present conditions.

All the forecasting indications from high cloud movements are summarized in the chart on Upper-Air Indications.

Once you have made an inference concerning the future movements of a weather system upstream of you, you can check that inference by observing how the winds and barometer behave in the next few hours. In general, falling barometers and rising winds confirm the departure of a high-pressure system and the approach of a low-pressure system. Rising barometers and rising winds confirm the departure of a low-pressure system and the approach of a high-pressure system. But you can tell a bit more. If the winds remain steady from one direction as the system approaches, you can be sure that it is approaching you straight on. If, on the other hand, the wind shifts, then the manner in which it shifts will tell you whether the low-pressure system is passing off to your north or to your south. A northward passage is indicated by a clockwise shifting of the winds, a southward passage indicated by a counter-clockwise shifting of the winds.

Upper-Air Indications

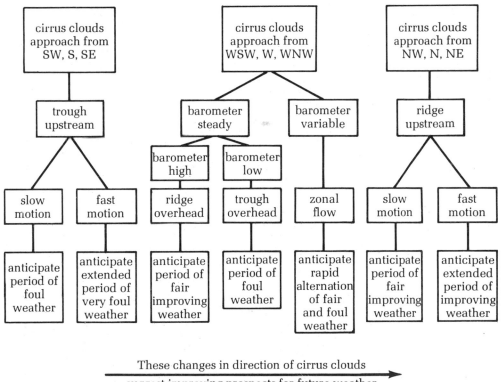

The combination of wind and barometer observations can also be used to infer how intense an approaching low-pressure system is and how rapidly it is approaching. The problem in making such an inference is separating out the effects of rapid movement and great intensity. A shallow low moving rapidly, or a deep low moving slowly both produce a rapidly falling barometer, winds shifting from the foul weather half of the compass, and rapidly increasing cloud cover. But the two situations will bring dramatically different weather. A

Barometer and Surface Wind Indications

WIND			BAROMETER				
			RISING		FALLING		STEADY
			RAPID	SLOW	RAPID	SLOW	
Shifting	Clockwise	Light	⇒ℓ (x)	→ℓ (x)	ℓ⇒ (x)	ℓ→ (x)	?
		Brisk	⇒L (x)	→L (x)	L⇒ (x)	L→ (x)	?
	Counter-clockwise	Light	(x) ⇒ℓ	(x) →ℓ	ℓ⇒ (x)	ℓ→ (x)	?
From foul weather half toward fair		Brisk	(x) ⇒L	(x) →L	L⇒ (x)	L→ (x)	?
Not shifting, steady: From single direction		Light	x⇒ℓ	x→ℓ	ℓ⇒x	ℓ→x	ℓ nearby or L at distance
		Brisk	x⇒L	x→L	L⇒x	L→x	L nearby

→x north passage   →x direct approach   x→ south passage

L strong low   ℓ weak low   ⇒ rapid movement   → slow movement

L→x low approaching   x→L low departing

rapidly approaching weak storm will bring a few showers soon. A slowly approaching, intense storm will strike less quickly but will bring a sustained period of precipitation and strong winds.

The clue to telling the two situations apart is the wind speed. The wind speed at your location is determined by your local pressure gradient. That gradient is the "slope" of the pressure difference across your region. Just as a hiker might move faster down a steep mountain, the wind moves faster down the "slopes" of a steep high- or low-pressure area. Consequently, a high wind speed accompanied by a slow and sustained barometer drop is an almost certain sign of the slow approach of an intense system; on the other hand, low wind speeds accompanied by rapidly changing barometer is an almost certain sign of the rapid approach of a weak system.

The chart on Barometer and Surface Wind Indications summarizes these relationships. The chart gives you what may be inferred from various combinations of barometer and wind observations. To figure out what's going on with your weather, look at the cell of the chart that corresponds to your present circumstances. Is your barometer rising or falling? Rapidly or slowly? Is the wind light or brisk? Is the wind steady or shifting? Is the shift clockwise or counterclockwise? When you know the answers to these questions, find the cell in the chart that corresponds to these answers. Each cell is like a little schematic map with you at the "X" in the center. The map is designed to show you whether the low is making a northward or southward passage and whether it is approaching or departing.

Inferring the Weather an Approaching System Will Bring

Once you have determined that a low-pressure area is going to pass close to your location, your forecast will depend a great deal on whether you expect it to pass just to the north or just to the south of you. The weather near a low center can be extraordinarily diverse, and a few hundred miles north or south can determine whether you get blizzards or tornadoes out of the same storm. Once you have used your analysis of the surface winds and upper-air stream to predict a storm's passage, you should constantly update that prediction by watching the shifting of the winds as the storm develops; remember, clockwise shifting suggests a northward passage, counterclockwise shifting, a southward one.

When a low-pressure system is passing to the north of you, the critical issue for you to bear in mind is your position with respect to the storm's warm sector. In such a northward passage, most of the precipitation will occur in advance of the warm front. After the warm front goes by, the weather will become mild and showery at worst, possibly sunny and warm. With the approach of the cold front, you can anticipate showers, squalls, thunderstorms, and a rapid drop in temperature. Barometric pressures usually fall most rapidly in advance of the warm front, rise most rapidly behind the cold front, and are comparatively steady in the warm sector, since the storm is moving more or less parallel to your location.

One factor that is extremely difficult to judge from the end of your garden is the size of the warm sector that is going to pass over you. The warm sector, you will recall, is the part of the cyclone where the warm, moist air is at the ground. Warm sectors can vary from week-long baths of unseasonably balmy air at one extreme, to a momentary sunny hiatus between the warm front rains and the cold frontal squalls. Or the warm front may be occluded and therefore not observable at ground level at all. The only surface indications of such an occluded warm sector may be an hour or so of amorphous weather accompanied by a bottoming-out of the barometer as the low slips by.

On a southward passage, the weather is more homogeneous than the weather on a northward passage. In general, as the winds move counterclockwise and increase, the barometer falls, the temperature may rise a little, and the precipitation intensifies. About halfway along in the storm's passage, these trends reverse: the temperature begins to fall again, the barometer to rise, the precipitation to taper off, and then finally, the winds begin to diminish.

This transition occurs approximately at the point that the low center is "beside" you in the stream. One way to identify this point in the passage of the storm is to compare the movements of the upper-air stream with the position of the low center estimated by surface winds. The high clouds may be difficult to see in the midst of a storm making a southward passage, so you may have to rely on your memory of the direction of the stream. Remember that the worst weather often occurs just as the storm is beginning to pull away. This warning is particularly appropriate for the "backside" of a winter storm in which the combination of falling temperatures, increasing winds, and high moisture aloft may generate blizzard conditions.

The more intense the low-pressure system, the more intense will be each of the phases of its passage. The warm front will produce more general rain, the warm sector will be more unseasonably warm, the cold front will be more squally, and the cold air behind the front more unseasonably cold. Consequently, it is important to try to estimate the intensity of the weather systems that are approaching you.

It is also important to try and discover how rapidly the system is moving. A rapidly moving low center can pass over a location, from its beginnings to its very end, in about twenty-four hours. This means that the actually bad weather associated with a fast-moving low may only occupy six to ten hours, even if the low passes directly overhead. Slow-moving lows, on the other hand, can take days to pass by a particular location. Any clues you can derive to tell you how rapidly a storm is moving will be important in determining your forecast.

One good forecasting rule is "slow to come, slow to pass." Since the winds and pressures of a weather system are more or less symmetrical, you can expect to spend about as much time coming out of the system as you took to get into it.

Usually I do my observations and forecasts informally. But every once in a while, I like to be more organized about my meteorological studies and use an observation and analysis format that stays the same from day to day. For these occasions, I made myself up a form like that shown below and photocopied a

Weather Observations and Analysis

Date: _____ Time: _____ Location: _____

Temperature: Current: _____ Last 24 hrs.: _____ _____
                                                        high   low

Humidity (visibility, etc.): _____

Barometer: _____ inches and _____
                                                          trend

Surface wind: _____ mph from the _____
                                                              direction

Clouds: Low _____ moving from _____ at _____
                       type   direction   hands/min.

        Mid _____ moving from _____ at _____
                       type   direction   hands/min.

        High _____ moving from _____ at _____
                       type   direction   hands/min.

Map: N ↑	Analysis:
x	

Predicted: Observed:

Next 6 hrs. _____   Next 6 hrs. _____

_____   _____

6 to 12 hrs. _____   6 to 12 hrs. _____

_____   _____

12 to 24 hrs. _____   12 to 24 hrs. _____

_____   _____

_____   _____

bunch of copies of it. The form has a place for me to enter all my observations so I don't forget any. Also there's a place for me to write down what I think the current weather situation is and a little map for me to sketch where I think the highs and lows and fronts are. I indicate with an arrow, after I've placed the highs and lows, how I think they are going to move, based on my high-cloud observations. Down at the bottom of the form is a place where I can write my six-hour, twelve-hour, and twenty-four-hour forecasts. Beside this is a space where I can write down what actually happened.

Don't get discouraged if the forecasting system doesn't work for you the first few times you try it. You will have to learn to fine tune your forecast to your local conditions. As we discussed in chapters 8 and 9, on eastern and western regions, some local geographic features are powerful weather-makers in their own right. And some weather situations are just too tough to predict from a garden. And remember, even the professionals get their forecasting wrong, sometimes.

Testing Out Your Forecasting Skills

Now that you are a skilled forecaster, your neighbors will flock to your door to get advice on planting and such matters. Here are some forecasting problems to practice with.

Problem #1

The Problem: Overnight you had some June showers, and this morning there is a low overcast with the sun dimly visible through occasional thin places. The air is warm and sticky. The barometer fell overnight and hasn't changed much since. Temperatures are in the middle seventies. The wind was southeast yesterday and is southwest today. Last night as you went to bed you noted that the high clouds were moving from the west-southwest against the moon. What will today's weather be?

Your Analysis: There is a low-pressure area to the north of you, moving east-northeast. The chances are that you are in the warm sector and that you have a cold front to the north and west of you. Your air is moist and your dew point is high, but the sun is gradually heating this air and evaporating the moisture.

Your Forecast: The sky should clear in a few hours, but afternoon showers are likely, possibly accompanied by severe weather as the cold front comes through. Look for signs of vigorous vertical cloud development, with towering cumulus clouds capped by anvils. There are real risks here. Check an afternoon radio or TV weather broadcast for severe weather warnings.

Problem #2

The Problem: Yesterday you had exceptionally mild winter weather and southerly winds. But overnight the wind shifted to the northwest and this morning is blustery and cold. The sky cleared of low clouds before sunrise, but all morning long there has been a procession of high clouds marching rapidly from southwest to northeast across the southeastern sky. About midday you notice that the wind is diminishing. The barometer, which had been rising, now has leveled off. The sky is a beautiful blue to the northwest of you. Should you expect a nice day tomorrow?

Your Analysis: There is a low-pressure system moving away from you toward the northeast. Its cold front passed through last night. The cloud bank you see on your southern horizon is likely the warm air over the cold front. The upper-air westerlies continue to blow from southwest to northeast behind the cold front. The low which passed you has pulled in a cold high-pressure area at the surface. But there is every reason to believe that there is a deep trough in the upper-air westerlies upstream of you. It is only a matter of time before that trough generates another low-pressure area and sends it off in your direction. With the cold air at the surface, a whole range of hazardous winter weather is a possibility.

Your Forecast: Winds will go variable and then easterly within a few hours. Watch the cloud band to the southwest. If it begins to thicken and spread over the western horizon, then some bad winter weather is likely. Check the wind and barometer. If the winds pick up from the northeast and the barometer falls off, then you can be pretty sure that conditions are setting up for a bad winter storm.

Problem #3

The Problem: Yesterday you had your first fall storm, but this morning dawned beautiful and clear, with just a few wispy, high clouds moving across the sky from north to south. The barometer is very low and steady. The wind is light northerly, but has been picking up ever since sunrise. The temperatures are in the low sixties. You planned to take a group of friends on a tour of local organic gardens and you expected to eat a picnic at a local park. Should you cancel your plans?

Your Analysis: There is a deep surface low-pressure area to the east of you and a deep upper-air trough to the east of you. You probably also have a steep upper-air ridge to the west of you and an intense, cold high-pressure area upstream.

Your Forecast: I wouldn't go on a picnic on a day like this. Look for "fair" weather clouds to form in a few hours and to rapidly thicken. Expect strong northerly winds, cloudy skies, and drizzle by noon with a possibility of intense, brief rainshowers. Look for the pattern to persist until the upper air turns more westerly and the barometer moves up to 30 inches or so. In short, I would recommend rescheduling the trip.

Problem #4

The Problem: Today dawns as a mild and misty October morning with lots of high, thin clouds in the sky. All morning long these high clouds have been slowly increasing and lowering from the northwest while the wind has been increasing from the southwest, until now it's blowing quite briskly. The barometer is falling slowly. Is a storm on the way?

Your Analysis: Yes, but probably not a very big one. The northwest movement of the high clouds suggests a ridge to the west of you. The southwest winds and falling barometer suggest a low approaching from the northwest. Since the low is approaching off a ridge (and ridges discourage the development of surface lows), I wouldn't expect much storminess. However, the same northwest flow aloft that is discouraging the development of this storm is likely to bring a cold high-pressure area along behind it. Also, the chances are good that a trough lies to the east of you so that the low, once past you, may develop dramatically.

Your Forecast: Increasing and lowering clouds with showers overnight. Winds becoming northwesterly and increasing possibility of snow flurries. Much colder tomorrow, with northwesterly winds, perhaps strong.

Problem #5

The Problem: Yesterday was a stinking hot summer day and last night you had thundershowers. This morning the air near the ground was all misty, but the sky is blue, not bronzy, and there is a cool, light northwest breeze. There are a few high clouds overhead, and they are moving rapidly from west to east across the sky. You were planning to have an outdoor party in your garden late this afternoon. How sure can you be that the weather will hold?

Your Analysis: The northwest wind suggests high pressure to the southwest, and the rapid eastward high-cloud movement suggests that the high will move swiftly to a position due south of you.

Your Forecast: I wouldn't make any bets for tomorrow's weather, but this afternoon should be safe. If there is rapid high-cloud development to the west, you might expect showers overnight.

Problem #6

The Problem: As the sun sets this evening you notice dense high and middle clouds across the sky moving from south-southwest to north-northeast. Winds are picking up from the southeast and the barometer is falling slowly. You're going to have a storm tomorrow, right?

Your Analysis: Yes, almost certainly. The direction of high clouds however, suggests that the center of the low which is to the southwest of you will pass to the west and north of your position, so you should pass through its warm sector. In addition, the deep trough which appears to be to the west of you will almost certainly mean that the high-pressure area that reaches you after the storm passes will be relatively warm.

Your Forecast: Expect a couple of days of mild, showery weather with winds from the south and southwest. Be on the lookout for any sign that your high clouds are moving in a more westerly direction. This will suggest that the upper-level trough is moving easterly and that much cooler weather is soon on the way.

A Cautionary Conclusion

I have been an amateur forecaster for more than thirty years, and since the age of eleven I have been offering to friends, siblings, parents, and strangers on trains my homegrown weather forecasts. I soon learned—as I suppose all forecasters do—that it is a short step from the flattery of being asked one's opinion about tomorrow's weather to the misery of being blamed for it. In short, offering weather advice to neighbors can be a perilous business.

I think making one's own forecasts is great fun and very useful. I never take a stroll outside but that I take a crack at it. But I would never advise anybody to take chances with my homegrown forecast in a situation that is important. If your neighbor is planting tomatoes, flooding cranberries, pouring cement, spreading grass seed, or any one of a myriad of operations around the house and garden where the weather makes a major difference, have him double-check your prediction by getting a fresh and timely forecast from a professional forecaster in your region. It is not so much a matter of forecasting skill—although many of these people are enormously well trained and experienced. It is mostly a question of information. No professional forecaster, no matter how well trained and experienced, would attempt to make a forecast on the basis of information from a single observation point. Without an actual weather map, most forecasters would just throw up their hands in despair. Unless you are willing to go to the trouble of setting up your own network of gardeners and getting a teletype, and a radar antenna, and one of those devices that receives satellite pictures, you will always need the professional forecasters because they have so much more information at their disposal than you do.

So, when it *really* matters, call the Weather Service office, listen to your weather radio, or watch a TV weather broadcast and be grateful that these services are as excellent as they are. But then, after you've got your tomatoes planted or your cement poured, go ahead and make your own forecast. If the official forecast comes out right, you'll have your tomatoes in. If your tomatoes get nipped, well then, you knew it all along, didn't you. You must be a pretty good forecaster, too!

And if, by now, you've been bitten by the forecasting bug, then read on. In the next several chapters there are many hints on how to predict specific weather situations—like frosts, or thunderstorms, or hurricanes, or other weather events that may be important to you or your garden—as well as lots of information about how to cope with these situations when they come to you in the garden.

12

FROST

I do my organic gardening in a frost pocket. My garden is in a valley that is 600 feet above sea level. At this altitude, the air cools just a bit quicker than at sea level, and on still nights, the cool air puddles at the bottom of the valley. My garden is low enough in the valley to be in the puddle of cool air but not so low that it gets some of the moderating effects of the river which flows across the valley's floor. So, when I listen to weather forecasters at night, I have to subtract about 15 degrees from their lowest temperature estimates.

Still, I get fooled. I wish I had a dollar for every time I've stood at the foot of my garden watching the sun descending to the west wall of the valley, trying to figure out how low the temperature would go. Covering the plants is such an aggravation. In the spring, the tender bedding plants resent all the handling. In the fall, when there are so many big plants, I never have enough covers for them all. Terrible ethical decisions must be made. Whom shall I let in and whom shall I leave outside the shelter?

The big-city forecasters are never much help. Where I live, the forecasts come from Boston. The forecaster sits in the midst of the city "heat island," next to a warm, wet ocean. He is forecasting mostly for the million people who live in the city and its suburbs. *They* won't have a frost tonight. The forecaster gives low temperatures for the "outlying" areas, but even these are too conservative. If the forecaster were to give a realistic forecast for my valley, cautious gardeners all over the state would be thrown into a panic. Late tomatoes and peppers would be harvested long before they needed to be. Indian summer harvests would be forfeited. A city forecaster can't forecast for my garden. He has to play the averages. My garden is not in an average location.

How to Predict Frost

In matters of frost prediction, there's practically no substitute for knowing your own situation and knowing it well. So, when you're standing at the foot of **151** your garden, watching the sun descend to the horizon, the following are some of the things you should be wondering about.

What's the Temperature?

When the temperature of the air around your plants falls to 32 degrees, you have a frost. As you stand in your garden in the evening, it's obvious that the temperature at sunset is going to have something to do with the temperature at dawn the following morning. But there is tremendous variation in how much the temperature falls during the night. Sometimes it even rises. Where I live,

Using Phenology to Make Planting Decisions

One traditional way to make decisions about planting times is to look to the wild plants in your neighborhood for advice. After all, aren't the lilacs and the elm trees and the forsythia in your neighborhood adapted to live successfully in your location? Every year, they decide when to blossom, when to put out leaves, and when to fruit without any assistance from you. Most years they get it right. Why shouldn't you follow their lead? This sort of study of the growth stages of natural plants is called phenology. Many old sayings are based on phenology. There is a network of people who make phenological observations of certain widely distributed plants called indicator plants. The most commonly used plants as indicators are the honeysuckle and the purple lilac. Careful observations of the various stages of growth of these plants are made each year at loca-

tions widely spread across the country.

Honeysuckle and lilac are used in making phenological predictions because of their wide adaptability to different geographical areas and their reliability in making consistent responses to varying weather conditions. Observing the time that these plants bloom each year gives you a good indication whether spring is earlier or later than previous years. They can be helpful in determining when to plant certain crops by noting the emergence times of their leaves and flowers.

For over ten years, it has been observed in New England that cool-season crops such as lettuce, peas, and spinach can be sown in the garden when the lilac shows its leaves in early spring. Tender or warm-season crops like corn, peppers, and tomatoes can be safely planted when the lilac opens its the following rule of thumb works pretty well: if the high temperature for the day is above 75 degrees, I don't have to think about the possibility of frost. In drier climates cautious gardeners might have to use 80 degrees, or even 85 degrees as their guidelines.

How Fast Is the Wind Blowing?

If as the sun sets, the wind drops off to a calm, then I really worry! On a still, cool night, the air tends to sort itself out into layers, warmer layers on top, colder layers at the bottom. The longer and stiller the night is, the more time the

blooms. The lilac refuses to display its delicate flowers until all danger of bad weather has passed.

The lilac as well as the dogwood can also give you a helpful clue where to select a planting site for tender fruit trees such as apricots and peaches. Their success in blooming year after year in a particular spot indicates the microclimate of that immediate area is conducive to nurturing tender fruit trees.

For many years, New Englanders have relied on the elm to tell them when to plant their corn. Their rule is to plant corn when the elm leaves are the size of a squirrel's ear. At this time the soil has warmed sufficiently to ensure successful germination of the corn seeds. Elm trees aren't as common as they used to be, but maple and oak trees make good substitutes.

Phenological observations can also help you avoid harmful attacks by insects. Gardeners in North Carolina have found that if cabbage, broccoli, Brussels sprouts, and other brassicas are not planted until the dogwoods are at their peak bloom, the cabbage maggot won't attack them. Farmers in Montana also use the blooming of lilac to warn them that they must harvest their alfalfa in ten days in order to avoid an attack from the first barrage of alfalfa weevils.

The only problem with using phenological indications to guide you in picking your planting dates is that the practice is based on the assumption that plants are conservative creatures that never take risks and never make mistakes. In fact, plants may be more daring than we suppose. Natural selection constantly presses plants to be first to get their leaves out in order to cast shade on their neighbors and grab more than their share of the nutrients from the soil. Wild trees and shrubs seem to get fooled into premature growth often enough so that I'm not sure I would completely trust their advice on when or when not to set out my tender bedding plants.

air has to do this. Unfortunately, the wind at sunset isn't a very good indication of what the wind will be like at dawn. Afternoon sunlight roils the atmosphere; during the night, the atmosphere settles down and the winds diminish. The wind can be vigorous enough at dusk to make it difficult to cover the garden, yet still enough by the following dawn to permit a murderous frost. Thus, when I'm making my decision to cover or not, I only take the evening wind into account if it's blowing vigorously and I have very good reasons to believe it will continue to blow all night.

What Sort of Cloud-Cover Is There?

Clouds, even very high clouds, can keep temperatures from falling further than they might otherwise. In the same way clouds reflect the light from a distant city, they reflect the heat radiated by the earth and shine it back down. "Cloud shine" may not give your garden very much heat, but it is usually enough to keep the temperatures from plunging. Remember, though, that the clouds at sunset may not be the same as the clouds at dawn. The effect of the sun on the atmosphere is often to *make* clouds; when the sun goes away, so do the clouds. Notice the trend of the clouds. If the sky has been covered by low, grey clouds all day, which begin to break and thin as the sun sets, *then* I worry. On the other hand, if the sun falls toward the horizon through an increasingly dense network of vapor trails and mare's tails, then I don't worry.

What Is the Condition of the Ground?

The temperature and moisture of the soil affect the atmosphere near the ground, particularly on cold, still nights. If the soil is cold and dry, the atmosphere near the ground can cool more rapidly. If, on the other hand, the ground is moist and warm, then it lends its heat and moisture to the atmosphere, raising the temperature of the air. But there's another factor to be kept in mind. Plants seem more vulnerable to frost when the soil has been recently wet. It seems as though the fluids in the plants are thinner then, and the plants are more likely to freeze.

So, I try not to let soil warmth and moisture influence my decision unless the soil temperature is well up in the seventies. Generally speaking, you can count on the soil temperature to give you a little help in the fall, and not much help at all in the spring. And don't count on soil temperature to help you out in a deep mulch garden. The same insulating effect which helps protect your plants' roots in the hot summer also insulates their leaves on cold fall nights from the protective effects of the warm ground.

How Long Will the Night Be?

The longer the night, the more time there is for the earth to lose heat to the sky. During the fall frost season, nights can be as much as two hours longer than nights in the spring frost season.

What Is the General Weather Situation?

Despite the diversity of local factors which determine frost possibilities over most of the United States, unseasonable frosts commonly occur in only one meteorological situation: under the crest of a continental polar or arctic air mass that follows the passage of a low-pressure area. In these circumstances, skies clear, winds diminish, the air is dry, and nighttime temperatures fall. But weeks of weather can go by without this meteorological situation occurring. One year, I remember we had our last spring frost in late March. The weather was hot in April with temperatures reaching the nineties. Summer came on June 21. The following week a northeast storm came up the coast, gave us two or three miserable cold, rainy days and, as it departed, released an arctic air mass that had been bottled up in central Canada all that time. That arctic air mass poured down over my garden, and on June 25, long after I had put all my covers away, I lost several bean plants at the low end of my garden. My neighbor said it was some kind of leaf disease, but I knew the awful truth. We had had a *summer* frost.

Is the Moon New or Full?

Whatever the professionals say, I believe that frost is more likely under the full or new moon. I used to think that it was just that you could see the moon—meaning that there were no clouds in the sky and that therefore the temperatures were likely to fall. But that theory doesn't explain new-moon frosts. Partly I believe that the moon increases likelihood of frosts because my experience seems to suggest it; partly I believe it because the idea makes sense to me. The moon makes tides in the atmosphere, just as it makes tides in the ocean. Presumably, the moon makes the highest tides in the atmosphere at the new and the full moon. Frosts occur under high-pressure areas. A high-pressure area is sort of a tidal bulge in the atmosphere. Doesn't it seem reasonable that if the moon tide effect is added to the effects of a high-pressure area, that frost might be made more likely? Whatever the reason, those long, dark nights when there is no moon at all and those high, bright nights when the moon illuminates every detail both seem to be particularly dangerous nights for frost.

What Is the Dew Point?

Dew point is more important than any other factor in determining the likelihood of frost. The dew point temperature is the temperature at which the water vapor in the air condenses into water droplets or ice crystals. Unlike the air temperature, which falls during the night, the dew point temperature remains about the same. As the air temperature falls, it approaches the dew point. When the dew point is reached, water starts to condense on the ground in the form of dew or on microscopic particles in the air in the form of fog. But the condensation of water in the air has two important effects. Most important, it releases heat. For each small quantity of water that becomes a fog or a dew droplet, a small amount of heat is released into the atmosphere. Once the dew point is reached, the condensation of the water vapor tends to heat the air as it cools. Second, the condensed water vapor in the air tends to reflect heat and to serve as a blanket over the ground. Unless the ground is already frozen (in which case your tomatoes are long since gone to your kitchen windowsills), the ground will tend to heat the air around your plants and protect them.

Important as the dew point is, it's not all that easy to discover. Most gardeners don't own a sling psychrometer. (See chapter 17.) Radio forecasts and recorded telephone forecasts don't always give dew points. Newspaper daily almanacs often contain the dew point, but by the time your cold dawn rolls around, that measurement will be too old to be of much use to you. The best source of the dew point is a TV weather broadcast. Many TV forecasters do give you the dew point. In fact, there seems to be an educational campaign on among these forecasters to teach the public about the usefulness of knowing the dew point. If they don't give the dew point, they usually give the relative humidity, from which the dew point can be estimated. (See the chart on estimating the dew point, in chapter 10.) In most broadcasts, the dew point is given right at the beginning of the broadcast, usually as part of a printed display describing current conditions. It's not on the screen long, so you have to be ready for it.

My rule of thumb is not to worry about frost if the dew point is above 45 degrees on the six P.M. weather report. Well, not to worry much, anyway. Why so much leeway? Actually, a dew point 1 or 2 degrees above freezing should be enough to protect my garden. But remember, it's not the dew point at the airport in the big city at five P.M. that determines whether my garden has frost, it's the dew point one or two feet above the surface of the ground in my garden at dawn. Dew points may be much more stable than temperatures, but they do change over time and over distance. The airport may be near some ameliorating influence like a body of water or a factory steam stack. Or weather conditions may change overnight and dry air may move in, lowering the dew point. Tonight's dew point is only useful as a guide to tomorrow's dew point.

I remember one night in early September a few years ago, I decided not to cover the garden. After all, the season was yet early, the temperature was in the low sixties, the sky was cloudy, the wind was blowing, and there was a warm rain falling. Not a chance of frost on such a night! Unfortunately, weather systems were moving quickly that night. In the twelve hours between sunset and dawn a small high-pressure area moved in and crested over us: the sky cleared, the moon came out, the dew point fell, the wind fell, and so did some of my tomato plants.

Predicting dew points in your garden is no easy task. One trick I've used sometimes is to call the Weather Service and ask them for the dew points of cities 200 to 300 miles upwind of my garden. The air over those cities at ten P.M. is likely to be the air over my garden at six or seven o'clock the next morning. If my dew point is near 40 and the dew points in these places are lower than my dew point, then I worry. If the dew points in these places are higher than my dew point, then I quit worrying. The cost of a toll call to the Weather Service is not much to pay for a peaceful night's sleep.

One thing more. If you don't have a sling psychrometer and you miss the weather broadcast, then you can still guess the dew point. If the air is murky and the horizon ill defined, if distant hills march away into a veil of haze, stars are indistinct and few in number, then you know the dew point is high. But if the atmosphere is lucid and distant hills are the same color as near ones, if you can see every detail of distant structures, if the sky is a purply-blue at the zenith, if the sun sets to the horizon without changing color and the moon comes up the color of platinum and the stars come out in thousands, then you know the dew point is low. On such a night the wise tomato cringes.

Decision Time

Well, there you are. You're standing at the end of the garden. The sun is plunging toward the western horizon. Your spouse is waiting your dinner, or perhaps you yourself are burning it, right there and then, as you stand in the garden. You've asked yourself all the questions and you don't like the answers. The temperature is under 70, the soil is cool, the winds are light and variable, the sky is cloudless, and the horizon clear and sharp, and the night will be long. What do you do? "To cover or not to cover?", that is the question.

I'm afraid the best advice is to put down your hoe, walk indoors, and turn on the television. Uncertain science as meteorology is, it's a lot better than anything you can do from the end of your garden. As you listen to the broadcast, take note of the current temperature, the current dew point, the low temperature for the previous day, the general organization of the map, and lastly, the forecast.

If the dew point is near 40 degrees, protect your garden unless you can see a good reason not to. For instance, a low-pressure area might be rapidly approaching from the west. Under those circumstances, you might not cover because the wind will go southerly overnight and pick up; dew points will rise; and a cloud cover will move in. Or, a low-pressure area might be forecast to linger to the east of you. The air might be cool and the dew point and temperature low, but gusty north winds could be expected to persist overnight. In such circumstances, you might save the effort of covering.

Why, you might ask, do I recommend that you go to all this trouble about the dew point? Why not listen to the forecaster's prediction of the overnight low temperature and trust it? You can do this, but then you have to take into

(continued on page 160)

Frost Damage and How to Prevent It

A plant cell consists of a finely differentiated tissue, called protoplasm. Distributed through the protoplasm are pockets of fluid contained within membranes. Frost can damage this structure in two quite different ways. Very severe frosts can actually tear the membranes that keep the various parts of the cell separate. Usually, however, the damage-causing mechanism is more insidious. When the temperature falls below freezing, ice forms in the pockets of fluid inside the cell. Now the osmotic pressure forces water out of the

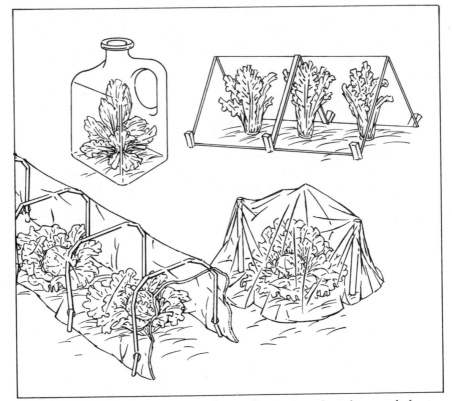

An assortment of simple devices can be used to protect plants from early frosts. Shown here are, upper left, a bottomless plastic milk jug that is set over an individual plant; upper right, a glass cloche; lower left, a sheet of plastic stretched over wire hoops to cover a whole row of plants; and lower right, a plastic cover for a single plant.

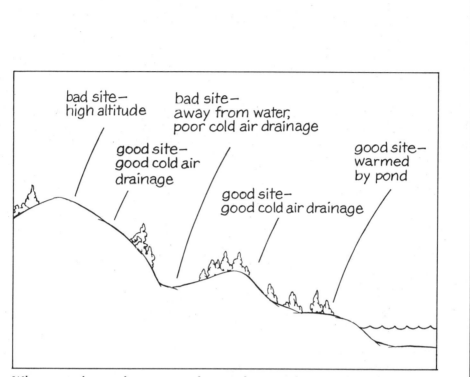

Where exactly you place your garden in relation to slopes and bodies of water can dramatically affect your growing season, as shown in this diagram.

protoplasm and into the fluid pockets, dehydrating the protoplasm just as severely as in a drought. Like a house plant that has been left unwatered too long, a slightly frost-bitten plant may suffer no damage so long as it is not stimulated into activity by strong light. As long as the plant is kept in the dark, the demands of its cells for water and for the nutrients are minimal. But as soon as the sun falls on the leaves and the cells spring into metabolic action, the plant suddenly begins to show the effects of dehydration. Before the ice crystals can melt and the protoplasm reabsorb the water, the cells have been irreversibly damaged.

The fact that frost damage arises from dehydration of living parts of plant cells is probably the basis for many of the tricks that gardeners use to rescue their plants from frost. Several strategies involve watering the plants or washing the frost off their leaves before the sun gets on the plant in the

(continued on next page)

Frost Damage and How to Prevent It *(continued)*

morning. The comparatively warm water from the hose helps to melt the ice in the plant and begin the return flow of life-giving water into the protoplasm of the plant before the sun falls on the plants and stimulates them to begin to metabolize.

But of course the best frost cure is frost prevention. Any device which holds an insulating layer of warm air around the plant will offer considerable frost protection. Covering your plants with old milk cartons, sheets of plastic, moth-eaten blankets, bedspreads, anything to retard the escape of warm air from the surface of the earth and contain it around the plants will help. Just remember to remove the covers in the morning when the temperature gets above the freezing point.

Also, you can save yourself a lot of grief in frost season by choosing carefully the site of your garden. Slopes help because they keep the cold air from puddling in your garden. Remember, cold air is heavier than warm. As the air cools in your garden, it slides downhill to your neighbor's garden and is replaced by warmer air from above. Water sources also help by supplying warmth by raising dew points, and sometimes by enveloping your plantings in a protective mist. Believe it or not, a well-sited garden can have a month more of growing season than a poorly sited garden down the hill or away from the pond.

account the differences between your garden's position and the position from which the forecast is made. Forecasts are usually made on the basis of data from airports. Is your garden higher than the airport? All other things being equal, temperatures are a little cooler where it's higher. Is your garden in a valley, whereas the airport is on a plain? All other things being equal, the bottom of a valley will be cooler than the plain. Is your garden in a suburb, and the airport out in the countryside? Cities, even suburbs, give off heat and moisture. Is your garden near to or downwind of a body of water and the airport not? Water keeps temperatures up and dew points up. Is your garden northwest or southwest of the airport? Cold weather changes usually arrive from the northwest; changes for the milder usually arrive from the southwest. For instance, if the forecast at the weather station calls for clearing overnight and sunny and cool tomorrow with gentle winds, and if your garden is one or two hundred miles north of the forecasting station, then I would worry about frost, even if frost is not predicted at the forecasting station. Clearing will very likely take place several hours earlier over your garden and the forecast suggests that there is no big rush of cool air which will keep the air mixed. Cover your plants. You'll be glad you did.

Over the long run, if you want to make use of temperature forecasts, it's wise to do a little research on the relationship between low temperatures at the forecasting station and low temperatures in your garden. You can do this by watching the weather broadcasts during some quiet early spring nights and keeping track of the forecasted low temperature, the actual low temperature at the forecast station, and the low temperature in your garden. Very quickly a pattern should emerge, and you can develop a rule of thumb, such as "subtract 10 degrees from the lowest forecasted temperature," or "take the highest number from the range of low temperatures forecasted" or some such.

It's distressing to have to worry about frost. But if your garden is in a frost pocket like mine, you are going to have to face the fact that you'll cover it on lots of nights when hindsight reveals you didn't need to. There will also be nights when you will wish at midnight you had covered it at dusk. Two or three times

Relative Hardiness of Common Garden Plants

Hardy: able to withstand freezing temperatures	Half-Hardy: can withstand some light freezing (short-term exposure to subfreezing temperatures)	Tender: fruit and leaves injured by light frosts	Very Tender: need hot temperatures (above 70°) for growth
Broccoli	Artichoke, Jerusalem	Artichoke, Globe	Beans, lima
Brussels sprouts		Basil	Coriander
Cabbage	Beets	Beans, snap	Cucumbers
Chives	Carrots	Corn (depending	Cumin
Collards	Cauliflower	on variety)	Eggplant
Garlic	Celeriac	Marjoram	Luffa
Horseradish	Celery	Soybeans	Melons
Kale	Chard	Squash, summer	Okra
Kohlrabi	Dill	Tomatoes	Peanuts
Leeks	Endive		Peppers
Onions	Escarole		Potatoes, sweet
Peas	Fennel		Pumpkin
Rutabagas	Lettuce		Squash, winter
Sage	Mustard		
Salsify	Parsnips		
Scallions	Potatoes		
Spinach	Radishes		
Tarragon	Rosemary		
Thyme	Sunflowers		
Turnips			

a year I find myself out in my garden at 11:30 at night in my Wellington boots and my pajamas spreading covers on the plants by the light of the car's headlights. The dog takes great pleasure in these late-night outings and bounds around the garden; the cat chases the corners of the plastic covers as I drag them over the grass.

As I crawl into bed with my cold, damp pajamas, I console myself. The rewards of being a frost-conscious gardener are tremendous. Here in my valley, the absolute frost-free period is barely seventy days. For most of my neighbors, the tomatoes and peppers are pretty much done by the middle of September. But by watching the weather and carefully covering my plants when frost threatens, I can have peppers and tomatoes from mid-July until the middle of October, sometimes even beyond. It's a faint-hearted gardener indeed who wouldn't trade a pair of dry pajamas for a forty-day extension of his growing season.

13

DROUGHTS AND DRY SPELLS

Hurricanes, tornadoes, and thunderstorms are things that nature does *to* us. They are calamities that are pretty much beyond our control. We can, to a degree, control how much damage they do, but we cannot control whether or not they happen. A drought, however, is mostly something we do to ourselves. We make droughts happen by how we use water, by how we cultivate the soil, and by the species and varieties of plants we decide to grow in a particular region.

To assert that droughts are caused by people may seem odd. But think about it for a moment. Boston has more than forty inches of rain a year; San Francisco has around twenty. Nobody would say that San Francisco is in a permanent drought. But if Boston had San Francisco's rainfall for one year, Boston tomato-growers would surely complain that they had a drought. Obviously, the amount of rainfall by itself does not define a drought. A drought is not simply a period of low rainfall; it is a period of rainfall lower than farmers and gardeners *expect*. Understanding and coping with drought may be as much a matter of dealing with these expectations as it is of monitoring water supplies.

The fact is that periods of low rainfall are inevitable. The area of heavy precipitation in a storm is a very small part of its whole area, perhaps as little as 5 percent. Even in a huge storm whose circulation is affecting most of the country, heavy rainfall may be localized in a narrow band fifty to a hundred miles in advance of the warm front and in patches around the cold front. Everywhere else will be having drizzle or light rain or perhaps just plain clouds.

The reason that rainfall gets spread around the country as equitably as it does is that storms move across the country pushing their areas of maximum **163** rainfall along ahead of them as they move. Moreover, storms do not always travel in the same track or develop at the same rate. Different storms spread their rain across different parts of the country, with the result that the gardeners of every region eventually get the rain that is due them.

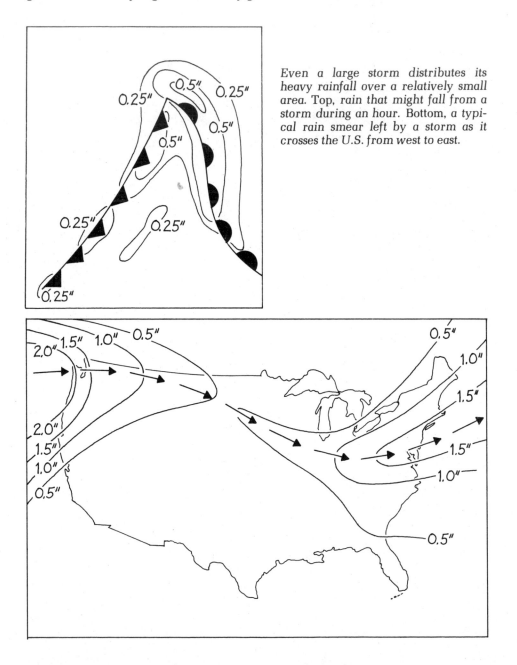

Even a large storm distributes its heavy rainfall over a relatively small area. Top, rain that might fall from a storm during an hour. Bottom, a typical rain smear left by a storm as it crosses the U.S. from west to east.

The problem is that eventually may not be soon enough. In some years, the storm track gets stuck. Month after month, the storms travel the same track across the country, repeatedly laying down their rainfall in the same places. In these areas, rainfall totals build up. Here, gardeners curse the foul weather that keeps their soil waterlogged and prevents them from getting in the garden to plant or till. But these gardeners are the lucky ones. Elsewhere, the ground cracks and the plants wilt and the gardeners till and plant in vain. Eventually, the storm track will come unstuck and the weather pattern will break down and be replaced by another. But that knowledge is small comfort for a wheat farmer who has lost his crop or a gardener whose broccoli plants lie flopped on the ground like tired dogs. A promise of a December deluge is no help to a gardener suffering from a July dry spell.

Plants' Needs
in Dry Years and Wet

The variation in rainfall patterns in the United States is enormous. Some desert regions receive as little as four inches of water over a year, while parts of the mountain rainforests of Washington State receive as much as ten feet. Only the eastern quarter of the country is lucky enough to have its rainfall spread pretty evenly throughout the year. Some regions, such as the Plains states, have most of their rain in the summer; other regions, such as California, have their wet seasons in the winter.

The amount of rainfall varies from year to year as well. Working with the Kansas Agricultural Field Station, Professor L. Dean Bark has assembled the annual precipitation totals for Manhattan, Kansas, from 1858 to 1976. In those 118 years the gardeners of Manhattan, Kansas, suffered through 34 years that were at least 6 inches short in rain. Manhattan, Kansas, gets barely 33½ inches of rain in an average year, so in those years they were missing at least a sixth of their rainfall. Some years were even worse. In 12 of those 37 drought years, rainfall totals were more than one-third short. In those years, the people of Manhattan, Kansas, were trying to conduct midwestern agriculture in a climate nearly as dry as that of San Francisco. Anyone who has seen in summer the bare, brown hills of the Bay region of northern California knows how difficult those years must have been for Manhattan gardeners.

Most garden plants are as fussy in their water needs as the North American climate is unreliable in providing for them. Traditional garden plants do not tolerate much climatic frivolity. They must have an uninterrupted water supply. They require water not only to maintain their structure but also to supply themselves with nutrients. Plants feed their cells by flushing nutrient-containing water from their roots through their stems to their leaves and back. Much of the power for this movement of water is provided by the evaporation of water from the leaves of the plant, called transpiration. A full-grown tomato or corn plant may require up to a gallon of water a day to meet its transpiration needs. Without this water, the plant begins to lose its structural rigidity (it wilts), and it begins to starve for lack of the nutrients that the water supplies.

Whatever the uncertainties of the weather, therefore, the gardener must never allow the plants to exhaust the water supply stored in the soil. Indeed, for best growth, the gardener should not permit any part of his soil to dry out. The roots of the plant require water in order to forage. When the water in any part of the soil, say the top two inches, is exhausted, then the plant cannot feed from the nutrients in this part of the soil. Allowing any part of the soil around a plant to dry out is like cutting off some of its food supply.

But plants also demand that they not get *too much* water. The bacteria which most actively supply nutrients to the plants' roots are *aerobic:* they require oxygen to do their work. A waterlogged soil lacks adequate oxygen for a healthy population of microorganisms. Thus, a drowned plant may suffer from starvation just as surely as a thirsty one. So, when the climate varies whimsically the amount of rainfall it provides, the gardener has to respond to its whimsy with caution. Too small a response or too large a response, and the garden suffers.

How Much Water Must Be Added?

When a dry spell strikes, a gardener needs to know how much moisture is depleted from his soil, so that he knows how much moisture must be replaced to maintain the soil stores at full capacity without overloading it. But the rate at which moisture escapes the soil through transpiration and through direct evaporation varies from region to region, season to season, and day to day almost as much as rainfall itself. Where temperatures are warm and relative humidity is low, as in the Southwest, the replacement needs of plants may require the equivalent of over one hundred inches of rain a year. On the other hand, cloudy, cool, humid places such as coastal Washington or coastal Maine require less than twenty inches of rain to balance their annual water loss. Unfortunately for gardeners, demands upon the soil's water reserves are usually greatest in those places and in those seasons when growing conditions are otherwise the best.

The meteorologist Joe R. Eagleman has developed a method for estimating the number of inches of rain required by the plants in a particular region and time of year.* How much water plants draw out of the ground depends on the

*See his interesting book, *The Visualization of Climate* (Lexington, Mass.: Lexington Books, 1976).

Relative Water Needs of Vegetable Crops

Plants that like frequent watering. Need copious amounts of water during dry conditions	Plants that respond best when watered during flowering and pod/fruit production	Plants that do not respond favorably to frequent watering. Should be watered only before the soil becomes too dry
Cabbage	Beans	Beets
Cauliflower	Corn, sweet	Broccoli
Celery	Peas	Brussels sprouts
Lettuce	Potatoes, main crop	Carrots
Potatoes, early	Tomatoes	Onions
Spinach		Parsnips
Squash, summer		Radishes
		Rutabagas
		Turnips

rate at which water escapes from their leaves and that depends on temperature, humidity, and wind velocity, among other things. By comparing Professor Eagleman's estimate of the moisture used by the plants in a particular region with the average precipitation for the same region, a gardener can get a sense of how many inches of rainfall equivalent the gardener will have to supply from other sources. For instance, gardeners in Chicago can expect 19.9 inches of rain over their growing season. (By growing season, in this case, I mean the period from the planting of the first peas, to the time when cool-weather fall crops stop putting out new leaves.) During the same period, the soil and plants in Chicago, according to Eagleman, will evaporate 31 inches of water. Thus, Chicago gardeners can expect a water deficit of 11 inches over their growing season, a little under 2 inches of water shortfall per month. This means that a Chicago gardener must expect to provide nearly 2 inches of rain equivalent a month from somewhere.

Gardeners who get a lot of rain on their gardens may still have a water deficit. The gardeners of Savannah, Georgia, get lots of rain during their growing season—more than enough to fulfill the needs of a gardener in Chicago. But because the weather is warmer in Savannah, the gardeners there need an average of 5 inches a month. So even though it rains more, almost 4.5 inches a month in Savannah, Savannah gardeners still must pay attention to the water needs of their plants.

Remarkably few places in the United States get enough rainfall in a growing season to replace the water that is evaporated from plants and soil. One of the few that does is Caribou, Maine. Over Caribou's short, cool, and damp growing season almost 4 inches of rain falls a month. During the same period, Caribou's gardens require only 3.5 inches per month of rainfall. Unlike most other gardeners in the United States, Caribou gardeners have the unique distinction of gaining ground in the water department all summer long.

Gardening in Water-Deficit Regions

So, unless you are one of the lucky few readers that lives in Caribou, Maine, you are going to have to see to your garden's water needs during most growing seasons. One way to provide water to your garden is to store it in the soil. All but the driest sections of the country experience a water surplus during the nongrowing months of the year. This surplus is like a savings account that your plants can draw on during the growing season.

The question of how much water is stored in your soil is a complicated one. Obviously, the soil cannot hold all the water that falls on it, or streams would not flow and lakes would be empty; every soil has a limited capacity to hold water. If more precipitation falls than the soil can hold, then the water runs off into rivers and lakes and is lost to the garden. Furthermore, the total capacity of soil to hold water may be less important than the capacity of the top few inches. Most of the biological action occurs in the upper six inches of the soil where oxygen levels are highest. Consequently, the effective water reserve might be something considerably less than total capacity.

The Role of Organic Matter

The moisture-holding properties of soil vary considerably with the properties of the soil itself. Small-particled soils such as clay can hold three times as much water as coarse-particled soils such as sand. The problem with clay is that it's reluctant to release all that moisture to plants. Organic matter in the soil improves dramatically the capacity of any soil to hold and release water. The particle size of a garden's basic soil may be out of the gardener's control, but the organic matter content of the soil is something every gardener can control. Increasing a soil's organic matter from 2 to 5 percent can quadruple its water-holding capacity. Particles of organic matter act like microscopic sponges. They help soak up and hold water in sandy soil, and help open up pore spaces in clay soils to permit easier passage of water.

By controlling the amount of organic matter in the soil, gardeners can determine how much of a drought occurs in the garden. To illustrate this point, let us compare the gardens of two neighbors in Chicago, Hugh Mus and Celia Ment (known to her friends as "Cee"). Hugh Mus incorporates lots of organic matter into his soil each year and has built up its storage capacity to the equivalent of 6 inches of rainfall. Cee Ment has, however, only 3 inches of soil water capacity in her soil. Since Chicago winters have a water surplus, both gardeners start with their soil storage at full capacity. During the month of May (using Professor Eagleman's figures), we can estimate that both gardeners will need 3.25 inches of rain to balance evaporation, and will get 3.5. So far so good. In June, both gardeners get another 3.5 inches of rain. But June is hotter and the need for water goes up to 5.8 inches. Each gardener thus borrows 2.3 inches from his or her reserve. At the end of June, Mus has more than 3 inches left in his reserve, but Ment has used all but 0.7 inch of hers. In fact, Ment's plants will already be starting to slow down their growth. Their roots cannot find and extract water as rapidly as those in Mus's garden.

In July, the difference between the two gardens really becomes evident. Both receive 3.3 inches of rain and use up 5.8 inches. By the end of July, Ment is experiencing a serious drought. If she has not watered, her plants are looking poor. She complains across the backyard fence to Mus about the terrible drought. "Golly, Cee," Hugh says, "I hadn't noticed." In Mus's garden, no drought is in progress. As a matter of fact, he still has more than an inch of water in reserve in his soil. August continues the trend. Over August, the two gardens receive 3.3 inches of rain and expend 5. The drought continues in Ment's garden. Over in Mus's garden, the dry weather begins to take its toll. By the end of the month, Mus has exhausted his soil reserve and his plants are beginning to look unhappy.

When late September frost finally brings the growing season to a close for most plants, both gardens are suffering seriously from lack of water. In September, both gardens got only 2.9 inches of rain and used 3.7, for a deficit of 0.8 inch. When the summer is over, Ment has had a "drought" of almost three months' duration whereas Mus has had barely a month of drought. Over the whole season, Mus's garden exceeded its soil water storage by just over an inch of rainfall. He replaced his deficit by an evening of watering and still harvested a good crop. Ment's garden exceeded its capacity by more than 4 inches. Her harvest was very poor indeed, and she lost a lot of plants entirely.

How Helpful Are Mulches?

The parable of Mus and Ment illustrates how important it is to keep high levels of organic matter in your soil. Your bookshelf is probably full of organic gardening books that tell how to go about increasing soil organic matter, so I won't labor that point here. But let me say a word about mulches. Regular use of mulch obviously plays a role in increasing the organic matter of the soil and as such, the use of mulches can, over a period of several years, improve the water-holding capacity of a soil. However, most gardening books will assert that mulches help to conserve the supply of moisture in the soil. This I doubt very much. Mulches may slow direct evaporation from the soil. But in the peak of the growing season, when the days are long, the sun is hot, and the plants are large, direct evaporation accounts for only a tiny portion of soil water loss. Most

(continued on page 172)

Some Guidelines for Gardening during Dry Spells

You don't have to feel frustrated and defeated when the temperature soars and the unrelenting sun beats down on your garden, causing the soil to dry out and the plants to wither. There are several measures you can take to help your garden get over this climatic hurdle so you and your plants won't suffer any loss.

Helping your garden survive dry spells starts well before the dry weather arrives. In fact, it begins in the planning stages and continues throughout the season until the crops are harvested.

If dry conditions are a problem in your area, you might want to consider what kinds of vegetables to grow. Some vegetables, such as squash and tomatoes, don't demand as much water as the leafy, shallow-rooted types like cabbage and celery. You may want to plant only a few of the water-demanding crops if water is scarce. Low-growing crops are less subject to loss of water through transpiration than vining crops that have more leaf surface exposed to the wind and sun. Many vining vegetables are available in the compact bush varieties that conserve both space and water. Also, some varieties of vegetables are more drought tolerant than others, so read your seed catalogs thoroughly and note which varieties perform well in dry conditions.

Now that you have chosen the types of plants you want to grow, there are a few things to take into consideration when picking a site for your garden. First, don't plant your garden near big trees that have sprawling roots which can rob your plants of water. Look for areas that can provide protection from the wind. Locating the garden near a building or erecting barriers near the garden will help to shield your plants from the wind. A fence or natural barrier such as a hedge or a row of trees will provide protection from the wind. Just make sure the windbreaks don't shade the garden.

Consider planting some of the vegetables in an area that receives partial shade (full sun only part of the day). Shaded soil loses less moisture through evaporation than soil that receives full sunlight all day. Leafy vegetables such as cabbage, lettuce, spinach, and Swiss chard do well in partial shade. Herbs such as basil, mint, parsley, and tarragon will also tolerate a shaded area. But not all plants thrive on less sunlight. Tomatoes, peppers, and vine crops require lots of direct sunshine to produce an abundant crop.

The most important principle in drought gardening is to make sure your plants don't have to share their precious water supply with any weeds. Space your plants closely together. When they get bigger the foliage will form a natural canopy that keeps down the weed population.

Mulch is an asset for discouraging weed competition. A three- to four-inch layer of grass clippings, straw, salt hay, compost, or partially decomposed leaves will keep the soil surface moist and also keep down most weeds. Several sheets of newspapers or plastic weighted down with soil or rocks also makes a good mulch. Just remember that the soil must be moist before you put the mulch down, and remove any weeds that pop up from underneath the mulch.

If you get a long dry spell, your plants are going to need to be watered. There are a few rules to keep in mind that will help you make the most of your watering.

Only water very late in the afternoon or very early in the morning. This is the time when the least water will be lost to evaporation.

One good soaking is better than several light waterings. The surface layer dries out the quickest and sometimes the water never reaches the plants' roots. Deep watering encourages the plants to send their roots deep into the soil where water supplies are usually more reliable.

When choosing a method of watering your garden, drip irrigators are the most efficient means. They provide a slow, steady supply of water that penetrates deeply in the lower layers of the soil. Oscillating overhead sprinklers are the least efficient since a lot of the water evaporates before it even reaches the plants. Plastic perforated soaker hoses can be purchased at many garden centers but you can make several different homemade versions of drip irrigators in just minutes.

Save your empty plastic gallon milk jugs or bleach containers and punch holes in their bottoms. Bury the container partially in the soil between two water-needy plants and then fill with water. The water will seep slowly out of the holes in the bottom of the containers and will give the plants a thorough soaking.

Gallon-size glass jugs can also be used as drip irrigators. Remove

(continued on next page)

Gardening during Dry Spells *(continued)*

the lid from the jug and punch several holes in it with a hammer and finishing nail. Fill the jug with water, screw on the lid, and lay it on its side next to a plant so that the lid is pointing toward the base of the plant. Water should slowly drip out of the holes in the lid.

Clay pots and tin cans can serve water-demanding plants like tomatoes and cucumbers. Clay pots come equipped with holes but you will have to punch several holes in the bottom of the tin cans. At planting time sink a clay pot or tin can in the soil between two plants (allow at least three inches between the edge of the container and the plants) so that all but one inch is submerged in the soil. The container can then be filled with water as the need arises.

Be alert at harvesting time and pick the vegetables as soon as they ripen. Letting them hang on the plants after they have matured drains the plants of water that could be used to ripen the younger fruits. Then remove the plants from the garden as soon as they are finished bearing. This will provide more water for the plants that are still producing.

Don't forget your fruit trees during dry spells. If newly planted trees are receiving less than one inch of water per week, soak them once a week to a depth of one foot. If the trees have been in the ground between one and five years, you should water them every two to three weeks during dry spells. Older trees need to be watered only every four weeks.

of the water is lost through transpiration, that is, through the leaves of the plants as they use the sun's energy to move nutrients around in their systems. Mulch does not affect water loss through transpiration at all.

Mulches *do* keep the top surface of the soil moist. Soil surface moisture is important because it is in the top few inches that the oxygen levels of the soil are highest and that the most vigorous and complex soil life is maintained. Mulches are useful because they help to keep this active layer of the soil from drying out and overheating. Cultivation does the job almost as well, however. By keeping the surface of the soil open, moisture seeps gradually upward from lower down in the soil and keeps the surface moist and biologically active.

I stress this point with such vigor because in my first years as an organic gardener I was much smitten with the mulches. Because I had read so often that mulches preserve moisture, I thought my extensive use of mulches would protect my garden from drought. But from this idealism of mine, my gardens really suffered. In the dry, warm summer months, I never thought to provide my plants with extra water. The plants never died but they did hang back reluctantly, waiting for more rain. I soon learned that mulches do not necessarily relieve the gardener from the responsibility of providing water to his or her garden.

When Can You Expect to Water?

You can use the map I have provided to get an idea of how much you should expect to water your garden during an average growing season. The map shows the weekly difference, averaged over the growing season in each area, between the amount of water needed by plants for best growth and the amount of water that can be expected from rainfall. If you want to know your total soil water surplus or deficit for your entire growing season, multiply the weekly number in your area by the number of weeks in your growing season. Wherever that growing season soil water deficit is more than six inches, gardeners will have to do some watering, unless they are able to develop truly extraordinary water-holding capacity in their soils. In regions without any soil water deficit in the growing season, gardeners will not have to water no matter how poor their soil water-holding capacity. Between these extremes each gardener can decrease the amount of watering the garden will need by increasing the proportion of organic matter in the soil.

So far in this chapter we have been talking mostly about *average* rainfall and *average* soil moisture needs. But as every gardener knows all too well, the weather is rarely average. Weeks can go by without any significant rain at all. The area in New England where I garden has the distinction of being a place with very even rainfall amounts over the year. In an average growing season, gardens around here get 19.6 inches of rain and use about 21.3, for a very manageable deficit of less than 2 inches over the whole growing season. But even so, I and my neighbors have to expect that one year in six our rainfall will average at least 1 inch short for every month of the growing season. Overall, that makes a shortfall of 5 inches of rain. Such years are also likely to be years in which the humidity is low and the temperatures are high. Thus, years in which the rainfall is unusually low are also likely to be years in which the water demands of the garden are unusually high. In such years, even good gardeners have to water frequently to keep their gardens growing well. In short, most gardeners in the United States should probably be prepared, at least from time to time, to provide supplemental water to their gardens.

The goal in watering a garden is to replenish the soil moisture reserve

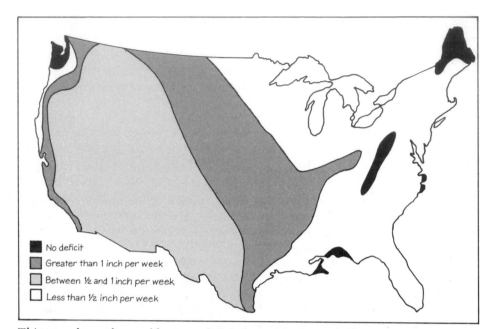

- No deficit
- Greater than 1 inch per week
- Between ½ and 1 inch per week
- Less than ½ inch per week

This map shows the weekly water deficit that can be expected by gardeners in the various parts of the country. Only a few places are free of a growing season deficit, and most have a deficit of ½ inch or more through the growing season. The deficits are more serious in Florida and the West because here the soil moisture storage is never fully replenished over the nongrowing season. Thus, these gardeners don't necessarily start with a full supply of moisture when they begin their gardening in the spring. Data taken from Joe R. Eagleman, The Visualization of Climate (Lexington, Mass.: Lexington Books, 1976).

without waterlogging the soil. In my garden, I've tried all sorts of ways of doing this, none of them altogether successful. The most efficient way in terms of saving water and protecting the soil from waterlogging is some sort of trickle irrigation system that delivers the water directly to the plants in small amounts. But except where moisture deficits are severe and perennial, many gardeners won't have the patience or desire to go to the trouble to set up such a system. Putting water into furrows cut alongside the plants is also an efficient way to deliver water to the soil, but in my garden at least, I always end up overwatering one end of the furrow and underwatering the other. So, after years of fooling around, I've gone back to overhead watering. I rationalize my methods by telling myself I am delivering the water to the plants in the way they "expect"—from the air. Surely a tropical plant like a pepper or a tomato needs a little water on its leaves from time to time!

How Much Water Should You Give?

The goal of watering is to put into the soil the difference between what the rain put in and what the plants took out. That way, your soil reservoir will always be nearly full. From the map, you can tell what the difference is likely to be in your part of the country. But remember, the weather is rarely average. You can make a rough approximation of the water needs of your garden in any particular week by keeping track of the average temperature. A good rule of thumb is, you will need an inch of rain a week plus an additional half inch for each 10 degrees the temperature averages above 60. During a cool spell, when nighttime lows are near 45 degrees and highs near 75 degrees (an average of 60 degrees), an inch of water per week might take care of your plants' moisture needs. But during a hot spell, with nighttime lows around 70 and daytime highs near 95 (an average of 82.5 degrees), two inches might be needed to maintain soil moisture levels. If you subtract from these numbers the amount of rain you actually received in a week, then you know how much water you have to add to replenish your garden's soil moisture reservoir.

How long do you have to water to get an inch of water on your garden? Well, you can find out by putting a pan in your garden and watering until the pan has an inch of water in it. Or you can calculate the flow of water through your sprinkler. If I hold my sprinkler nozzle still and direct it into a gallon milk pail, the sprinkler fills the pail in just twenty seconds. When the sprinkler is working, it waters about 1,200 square feet. In twenty seconds, therefore, it lays a gallon of water over 1,200 square feet. How long will the sprinkler take to cover the garden an inch deep in water? Sounds like one of those irritating rate-and-measure problems from high school, doesn't it? If you enjoy fooling with numbers, you can work it out yourself. It's helpful to know that a pan, one inch deep and one square foot on the bottom holds five pints of water. If you *don't* enjoy numbers, I suggest using the following rule of thumb: multiply the square footage covered by your sprinkler by the number of seconds it takes your sprinkler to fill a gallon container. Drop the last two digits of the number you get. The result is roughly the number of minutes you have to water your garden to put an inch of water on it. In the case of my sprinkler, the result is $1,200 \times 20 = 24,000 = 240$ minutes.

These calculations should convince you (they certainly convinced me!) what a lot of labor the atmosphere spares us by putting water on our gardens for us. To water my entire 4,800-foot garden I have to set my sprinkler four times. This means I have to water for sixteen hours just to get an inch of water on my whole garden. When I consider that in hot weather my plants can transpire two inches of water in a week, I begin to see why dry spells can put such pressure on me as a part-time gardener. Between the time when a gardener is not available for watering and the times when some gardens seem to resent being watered, there may be little time left to get the water on the garden that the plants need.

Droughts vs. Dry Spells

I started this chapter by arguing that droughts were man-made. A drought occurs in a garden when a gardener is unable to do something he or she normally does because of lack of rainfall. So much depends on what the gardener expects to do. If your normal gardening practice is to grow flowering cactuses, then you will rarely experience a drought. But if you are in the habit of growing the flowers and vegetables that are traditional in American gardens, then you have to expect to experience droughts and dry spells. The American climate is rough and unreliable, first hot then cold, first wet then dry. And most of our traditional garden plants originate from tropical or moist climates. Nothing reasonable tells us that we should expect plants originating in tropical or maritime climates to grow readily in our "temperate" climate. Only tradition and stubbornness make it so.

A gardener must think of himself as the curator of a collection of exotic plants. The garden is a little horticultural park, analogous to a zoo. A zookeeper would not throw a gorilla out in a Philadelphia snowdrift and complain that the poor animal died of a "cold snap." Nor should a Chicago gardener throw his tomato plants out in a Chicago summer and complain that they died of a drought. It is not the weather that is unreasonable, it is the gardener's expectations.

If a gardener's expectations with respect to his climate are reasonable, then his plants need never experience drought. Reasonable expectations for gardening in the United States include provision for wide variation in the amount of rain received from week to week. Let the gardener beware and his plants will flourish.

Some Comments
on Catastrophic Droughts

But what of *real* droughts? Not the suburban dry spells that irritate American gardeners, but real droughts. Like the Sahelian droughts in the 1970s. Like the Dust Bowl years. Droughts where agriculture fails, livestock dies, and people are driven off the land by starvation and diseases. Are these not meteorological calamities outside the control of human beings?

Not entirely. The first step in such a calamity is the extension of human population and traditional agricultural practices to a region that is not suited to them. The extension takes place during wet years. The intrusion is continued and extended by the drilling of wells into the water table. Population collects around the water sources. In grasslands, population means cattle. Cattle means grazing. Concentration of cattle means overgrazing. Overgrazing means destruction of the soil's capacity to hold water.

Now the stage has been set for a drought. A few years of low rainfall occur, back to back. The water table falls, surface water supplies are eliminated. The scarred soil dries out completely. Demand for water increases at the well heads and the pumps begin to have difficulty keeping up. Marginal agricultural plots fail and cattle begin to die. If the drought is severe enough, people go hungry. The desert begins to encroach on the once productive land. Newspapers rail against the unreliability of the weather.

But such calamities are entirely predictable. The same kind of tragedy has occurred repeatedly here in the United States, in the High Plains east of the southern Rockies where wheat is grown. The fact is that the Plains climate is not always appropriate for growing wheat. High Plains farmers can greatly extend the number of years when it is posible to grow wheat by how they grow it. But no matter how careful they are, there are going to be years when they cannot make a good crop. If our agricultural and food distribution systems are based on the assumption that abundant wheat can always be grown on the High Plains, then those systems are irrational.

One of my anxieties, as a gardener and as a person interested in the weather, is that we in the United States may now be setting the stage for one of the most calamitous droughts the human species has ever witnessed. A distressingly large proportion of the world's grain is grown in the area between the Mississippi River and the east face of the Rockies. Rainfall amounts in much of this area are variable and marginal, and over the years, farmers have learned to assure themselves of a crop by growing drought-resistant strains and by employing careful cultivation practices. Beneath much of this area is an underground reservoir of water, an aquifer that supplies the streams and wells of the area. In an attempt to assure crops in dry years, farmers began to tap this aquifer with deep wells. Of course, once the wells were drilled, it seemed reasonable to employ them all the time rather than just for emergencies. Consequently, agriculture has begun to shift away from a dry-land agriculture based on drought-resistant varieties and water conservation techniques to an agriculture that is really more appropriate to a humid climate.

This system would work just fine if the aquifer were inexhaustible. But it's not. We've all seen that engaging commercial on television by a company that manufactures pumps that can work deeper than conventional pumps. It's the commercial in which the little boy and his dog run joyfully in a shower of water pumped from deep under the ground. Did you ever question why markets exist for companies to drill and service very deep wells? Have you ever wondered what it means that the shallow wells are running dry?

A drought disaster on the American High Plains is almost sure to happen one of these years. Here is how it will come about. There will be a few years of very low rainfall. Traditional dry-land farmers will be unable to make a crop; they will either require emergency water supplies or their crops will fail. If the crops fail, the price of food is driven up; if emergency irrigation is developed, demands on the aquifer will increase. High food prices will increase the pace of agricultural activity in the irrigated areas. The pumps will work overtime. Water levels will drop in the aquifer; pumps will begin to fail. Once this happens, the collapse of Plains agriculture could be precipitous and total. Generations will write later about the great dustbowl of the eighties.

Water management is a simple business. It's a simple put-and-take proposition. But it requires clear thought. The water which we put on our plants comes from somewhere. If the source is not replenished, then eventually we will experience a drought. We have a lot of information about the rainfall that provides the sources for all our groundwater. It's easy to see that water use in an area should not be permitted to exceed the average input to the aquifer in the region. If such a policy is not followed, there will be a drought. And it won't be because the weather was extraordinary. It will be because people have been stupid.

14

THUNDERSTORMS

As a gardener, I have mixed feelings about thunderstorms. In many summers they provide the only rain my garden gets for weeks at a stretch. When the soil stiffens and cracks and the plants begin to look listless and thirsty, I long for a storm. But once the clouds actually begin to gather, I get uneasy. Some thunderstorms bring wind that batters the plants to the ground and driving rain that washes out the rows in the lower end of the garden. Worse, a thunderstorm can bring severe lightning strikes, which start fires in my neighbors' barns, or kill cattle as they shelter under the big trees that dot the pastures hereabouts. Some thunderstorms are accompanied by tornadoes big enough to twist the tops off some local trees as one might twist the tops off carrots before bringing them in to cook. Or worse.

So, as the sky quickly darkens and the roll cloud of the thunderstorm churns across the valley toward the farm, I hurry to get the last equipment under cover and the stakes and fences in the garden firmly set. And I run through a checklist in my mind of the hazards that a thunderstorm can bring.

Thunderstorms are one of many meteorological calamities that present more hazards to the gardener than to the garden. True, a thunderstorm's high winds and torrential rains can leave a garden looking whipped and drowned. And it's also true that a lightning strike in the neighborhood can do electrical damage to plants in a garden, stunting them or even killing them outright. True, too, a severe hailstorm can strip a garden in minutes. But a garden is relatively easily defended against wind and rain, and the odds are against a bolt of lightning directly striking the garden. Severe hailstorms are unusual except in the small portion of the High Plains just east of the Rockies. Hail has earned most of its awesome reputation as an agricultural wrecker because this area happens to be one of the world's most productive wheat growing areas, and wheat is a crop that is particularly vulnerable to hail damage.

For every way a thunderstorm can do damage to a garden, it can do more damage to the gardener. The most obvious of a thunderstorm's hazards for people is lightning. More than a hundred people are killed in the United States each year by lightning and about twice as many are injured. These numbers may not sound very large for a country of 220 million, but the numbers are a bit misleading. Two-thirds of the people who are killed by lightning are *outdoors*. If you begin to think about what a small portion of the population is likely to be wandering about outdoors in a thunderstorm, you begin to get the impression that lightning is a considerable hazard for anyone who is unfortunate or foolish enough to be caught out in it.

In fact, one of the most lethal temptations of country life is the impulse to help the neighbors get the hay in before a thunderstorm. Statistics show that over the last three decades, better than one in every fifteen people who were killed by lightning were on or near a tractor at the time of their death. Seeing the neighbors hurling bales of hay on the hayrick as the sky blackens overhead, it seems cruel not to send all the members of your family out in the field to help. And once out there, it's so hard to quit. You say, "Just one more swath of hay to bale," or "Just one more row of bales to pick up," until there you are, stuck in the middle of the haymow, a metal tractor by your side and lightning striking on every hand, and a quarter of a mile of exposed ridge between you and the barn. Whatever the lightning death rate may be for people in general, I don't doubt that the death rate for people who have let themselves get into that sort of predicament is pretty high.

Another serious hazard of thunderstorms is tornadoes. Unlike lightning, tornadoes aren't very common. But when they occur, they are unimaginably destructive. An average of a hundred people a year are killed by tornadoes, but these numbers understate the consequences of a tornado outbreak. One severe outbreak can kill dozens of people on a single afternoon. The damage inflicted on a residential area when a tornado touches down is comparable to severe earthquake damage or damage from aerial bombing in wartime.

I have the feeling that more people should be aware of the danger of tornadoes. Their occurrence is by no means confined to the traditional "tornado alley" states of the Midwest. True, the traditional tornado states such as Oklahoma, Indiana, Texas, Illinois, and Nebraska all have high tornado rates, ranging from four to eight tornadoes per year in an area equivalent to a square measuring one hundred miles on a side.

But some other states also have high tornado rates. For instance, parts of Delaware, Florida, Louisiana, Massachusetts, Mississippi, and Missouri all have rates nearly as high as some of the tornado alley states.

The statistics for Delaware and Massachusetts are particularly unsettling because these states have relatively few thunderstorms in an average year. Massachusetts and Delaware residents experience just about twenty-five days with thunderstorms in an average year, and these yield about five tornadoes per hundred-mile square in Massachusetts and three to four in Delaware.

Oklahoma has many more tornadoes—nearly eight per hundred-mile square—but Oklahoma has more than twice as many days with thunderstorms as Delaware or Massachusetts. These statistics are difficult to evaluate, but surprisingly, they suggest that the risk of getting a tornado out of a particular thunderstorm may be as great in Massachusetts as it is in Oklahoma. The same generalization seems to apply to Delaware, and may apply to a great many places in the United States that don't think of themselves as places that have a tornado hazard. Thus, I think it's prudent to believe that wherever severe thunderstorms can be found, residents should keep in mind the *possibility* of tornadoes.

Even if a thunderstorm doesn't have a tornado, its winds can be destructive. Every summer we get gale-force winds out of at least one or two thunderstorms. To trees heavily laden with leaves, such gales can be quite a shock. Sometimes limbs are torn off and whole trees uprooted by these violent squalls. Cornstalks, bean poles, and tomato trellises are smashed to the ground, and leaves of tender greens like young chard and spinach and lettuce get torn and bruised.

Flash flooding is an additional hazard from thunderstorms in some parts of the country. In the desert a sudden thunderstorm can drop several inches of rain on a landscape impervious to water. In minutes, this water can be funneled into dry river beds and canyons and become a life-threatening torrent.

How a Thunderstorm Works

A thunderstorm is simply a cumulus cloud that has gotten out of hand. Recall the thermal over the hot cornfield we discussed in chapter 5. The air over the cornfield rises, because hot air is lighter than cool air. If such a rising packet of warm air is moist, and if it rises enough to release its moisture, more heat is generated by the condensation process. If the water in the air freezes, still more heat is released. All these events serve to make the packet of warm air warmer than the air around it and more inclined to push farther up into the atmosphere. In this manner, heating of moist air near the surface by the sun shining on the ground can trigger an atmospheric chain reaction that converts the potential heat in warm, moist air into wind, electrical, and sound energy. The result of this conversion we call a thunderstorm.

Just how far this chain reaction will continue depends on the structure of the atmosphere through which the warm, moist air must rise. The most crucial feature of the atmosphere from the point of view of the thunderstorm development is the environmental lapse rate. The lapse rate is the speed with which the temperature decreases as altitude is increased. If the temperature falls off slowly, then the lapse rate is said to be low. When the lapse rate is low, a parcel of air that is raised up for any reason will become cooler than the air around it and will tend to fall back down to the level from which it came. Under these conditions, the atmosphere will be very stable and convective clouds such as cumulus or cumulonimbus won't develop. If, on the other hand, the lapse rate is high and the temperature falls off quickly with altitude, then parcels of air that are raised up will be warmer than the air around them and will tend to continue rising. Under these conditions, the atmosphere will be very unstable and large cumulus clouds will develop readily.

Lapse rates are increased by two related kinds of circumstances. If the air above the ground comes from a cooler source than the air near the ground, then the lapse rate will be increased. Another circumstance that makes for rapid lapse rates is the presence of a low-pressure trough aloft. Under these circumstances, the unusually rapid drop of pressure from surface to high altitudes makes for more rapid expansion and cooling at higher levels, hence a higher lapse rate. Under both these circumstances, the atmosphere is unstable and cumulus clouds develop quickly.

Once the cumulus clouds are well enough developed to push through the freezing level of the atmosphere, the process of thunderstorm formation begins in earnest. During the thunderstorm season, the level at which water in the atmosphere freezes is generally found between 5,000 and 12,000 feet above the surface—or to put the matter more precisely, the 32-degree temperature line is found between 5,000 and 12,000 feet. The distinction between the freezing altitude and the 32-degree altitude is important because liquid water exists in clouds above the 32-degree altitude where temperatures are several degrees below freezing. The water doesn't freeze immediately because water in clouds behaves a little differently than the water we are used to. The air in clouds is saturated with water. For saturated air to condense into ice crystals, each crystal must have a nucleus—a smaller ice crystal or a minute impurity in the air—around which the water molecules can condense and freeze. When air is saturated, many of the water molecules can't find nuclei and thus cannot freeze immediately. In the powerful thermals of a developing thunderstorm, droplets of liquid water can be whooshed in a few seconds from warm altitudes to altitudes substantially colder than freezing. Physicists tell us that a water droplet that is rapidly cooled in this manner has a different electrical charge at its center than at its edges. Such droplets are charged negatively at their edges and charged positively at their centers. When these supercooled droplets find a nucleus and suddenly begin to freeze from the outside in, the stress on them is too great and they fly apart. When the droplet shatters, the shell fragments, carrying the negative charge, tend to end up at lower levels of the cloud, while the positively charged droplets of spray spilled out of the center of the droplet tend to be lifted upward in the thermal toward the top of the cloud. Thus a cumulus cloud which has built itself up beyond the freezing level begins to have a positive charge near its top and a negative charge near its bottom.

As the cumulus cloud continues its development above the freezing level, it begins to form hail. Ice crystals at the top of the cloud become larger and larger as supercooled water pumped up from the bottom of the cloud condenses on them. As these crystals get larger, they tend to sink to warmer regions only to be carried aloft again and receive a new coating of supercooled water or even snow. This tendency of hailstones to wander around in a thunderstorm accounts for their ringlike internal structure with alternate layers of clear ice, "snow ice," and grainy material like sleet.

The formation of hail in a cloud in which positive and negative charges are segregated in different parts of the cloud apparently contributes significantly to the further segregation of these charges. An ice pellet falling to the lower part of the thundercloud, where charges tend to be negative, will tend to have its positive charges on the lower outside surface (because unlike charges attract) and its negative charges on the inside and top surface. As its weight causes it to sink through the masses of upward-moving water droplets, the water will tend to wash the positive charges off the surface of the hailstone and carry them upward, leaving the falling ice pellet with mostly negative charges. The more hail that is formed, the more powerfully charged the thundercloud is likely to become.

If this process of segregation of charges within the cumulus cloud continues for long enough, it will be neutralized by a lightning bolt accompanied by thunder. Lightning bolts may pass from the positively charged top of the cloud to the negatively charged bottom, or from the negatively charged bottom to the positively charged earth beneath the cloud. At this point, the storm officially becomes a thunderstorm. A lightning strike to the ground usually begins with the cloud sending earthward a relatively weak and slow electrical impulse called a stepped leader; when contact with the ground has been established, the ground sends back a return stroke. This return stroke is by far the most violent part of the lightning strike, reaching potentials of 100 million volts, and may actually consist of several rapid strokes in succession. The whole process takes barely a second. The violent heating of the air produces shock waves in the air that spread outward from the conductive pathway of the lightning, producing thunder. If the path of the lightning is all about the same distance from the observer, then the sound will arrive all at once and the thunder will be heard as a sharp "crack!" If the path of the bolt extends toward or away from the observer, then the sound will arrive a bit at a time and the thunder will be of the long, rumbling kind.

In its early stages of development, a thunderstorm is all upward motion. It's a bit like a juggler who has started hurling objects in the air just as fast as he can. For a while he can go on doing it, but eventually there are going to be more objects up there than he can catch and throw back, and they're all going to come tumbling down on him. A cumulus cloud can hold up all its ice and water and air only so long as the upper levels of the atmosphere permit it to continue its upward expansion. As soon as the cloud hits a layer of the atmosphere that won't support farther upward expansion, the drafts begin to falter. At this point, all the ice and cold water and cold air that the cloud has been holding up begin to sink. Once the cold downdrafts overwhelm the warm updrafts, the storm begins a precipitous collapse. Cold air, cold water, and sometimes ice, tumble from the top of the cloud to the ground. The ice and cold water deluge the ground and the cold air fans out ahead of the storm cloud as a powerful cold wind known appropriately as a "downburst."

Once a thunderstorm cloud reaches the downburst stage, it rapidly diminishes in intensity. But its downburst disturbs the lower atmosphere around it and encourages other convective clouds to develop in its neighborhood. These in turn rapidly appropriate the resources of moisture made available by the first cloud and go on to become powerful clouds in themselves. So even though the individual clouds themselves may come and go, the storm continues across the countryside unabated.

Super Thunderstorms

All thunderstorms are a bit unsettling. But some thunderstorms are truly monsters. We have already seen that the energy available to a thunderstorm depends on the height of the column of warm, moist air that supplies its energy. Most cumulus clouds disperse long before they reach the top of the lower atmosphere. But some thunderstorms grow so tall that they manage to penetrate all the way through the lower atmosphere and into the stratosphere. The thermal column of such a thunderstorm may exceed 50,000 feet. Such a column of rising air is an immense source of energy. It makes possible the lifting and accumulation of immense quantities of water and electricity for later delivery as cloudbursts, hail, and lightning. It also makes possible the development of tornadoes.

For a super thunderstorm to develop, all the conditions have to be just right. First of all, there must be a lot of warm, moist air available: dew points in the sixties and temperatures in the nineties, if possible. The best source of warm, moist air for tornadoes is a maritime tropical air mass moving northward from the Gulf of Mexico. The second important condition for a super thunderstorm is a stream of warm, dry air aloft flowing at right angles to the moist air at the surface. Thus, if the moist flow at the surface is from south to north, the warm, dry flow aloft should be from west to east. The dry layer aloft produces a dry inversion, a factor that temporarily discourages the formation of a convective cloud. Third, there should be something to make ripples in this upper-air flow: a mountain range or a cold front to the west will serve this function very nicely. Last of all, above the warm, moist air at the surface and above the warm, dry air farther up, a jet stream must be flowing overhead, preferably just emerging from a trough.

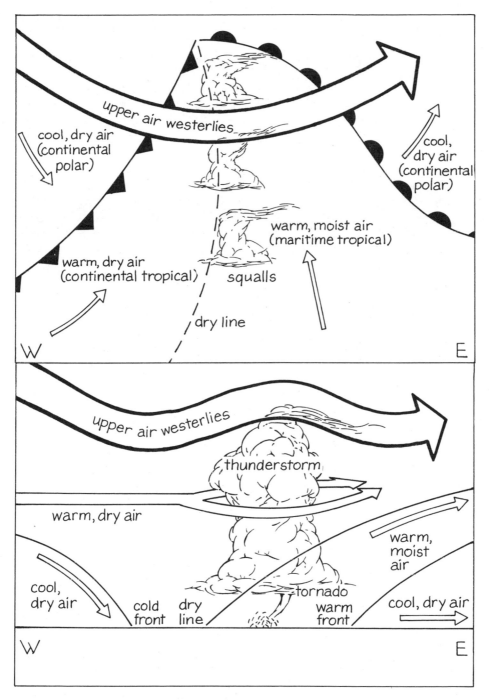

Two views of the development of a super thunderstorm. The upper illustration shows the top view. Below it is a side view, seen from the south. As shown in this diagram, these powerful storms may be accompanied by tornadoes. Adapted from Joe R. Eagleman, Meteorology: The Atmosphere in Action (New York: Van Nostrand Reinhold, 1980).

These conditions get together to produce monster thunderstorms in a manner every gardener will sympathize with. For super thunderstorms to grow, small thunderstorms have to be inhibited. It's like thinning your crops. If you want to have a large, healthy head of lettuce you have to thin out the smaller plants around its roots that might crowd it and compete for nutrients. To see how small cumulus clouds are thinned to make super thunderstorms, you can try a little "dishpan" experiment.

Put a colander and a funnel in a dishpan of water. When the colander has filled, remove it quickly from the water so that it brings a full load of water up with it. Watch the surface of the water in the colander as it drains away. It is turbulent, but the turbulence is in little bits. The surface of the water is bumpy and irregular. Now, quickly draw the funnel out of the water in the same manner. As the water streams out of the funnel, it forms one smooth vortex, swirling around a central point. What makes the single large vortex possible is that the funnel constrains the flow to a single outlet.

The way small thunderstorms get thinned to make super thunderstorms works on somewhat the same principle as an upside down funnel. The warm inversion serves to put a weak lid on the volatile moist layer below. The inversion suppresses convection because as packages of air move upward they are suddenly cooler than the warm air above the inversion layer and tend to sink back down again. As the lower atmosphere is heated by the sun it becomes more and more buoyant; it wants to go up, but it can't because of the inversion layer. One after another, the cumulus clouds try the layer and fall back. But each time they do this, they put a little moisture into the inversion layer, each time making it a bit more unstable. If one of those cumulus clouds can finally manage to break through the inversion layer, then the warm, moist air pinned to the ground by the inversion layer rises upward through the gap just as the water rushed downward through the funnel when it was removed from the basin.

If a particular thunderstorm is to puncture the inversion layer and become a super thunderstorm, it needs a little help. This help seems to be provided by the jet stream and by the ripples in the upper-air westerlies. The ripples have the effect of making places where the air in the westerlies is already headed upward. In these places, the thermals in the moist, warm surface layer may have an easier time getting through the inversion. Additional encouragement is provided by a jet stream. If a jet stream is just emerging from a trough, it exerts a gentle sucking effect on the atmosphere below it. In these parts of its wanderings, the jet stream is rising slightly and spreading out. Since the air in the stream is now distributed over a larger area, the pressure falls within it and air is drawn in from below to equalize the pressure. If such a region of the jet stream overlies a region where thunderstorms are trying to puncture a dry inversion, then all the conditions are present that make for truly violent thunderstorms.

These conditions are commonly met when a low-pressure center with accompanying upper-air low moves through the Mississippi Valley. Warm, moist air feeds in from the soupy waters of the Gulf of Mexico; warm, dry air filters in aloft from the southwest to provide the inversion; a cold front presaging an advancing continental polar air mass pushes in from the northwest to provide the rippling effect in the westerlies; and the westerlies sweep around the low in a great U, taking their northward turn as they pass over the warm sector of the low. When this combination of conditions occurs, tornadoes break out in the lower Mississippi Valley.

But the conditions are also frequently met on the east face of the Rockies in a different meteorological situation: a small low center in the west Texas/ west Oklahoma region draws warm, moist air westward until it washes up against the east face of the Rockies; warm, dry air from the Great Basin flows out of the high country and instead of sinking, it flows out on top of the warm, moist air, making the inversion. Overhead, the jet stream lies on a southwest to northeast track, arching northward from Arizona to the northern Great Plains. With the stage thus set, a little ripple that flows along the jet stream will provide the necessary upper-air weakness to cause spectacular thunderstorm development along the east face of the Rockies.

Given the specificity of these conditions, it's no surprise that tornadoes occur so rarely outside the United States. A world map with tornadoes dotted on it shows the eastern half of the United States to be the Saudi Arabia of tornado production. Once again, the unique configuration of the North American continent serves to make us the severe weather center of the world.

What Can You Do about a Thunderstorm?

Knowing how a thunderstorm works and what hazards it presents helps one to take precautions against those hazards. For gardeners living in New England or on the West Coast, where thunderstorms are comparatively unusual, such precautions might not seem to be worth the effort. But in such places as Indiana or Florida or Oklahoma, which have as many as sixty thunderstorms in an average year, some long-term precautionary efforts seem sensible.

In such climates, for instance, a gardener might particularly consider laying out the garden on a flat spot, or terracing it, or following the contours of the land to minimize the possibility of washouts. An inch of rain in ten minutes can make an awful mess of a badly laid out garden. The garden might also be sheltered from the west, since the strongest thunderstorm winds usually come from the west. Large trees in the neighborhood of the garden should be kept well pruned, and dead or weakened trees that might fall in a gale should be removed. Stakes and trellises should be anchored securely in the ground.

Perhaps more important than precautions that protect the garden are precautions that protect the gardener and his or her family. Lightning protection to buildings not only protects the buildings but the inhabitants as well. It

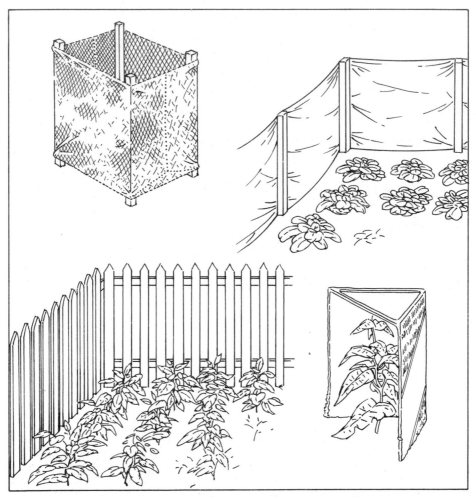

Here are some windbreaks you can use in the garden. Upper left, a favorite shrub or plant can be surrounded with burlap; or, upper right, a screen can be made with wooden stakes and a sheet of burlap or plastic and positioned between the garden and the prevailing winds. Lower left, a picket fence makes an excellent permanent windbreak. Lower right, a cutaway cardboard milk carton can provide an emergency shelter for a single plant.

might be wise to scout the basement for the best place to take cover if a tornado ever comes your way. It might also be wise to get hold of one of the excellent pamphlets put out by NOAA on tornadoes and on lightning and go through them with members of your family. (See chapter 17 for the address of NOAA.) Certainly, children should have a plan of action which they put into effect when caught away from home by a storm, so that people are not rushing around in cloudbursts and tempests looking for each other.

On the day a thunderstorm is expected, additional precautions are desirable. Sultry early morning weather is a pretty sure sign that late afternoon thunderstorms are likely, but if you are in any doubt, check a morning weather forecast. If NOAA considers that severe thunderstorms are likely in your area, then by morning it should have issued a "severe thunderstorm watch." These watches emanate from the Severe Storm Forecasting Center in Oklahoma. They mean that the forecasters have determined that many of the factors which encourage the development of severe thunderstorms are present in your area. Whenever such watches are broadcast in the morning, I plan to check in again later in the day. I generally also alert members of my family to the possibility of severe weather.

Unless the watch has been cancelled by midday, I begin to think about buttoning down my garden. It doesn't pay to wait too long. There are always more things to do than I anticipate, and I don't want to be running around outdoors as the lightning is striking all around. So, I put away the tools and equipment, drive in any poles that are loose, make sure all the tall plants are well fastened to their supports, and make sure that shed doors are fastened and greenhouses secure. A gardener who has livestock might want to make sure it has a place to shelter. Family members who are at home should be urged to stay close by, and family members away from home should perhaps be telephoned and warned.

During the afternoon, if the severe storms materialize, your local weather office will issue a severe thunderstorm warning. These warnings indicate that severe weather is already in progress nearby and is moving in your direction. Depending on how far away the storms are and how rapidly they are moving, they should be upon you in one to a few hours. Soon, the western sky will begin to darken, the radio to crackle with static, and distant rumblings of thunder to be heard.

On rare occasions, NOAA will also issue a tornado warning. These warnings indicate that there is a tornado on the ground or showing up on radar, and that it is headed in your general direction. In case of such a warning, I would take particular care to keep children at hand.

As the thunderstorm approaches, you will notice its roll cloud. The roll cloud is a band of darker cloud, parallel to the ground, with lighter grey behind it. It usually appears to churn horizontally like an old-fashioned reel lawn mower. By the time that cloud gets to you, you should be *indoors*. The cloud marks the edge of the downburst surge of cold air. Lightning and rain are moments away.

Once indoors you are reasonably safe. Relatively few lightning deaths occur to people in dwellings, and most of these befall people who are electrically connected to the outside, in some way. A severe thunderstorm is not a good time to reroute your TV antenna, chat on the telephone, or even to finish the washing up. Two summers ago, I was washing spinach in the kitchen sink during a lightning storm. Feeling a bit uneasy, I removed my hands from the water and shook the water off my fingers, spreading them apart as I did so. At that precise instant, lightning struck outside. Ten little bolts of lightning jumped from the ends of my outspread fingers to the water in the basin, making a little "FFFTT" noise like the spitting of a cat. It didn't hurt me, but since that time, I don't wash spinach during lightning storms.

If the window is closed, there's no harm in standing next to it to watch the storm. People near windows are not more susceptible to lightning strike than anywhere else in the house. There is so little one can do about a lightning storm and so much one *shouldn't* do while it's in progress, I generally take them as an opportunity to contemplate the raw power of nature. As the roll cloud surges by, you can often look into the maw of the thunderhead where clouds are tortured and twisted by the immense forces of the wind. There is so much that is unknown about these great storms.

Thunderstorm-watching is interesting even at night. As soon as the storm is close enough so that its flashes of lightning and rumbles of thunder are heard distinctly, you can begin to mark its approach. The thunder associated with a particular lightning flash arrives at your ears substantially after the flash of light. The longer this delay, the further away the flash of lightning was. As a child I was taught to "count alligators and divide by five" to find out how many miles away the lightning strike was. I would chant resolutely, "one alligator, two alligators, three alligators," until the thunder came. As long as there were enough alligators I didn't worry too much about lightning.

When a thunderstorm comes upon you in the night, you can lie in bed watching the flashes and counting the alligators. Each alligator is worth 1,100 feet, and there will be fewer and fewer of them until the thunder is coming so hard upon lightning that there is no time for alligators at all. Then, if you are like me, you will pull the covers over your head and wait until the alligators return.

My favorite time in a thunderstorm is just after it has passed. After a daylight storm, the air is suddenly bright and lucid, the great clouds go rumbling off to the east, and the birds sing at the return of the sun. From my safe vantage point behind the thunderclouds, I can now watch the fulminations with an easy mind. At a quick glance, such a line of receding thunderstorms seems as stable as a mountain range. But the individual "mountains" of the range are like billows of steam over a boiling pot; they surge up and fall back only to surge up again in another place.

As you can see, I definitely have mixed feelings about thunderstorms. But my dog feels only one way about them; he just doesn't like them at all. When all other warning systems have failed, when I haven't remembered to listen to the radio, or nobody has brought me word of the approaching storm, the dog provides me with my first warning. Long before the western sky begins to darken, the dog emerges from under the porch where he has been dug in all day, and comes to sit by me in the garden.

He knows he's not supposed to be in the garden. He's a willing enough old fellow, but try though he might, he just can't seem to get the hang of where he can walk in a garden and where he can't. So we agreed he shouldn't come in the garden at all.

If he wants to be near me when I'm weeding, he dozes in the grass by the side of the garden and doesn't try to come in.

Consequently, when he comes and flops down beside me in the garden, I know something is up. And sure enough, within fifteen minutes or so, I'll hear the first faint grumbles of thunder. First it's more a feeling than a sound, almost as if I am sensing vibrations too low or too high to hear. But soon enough, it is recognizable as thunder. The western sky begins to look ugly and I know the time is long past when I should have gotten in the tools and made ready for some rain and a bit of a blow.

15

HURRICANES

I grew up near the Atlantic Ocean among marshes and estuaries, only a few miles back from a low-lying coast. I remember the month of August with a special kind of pleasure. At this time of year, mainland, marshland, and ocean would blend together into a grey, hot, humid haze. My mother would open all the windows, pull all the blinds, and hope to catch a sea breeze, but no breeze stirred. The dogs lay under the tables and panted; the cats lurked in the cool tunnels of the earth cellar. August was a time to do nothing and be proud of it.

But I also remember August with a bit of anxiety. August was the time of hurricanes and polio. Hurricanes and polio were different in many ways but were alike in that both were very bad things that usually happened to other people. During my childhood, I was lucky enough never to get polio. But we had bad hurricanes three times.

The hurricanes were pretty scary for the adults, but for a child, they were mostly a lot of fun. First, there was all the getting ready: buying candles and flashlight batteries and food, filling the car with gasoline, helping the neighbors board up the only plate-glass window in the neighborhood, and making sure the buildings were closed up snug and everything loose was stashed away.

Then there was watching for the storm. I remember my father pointing out to me the eerie sky with its banners of cirrus clouds radiating out of the south, and I remember the strange feel of the air. The first breezes of the hurricane were so mild, so moist, so soft as to be barely distinguishable from the feel of one's own skin.

The storm itself wasn't so bad, except I had to stay indoors. I remember peering through the windows watching the water sheet down outside, the ocean tide creep up in the back marsh and the trees lash back and forth. Every time the wind let up I would say, "Is this the eye of the hurricane? Can I go outside and see the eye?"

Only one of the storms was frightening to me as a child. The lights went out and before my father could get candles lit there was a great tearing sound and a crunch and a shudder. And then a colossal crack followed by an awesome thud. We lit the candles and everybody peered out windows to see what had happened. But it was too dark to see and nobody dared to go outside.

After that I don't remember much: more wind and more rain, I suppose. My father put me to bed with a candle lantern. After he had told me to stay in bed and not to play with the candle he pointed out that the wind was blowing against my window. My window was on the west side of the house. He said that meant the hurricane was almost over.

Best of all, I remember waking up the day after a hurricane to a world transformed for the benefit of a child. The horse chestnuts were blown all over the ground so that I could pick up dozens in a minute. Wind-blown fruit trees lay on their sides, so that I might have the pick of the crop while standing on the ground. A tree leaned against the house so that I could clamber up it and gain the roof peak. A giant old poplar that I had always wanted to climb, lay flat on the ground so that its trunk was like an aerial roadway across the lawn. And wonder of wonders, the whole east side of the house was covered with a mass of powdery bits of leaves, as if somebody had mixed leaves in a blender and sloshed them all over the house.

No doubt my father took a different view of the hurricanes than I did. He has always been an avid gardener. All year long he worked planting his orchard, setting out rows of raspberries and blueberries, planting ornamental trees, mowing grass pathways that wandered here and there in the yard. Now that I am a gardener, I know how it must have broken his heart to see his world disordered so. When it happened twice in two weeks in 1955, he must have been devastated. If so, he never let me know of it. Fathers (or gardeners?) must have been a stronger breed in those days.

What Is a Hurricane?

A hurricane is a rotating wind and rain storm that arises over tropical ocean water. By comparison with the big storms that sweep across the United States every winter, hurricanes are small. Even a very large hurricane will influence only an area 500 miles in radius, and the zone of extraordinary storminess is smaller, extending out from the center less than 150 miles.

But by the standard of ordinary storms, hurricanes are incredibly intense. Even a weak hurricane may have a low-pressure center near 28 inches, rainfall amounts to over a foot in twenty-four hours, and storm tides of five feet above the sea level prevailing at the time of the storm. A severe hurricane may have central pressures approaching 27 inches, winds approaching 200 miles per hour, and storm tides over twenty feet!

The conditions in a severe hurricane are so far outside most people's experience that a simple recounting of the facts fails to make an adequate impression. Take the matter of wind velocity, for instance. For many places in the United States, a 40-mile-an-hour wind is the strongest wind experienced in an average year. Forty-mile-an-hour winds occur in big storms and in gusts from summer line squalls. A 40-mile-an-hour wind can gently flex the trunk of a largish tree, break twigs, make talking and walking difficult, and kick up twenty-foot waves at sea. An 80-mile-an-hour wind, such as might be experienced in a minimal hurricane, is twice as fast as a 40-mile-an-hour wind. But because of the physics of air pressure, such a wind is four times as powerful. Whole trees are uprooted, signs are flattened, antennas blown down, and anything loose—loose shutters, loose windows, loose doors, loose roofing—is torn off dwellings and destroyed. A 160-mile-an-hour wind, such as may be experienced in a very severe hurricane, is sixteen times as powerful as a 40-mile-per-hour wind. Objects in the environment behave in completely unexpected ways. Most houses are seriously damaged. Large objects, like roofs, tumble along over the ground. Planks fly along like missiles. If they strike a solid object like a tree or a house wall, they may plunge right through it like the blade of a knife. If any trees are left standing, the flat part of their leaves is dissolved as if sandblasted, leaving only the veins. People caught outside or flushed out of their shelters by the floods are often killed or injured by flying debris. Survivors report that in a wind of that strength, there is no sound.

The effects of hurricane storm tides are equally incomprehensible. All residents of coastlines have some experience with seasonal high tides. They know that several times a year the ocean waters pour inland over the marshes, and flood some of the lowest shore roads and beaches. But in a bad hurricane, floods will be as much as twenty feet above those seasonal flood tides. How bad could that be? No matter how hard I try to grasp it, I always draw a line in my mind twenty feet further up the shoreline. But of course the water is twenty feet deeper, not twenty feet farther inland. The twenty-foot height contour may be several *miles* inland. Moreover, in a hurricane, the surf line moves inland a corresponding distance so that waves may actually be breaking over the main streets of resort communities. Under these circumstances whole beach communities are set adrift from their foundations and brought miles inland in a storm rack that includes not only the usual seaweed, driftwood, and beer cans, but entire dwellings, pounding and bashing against each other as they surge along in the tide.

Perhaps the most inconceivable aspect of a hurricane is its capacity to produce rain. Under normal circumstances, a rainstorm which brings an inch of rain is a good, solid rainstorm. If it brings two inches, it is a real ground soaker. A six-inch rainfall is very rare—I do not think I remember one—but if it does occur, it is enough to saturate the ground. Any rainfall above six inches in a twenty-four-hour period will go directly into rivers and streams. Normal hurricane rainfalls exceed a foot. When a hurricane comes ashore and washes up against hilly terrain, the storm can unload all of its rain in a very limited area. Under these circumstances, rainfall totals can exceed 2 or 3 feet. To try and get a grip on what such rainfall totals might mean, I have done some calculations. There is a valley just to the north of where I live. The valley is about 200 feet deep. It has a stream running down the middle that drops about 50 feet over the whole length run of the valley. At the lower end where the stream flows out, the valley narrows into a tight V and here, there is a tiny village clustered around the remnants of an old mill. What would happen if 2½ feet of rain fell on that watershed? My calculations suggest that even if the first six inches of rain were stored in the ground, the water runoff would be enough to make a puddle on the floor of the valley that would be 30 feet deep. If all that water tried to get out the lower end of the valley at the same time, it would be 60 feet deep as it flowed through the village. Most of the houses in the village would be completely underwater.

How Do Hurricanes Form?

To make such extraordinary weather, extraordinary forces must be at work. The formation of hurricanes, like the formation of tornadoes, seems to have something to do with a dry inversion. The inversion in the case of the hurricane is the "trade wind inversion." The trade winds are two great currents of westward-moving air that flank the equator on the north and the south. The air in the trade wind zones is very moist and warm, just the sort of air that you would expect to give rise to constant thunderstorms and torrential rains. But trade wind weather is very tranquil. The reason is that overlying the moist, warm surface layer is a warm, dry layer that puts a lid on cloud development.

Everything about the weather in the Atlantic tropics is determined by the height and the strength of the trade wind inversion. The inversion is lowest near the coast of Africa and the weather is most tranquil near the coast of Africa. As the trade winds move west, they pick up moisture from the water below and become more buoyant. The further west they go, the higher up they push the inversion, and the more room there is for convective clouds to develop and showers and squalls to form.

The smallest ripple in the inversion can cause blemishes in the perfection of trade wind weather. Once or twice a week, such ripples set forth from the coast of Africa and plod along toward North and Central America. Each is like a little bump in the trade wind inversion where the moist surface layer pushes up a bit into the overlying warm, dry layer. These bumps are known as "easterly waves." Because the inversion is a bit higher in the easterly waves, they are accompanied by showery weather.

As an easterly wave proceeds westward up the sloping boundary of the inversion, there is more and more moist air below it. The clouds and showers that accompany it have more room to develop and the atmosphere below the inversion becomes more and more unstable. If some influence is encountered

(continued on page 198)

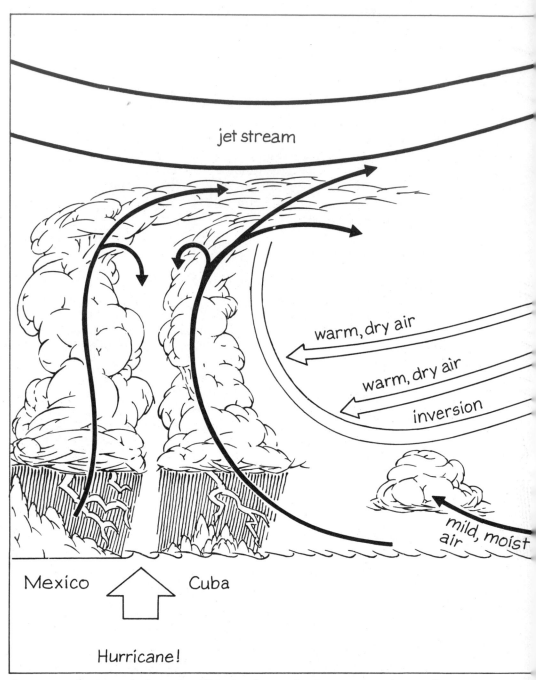

jet stream

warm, dry air

warm, dry air

inversion

mild, moist air

Mexico   Cuba

Hurricane!

As an easterly wave plods westward across the tropics, it may strengthen until eventually it develops into a full-fledged hurricane.

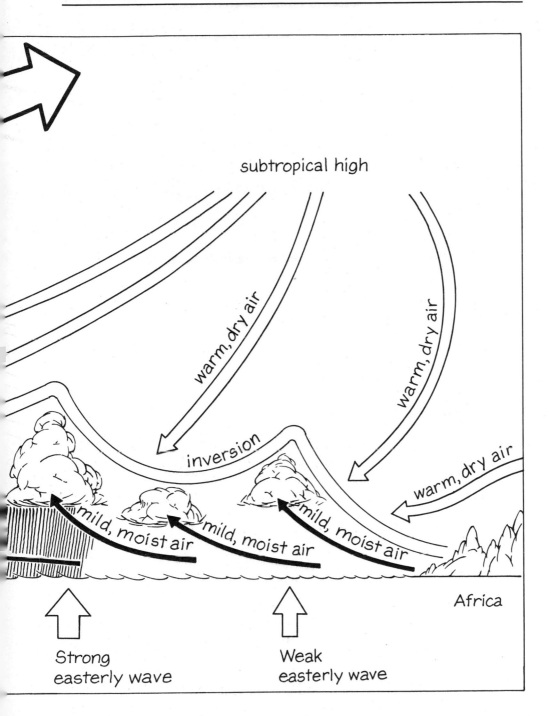

subtropical high

warm, dry air

warm, dry air

warm, dry air

inversion

mild, moist air

mild, moist air

mild, moist air

Africa

Strong
easterly wave

Weak
easterly wave

that weakens the inversion from above, then something spectacular takes place; the warm, moist air at the surface punctures the inversion and starts pouring upward through it. The effect is like the bursting of a dam. As the surface air rushes through, its moisture is converted to heat and its heat to more vertical motion. From every side, moist, soupy air rushes in to fill the vacuum left by the rising air. The coriolus force puts its sharp counterclockwise twist on the inrushing currents, and a tropical storm is born.

Although dozens of easterly waves set out from the African coast each year, and dozens more are formed elsewhere in the Atlantic, fewer than ten usually become hurricanes. The trade wind inversion is such a powerful force in tropical weather that it seems to break down only under very special circumstances.

First of all, the water surface and the air above it must be exceptionally warm and moist. These conditions are met in the western Atlantic in the late summer. During the ten weeks from mid-May to late July the sun stands nearly vertical over northern limits of the tropics. As it retreats southward in August, it leaves behind an exceptionally warm ocean. The temperature of the water and the dew point of the air above it may exceed 80 degrees, which is just about as high as dew points and seawater temperatures ever go. Once heated, the seawater surface is very slow to cool because each time the surface is cooled off a bit, warm water rises from below to replace it. Consequently, far into August and September, the northern tropical atmosphere retains its steamy summer heat.

The second special circumstance needed to break down the inversion seems to be the intrusion over tropical waters of some sort of upper-air disturbance from higher latitudes. Such intrusions are also likely to occur over the western Atlantic in late August and early September. The North American land mass cools much more rapidly than the ocean water. As it cools, the westerlies slip south and cold air masses intrude farther into the United States. As the westerlies wriggle and writhe over the United States, they send little eddies southward in the upper-air flow. These upper-air eddies apparently have the effect of weakening the trade wind inversion from above. So, with a little lift from above, and a big push from below, the inversion breaks down and the storm is formed.

If you have ever seen time-lapse satellite photos of a hurricane in action, you are in no doubt that a hurricane is a vortex. At the surface, long banks of tall rainclouds stream toward the center of the storm. Above the storm, a thin veil of cirrus spins outward as air at the top of the storm circulates away from the center. And at the center of the storm is the unmistakable eye. The eye of a hurricane is perhaps the most fantastic of all weather phenomena. As air rushes into the center of the storm, it spins faster and faster until its centrifugal force balances the pressures that pull the air in. At this point, the inrushing moist air can come no further and a slight vacuum is formed. Consequently, at the center of the hurricane is a circle perhaps ten to twenty miles wide in which there is barely any wind or clouds or rain at all. Because the air cannot enter from the sides of the eye, it is drawn down gently from the top of the storm. As it sinks down the eye, it is compressed and so is warm and dry at the surface, much like maritime air that has crossed a high mountain range.

How Hurricanes Move

The forces mustered by a hurricane are enormous. But, ironically, every hurricane seems to be at the mercy of outside forces that determine its direction of movement and course of development. At first, the young hurricane drifts toward the west in the steady westward-moving flow on the south side of the Bermuda Subtropical High. As it approaches North America, however, the steering influence of the Bermuda Subtropical High becomes less reliable. Sometimes the high is very strongly developed and the hurricane is carried far into the Gulf of Mexico; sometimes the high is moderately strong, and the hurricane turns northward around its west flank and strikes the Gulf States. Sometimes the high is so weak that the storm makes its turn early and strikes the Eastern Seaboard or misses land altogether. Since the Bermuda High is strongest in the summer and recedes eastward as fall comes on, the area of the coastline most often struck gradually moves eastward as the hurricane season progresses from the Mexican coast, to the Gulf coast, to the Atlantic coast.

Since the air currents that determine the movement of hurricanes in the western Atlantic are often weak and variable, the paths of hurricanes in this region are often highly erratic. Hurricanes can set off in one direction and then turn around and go back where they have come from. They can do loops and zig-zags. They can stop in their tracks for hours at a time. Weak upper-air troughs and the faint remnants of cold fronts hovering near a hurricane may quench it or may cause it to flare up. A hurricane can change from a dwarf into a giant overnight. And back again the next day.

That powerful hurricanes are affected by such atmospheric forces makes them a terrible forecasting headache. Each hurricane is tracked closely with satellite observations. Specially constructed airplanes fly right into the hurricane's wall and measure the conditions there. Each storm is given a name and the Weather Service issues regular advisories detailing the storm's progress and development. Still, the fact is that forecasters may have little way to know exactly where a particular hurricane is going to go or how it will develop. Therefore, if you live near a coastline where hurricanes prowl, you must keep your wits about you during the hurricane season.

Who Is at Risk from Hurricanes?

If you live in the eastern United States within 500 miles of a coastline, the chances are that at some time or other you will have some bad weather from a hurricane. What sort of bad weather, how bad it will be, and how often it will occur depends on what part of the coastline you are near and how near you are to it. Bear in mind that in general, while wind damage is the most dramatic and newsworthy feature of a hurricane, death from drowning presents the greatest risk for people.

Over the entire coastline of the United States from the Rio Grande to Eastport, Maine, two hurricanes can be expected to come ashore in an average year. Of these, one will, on the average, be severe. How often you will receive a visit from one of these hurricanes depends on which particular bit of coast you live near. In general, the places that "stick out" into an ocean have the highest

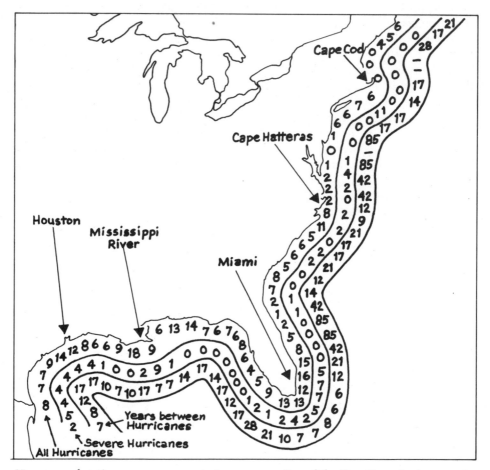

How many hurricanes can you expect on your section of the East Coast in the next 100 years? Data taken from Robert H. Simpson and Herbert Riehl, The Hurricane and Its Impact (Baton Rouge, La.: Louisiana State University Press, 1981).

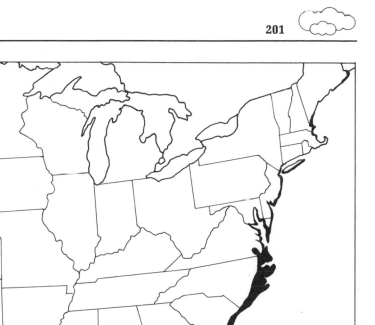

*How far do you have to go from the coast to be out of the reach of a hurricane flood
tide? Adapted from "Gulf and Atlantic Coastal Flood Plain; 10-Foot, 20-Foot, 30-Foot
Contours," prepared by B. Nadine Orabana for The Travelers Insurance Company.
Presented as an appendix in D. G. Friedman and R. S. Roy, "Simulation of Total
Flood Loss Experience on Dwellings on Inland and Coastal Flood Plains." Report
prepared for U.S. Department of Housing and Urban Development (Hartford, Conn.:
The Travelers Insurance Co., 1966).*

hurricane frequencies. If you look at the map I provided you can see that
places like the Louisiana delta, southern Florida, and the capes and islands off
the Eastern Seaboard get more than their share of hurricanes. Many points
along these coasts can expect a hurricane every ten years or so, and a severe
hurricane every twenty or thirty.

A hurricane brings three sorts of hazards: a coastal flooding hazard, a
wind hazard, and an inland flooding hazard. Of the three, the coastal flooding
hazard is the most narrowly confined. As the hurricane comes ashore, the
winds on its right side blow toward the coastline. Driven along ahead of the

wind, the hurricane's waves may reach heights of fifty feet or more. As the giant waves encounter the rising sea bottom, they are tripped up, so to speak, and fall toward the coastline. Their momentum carries them up on the shore, where they pile up on one another in a huge mound called a "storm surge."

Anybody who lives less than twenty feet above sea level should give some thought to the possibility of storm surge. For the United States coastline north of the Mason-Dixon line, the twenty-foot contour is mostly within sight of the ocean. Even so, it turns up in unexpected places, including parts of the metropolitan areas of New York, Boston, Baltimore, and Wilmington, to name a few. Along the southern coastline the twenty-foot contour often penetrates far inland. Deep penetrations occur along the North Carolina coast, south Florida, near Mobile, Alabama, around the Mississippi delta, and near Houston, Texas, including, as luck would have it, some of the most hurricane-prone portions of the coastline. Anywhere below the twenty-foot contour, hurricane flood waters may intrude. How deeply depends not only on the strength of the storm but on its speed as well. Slower-moving storms are more dangerous because they have more time to push the water inland.

Wind presents the most dramatic and obvious hazard of a hurricane, but like storm surge, it is a hazard somewhat limited in extent. In general, it is very unusual for hurricane winds to occur more than 200 miles inland. Usually, the penetrations are considerably less. How far they will penetrate in a particular case depends on the strength of the storm and how directly and rapidly it approaches the shoreline. Friction with the land surface and the deprivation of moisture supply from the ocean usually begin to take their toll on the strength of the hurricane as soon as the center encounters land. Hence, the deepest penetrations of hurricane winds usually occur with storms which hit a coastline very rapidly and directly. The map I have provided will give you some idea of where the wind risks lie from hurricanes and how the movement of the storm affects the risk. Bear in mind that the storm tracks I used in the map are only "for example." Just because I did not use your bit of coastline for an illustration, do not think that a hurricane cannot come calling tomorrow.

Of all the hazards of a hurricane, inland flooding is the most treacherous, because it can occur at such great distances from the coastline where all the maritime drama of a hurricane is unfolding. Hurricane Hazel (1954), which made landfall in South Carolina, brought floods to Toronto, Canada; in 1969, hurricane Camille, which made landfall on the Gulf coast, traveled up the Ohio River Valley and turned eastward to attack Virginia and West Virginia from the west. Hurricane Agnes came ashore in 1972 on the west coast of Florida, and devastated Harrisburg, Pennsylvania, more than 1,000 miles away.

Determining if you are in an inland hurricane flood hazard area may require a bit of research. During the 1960s, the Department of Housing and Urban Development prepared flood hazard maps for most floodprone communities and these maps should be available for study at your town or city planning department. You should also make inquiries of long-term residents

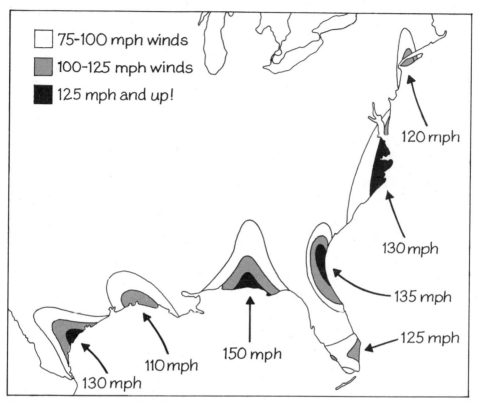

Some typical hurricane landfalls and how they would spread their winds inland. Adapted from D. G. Friedman, "Assessment of the Magnitude of Hurricane Hazard." Paper prepared for 11th Technical Conference on Hurricanes and Tropical Meteorology, American Meteorological Society, Miami, Fla., December 13–16, 1977.

and take a look at town archives. A good basic rule of thumb is, if there has *ever* been a flood in your area, then you have to expect that there will be a flood again. I would be most suspicious of reassurance such as, "Aw pshaw, M'am, there hasn't been a flood here since they built the Diddletown Dam in ought-six." Where *is* the Diddletown Dam? What's it made of? Has it been classified as unsafe by the Army Corps of Engineers? Has the lack of floods since "ought-six" been because of the dam or because no bad rainstorms have visited your hills since then?

What Do You Do When a Hurricane Strikes?

The best time to think about hurricane hazards is when you decide to make a commitment to a particular piece of land. If a hurricane disaster has ever come to a part of the world you are planning to give your heart to, then you can bet your mortgage that other hurricanes will come in the future. Hurricane hazard zones include some of the most tempting real estate in the world: white beaches with lashing surf, teeming marshes with great expanses of green and amber marsh grass, peaceful vales between picturesque inland hills. There are lots of reasons to live in such places, but long-term security of one's investment is not one of them. If you decide to stake your peas in a place like this, know what it is you are doing and make sure you have your priorities well thought out in advance. Nature may some day confront you with a choice: your land or your life. When that day comes, you may not have much time to ponder your decision.

Hurricanes are great media events and nobody who reads a newspaper, watches TV, or listens to the radio will be caught by surprise by an approaching hurricane. As for most meteorological hazards, the NOAA provides the media with three sorts of information about hurricanes. Hurricane *advisories* tell about the position, strength, and direction of movement of the storm. A hurricane *watch* is a message to the people of a particular area to be ready for a possible hurricane. Hurricane watches are issued to parts of the country which the NOAA feels have a better than even chance of being hit by a hurricane within forty-eight hours. If a hurricane watch is in effect in your area, make sure that you get up-to-date weather information at least every six hours. Do not go sailing or visit an isolated island or take a long hike in the mountains without a portable radio. The most serious of the Weather Service messages is a hurricane *warning*. A hurricane warning predicts the arrival of a hurricane in a particular region and stipulates particular hazards for the areas to be struck. A hurricane warning gives maximum predicted wind speeds, tide depths, and flash flood warnings. Such warnings may recommend evacuations or other protective courses of action.

A hurricane warning is a message to be taken very seriously. Listen carefully to the entire text of the warning. Make sure to take into account the location of the broadcasting station. Inland radio stations have been known to delete or deemphasize warnings which the Weather Service has directed toward coastline residents. If you are not sure you have heard the complete text of the warning, call the Weather Service or the broadcasting station and check it. Cross-check the message with one broadcast by a different TV or radio station. If you are not completely familiar with geographical places mentioned in the warning, get out a map and check them. Do not guess. Do not make assumptions.

When a hurricane warning has been issued for your area, obey it scrupulously. If hurricane winds are predicted, make preparations to be isolated for a time. You may expect to be without power, water, or transportation for many hours, perhaps for a few days. Store food and water, batteries, fuel, and other crucial materials. Batten down your property. Leave nothing outside that could blow around. Even large objects like picnic tables can become airborne missiles in an extreme hurricane. Make sure all doors, shutters, and other movable fixtures are secure, so that they cannot blow around in the storm. Board up large windows; tape or board up smaller ones, particularly those facing in the direction of the predicted wind directions.

Once the storm has begun, keep the windows shut and stay inside. Do not go rushing out in a hurricane gust to grab the lawn chair you forgot. You can monitor the progress of the storm by keeping track of the wind direction. Like any storm, a hurricane has a counterclockwise circulation. As the winds increase, they will do one of three things: (1) They will shift clockwise. This means that you will be on the right-hand side of the storm as it passes you. The right side of the storm is the strongest and you can expect the worst of the winds that the Weather Service is forecasting. (2) The winds will shift counterclockwise. This means that you will be on the left-hand side of the storm as it passes you by. The left-hand side of a storm is usually weaker and you can expect to be spared the worst of the storm. (3) The winds will remain about the same direction as the storm approaches. In this case, the storm is coming right at you. Once again, you should prepare for the worst.

Above all, beware of lulls in the storm, particularly if you are directly on the track of the hurricane. Hurricane winds vary as the spiral bands of the storm swing overhead, with gusts of great intensity followed by comparative lulls. Particularly treacherous is the hurricane's eye, where the wind may fall off almost completely, the rain may stop, and the sun may actually come out. Stay close to shelter. In general, a bad hurricane will not be over until the wind has swung around to the direction more or less opposite to the direction from which it started and then abated.

One last word. . . .

One of the hardest orders to obey is the order to evacuate. To leave a much-loved piece of property when it is at risk is a terribly difficult thing to do. There is no doubt that the dangers to the property are greater when you are not there to protect it. A window that pops open in a storm can be barricaded if there is somebody there to do it; if the house is evacuated, the wind and the rain can go to work on the opening they have created and worsen it.

But if an evacuation recommendation is given by disaster officials, then obey it. The people at the NOAA who make these decisions are fully aware of what they are asking. Disregard anybody who tells you about how in the last two warnings nothing happened. Every warning system must have false alarms if it is to provide timely advice to all who are in danger. Do not wait to see how the storm develops; by the time the storm develops, your escape routes will probably have been cut off. Do not hesitate. Almost every life that has been lost to hurricanes in the last two decades has been because of failure to understand or respond to evacuation orders. You must treat these evacuation orders with the greatest respect.

Remember, he who (or she who) gardens and runs away, lives to garden another day. Whatever havoc the hurricane may wreak on structures and plants, it cannot destroy the earth. And as every vegetable gardener knows, where there is earth, there is hope.

16

WINTER STORMS

I am surprised that the expression, "Happy as a meteorologist in winter," has not evolved to describe ecstasy. I have never known a meteorologist, amateur or professional, whose pulse did not quicken at the mention of a winter storm. Winter storms generate more intense and more variable weather than storms at any other time of the year. A single winter storm may bring rain, snow, freezing rain, ice pellets, thunderstorms, tornadoes, hail, floods, mudslides, and unseasonable heatwaves, and these effects may be observed over half the nation at once. Winter weather is the acme, the epitome, the quintessence of weather. So when a gale is blowing outside and frost and snow coat your windows and the power lines are down, remember: the weather-lovers of the world are in ecstasy.

How a Winter Storm Works

To call a winter storm a "snow" storm is to confuse things a bit. True, a tremendous amount of snow can fall from a winter storm in a very short period of time. But it is also true that the largest annual accumulations of snow do not come from storms—not directly, anyway—and it is also true that an awful lot of what falls from winter storms is not snow! Once this paradox is understood, then much that is puzzling about winter weather makes more sense.

The conditions that bring about a heavy snowfall are quite specific and not very common. For precipitation to be *heavy*, there has to be an ample moisture supply in the clouds where it is formed. For precipitation to be *snow*, the air at cloud level has to be cold. Heavy snow is unusual because air that is cold enough to make snow does not hold much moisture. Air at 30 degrees can hold barely a quarter of the water that air at 80 degrees can hold. Thus, for heavy snow to fall, there must be a steady injection of moisture into freezing layers of the atmosphere from warmer and wetter places. This sort of injection occurs in some parts of some winter storms and these produce heavy snowfalls. But it also occurs in two other situations that have more to do with local geography than they do with storms in the strict sense.

Injection of moisture into subfreezing layers of the atmosphere can occur when a subfreezing air current blows over an open water surface. Because the air near the water surface becomes warmer and more moist than overlying layers, the surface layer will tend to rise, forming convective clouds. If there is enough moisture available, these convective clouds will begin to shed their moisture as snow. Snow which falls downwind of large open bodies of water is named "lake effect snow." Lake effect snow can also occur as subfreezing air moves across the open ocean.

Moisture can also be injected into subfreezing layers of the atmosphere when mild, moist air is forced to ride up the side of a mountain range. As the air is forced up, it cools, eventually reaches its dew point, and its moisture begins to condense. If the temperature at this condensation level is below freezing, the precipitation will fall as snow. Snow falling on the windward side of mountain ranges is sometimes referred to as orographic snow, a term derived from an ancient Greek word meaning "mountain."

A map of annual snowfall shows that orographic and lake effect precipitation account for a very large proportion of snow that falls across the nation. If

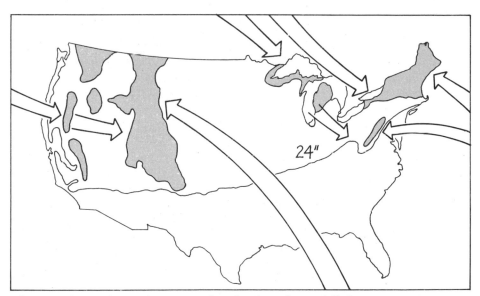

This map shows places where more than five feet of snow falls in an average year. The arrows indicate moisture-bearing air currents.

you draw a line from New York City to Los Angeles you have separated the parts of the country that annually receive substantial snowfall from those that do not. Almost anywhere north of the line residents can expect more than two feet of snow during the winter season.

The places that get more than five feet of snow in an average winter, however, form a very different pattern. These are found on the crests of the Sierra Nevada, Rocky, and Appalachian mountains, along the shores of the Great Lakes, and adjacent to the Gulf of Maine. The mountain accumulations are clearly examples of orographic snow, and the lake shore accumulations of lake effect snow. But what about coastal northern New England? The heavy snows in this region seem to be in part the results of a mixture of lake effect and orographic snow. In New England in the winter, arctic air often flows around a high-pressure area in eastern Canada, across the Gulf of Maine, and comes ashore along the northern New England coast. This coastline is dotted with small mountains, so that the precipitation produced may be orographic, lake effect, or both.

In parts of the United States where orographic and lake effect precipitation do not fall, snow falls primarily as a result of winter storms. Winter storms are frontal cyclones. A frontal cyclone (you will recall from chapter 6) is an engine that converts the latent energy in water vapor into work. The work a cyclone does is to move air and water around the countryside. The concentrations of water that are produced we experience as precipitation and the movement of air we experience as wind. The mechanism that converts latent heat into work in a frontal cyclone is the lifting of warm, moist air by cold, dry air. Warm air is lighter than cold air. When warm and cold air come in contact, the warm is lifted up by the cold. As it is lifted, the warm air expands, cools, and releases its latent energy and precipitation. The greater the temperature and humidity contrasts between the cold and the warm air, the more powerful the lifting action and the more energy and precipitation are released.

Winter storms are the most dramatic and powerful of storms because in wintertime, temperature contrasts across the Northern Hemisphere are at a maximum. In summer, the effects of sun altitude and daylength compensate for each other. As you move north in the Northern Hemisphere, the days become longer but the sun becomes lower, with the result that in the summer, temperature contrasts between north and south are minimized. In winter, on the other hand, the effects of sun altitude and daylength enhance each other. The farther north you move the lower becomes the sun and the shorter become the days. Thus, temperature contrasts between north and south are maximized. This generalization applies anywhere in the Northern Hemisphere in winter, but it applies particularly to the United States, where subtropical water masses lie directly to the south of subarctic land masses.

Because of these temperature contrasts, winter air masses which differ enormously in their temperature and humidity may come together on the North American continent. Because moist, warm air is lighter than dry, cold air, these differences in temperature and humidity may translate into substantial differences in weight between two neighboring air masses. The enormous forces generated by such a difference are hard to imagine. If you bear in mind the brisk sea breezes that can be generated in summer by temperature differences of a few degrees between, say, an ocean at 55 degrees and a neighboring shoreline at 70 degrees, then you can get some idea of the forces that can be generated by the contrast between a continent at 10 degrees and a tropical ocean at 65 degrees only 100 to 200 miles offshore.

When air masses from two such sources meet, they interact in ways that actually intensify the differences in their density. The colder, drier air mass slides under the warm, moist air mass, lifting it up. Once the moist air is lifted to its condensation level, its moisture begins to condense and release latent heat. Thus, the temperature of this air is increased relative to the surrounding air at the same altitudes, and its relative density is decreased. This drop in the relative density of lifted air means that areas where warm air is being lifted by cold air tend to be areas of low pressure. Into these areas of low pressure, air from the surrounding region tends to move. This air, of course, comes equally from the cold and the warm side of the line of interaction between the two air masses. The result is that the cold and warm air are drawn together more closely. Thus, until the warm air is cut off and the supply of latent heat is exhausted, the effect of the interaction of the two air masses is to pull them ever more closely into interaction.

As air streams in from the north and south to fill the low pressure, the coriolus effect takes over and a counterclockwise vortex is formed. On the east side of the low-pressure center, warm air pushes northward, riding up the rear of the cold air; on the west side of the vortex, cold air moves southward pushing under the warm air. It is in these bands of overrunning and undercutting that the varieties of precipitation characteristic of winter cyclones form.

Precipitation from Winter Storms

What kind of precipitation falls out of a winter storm depends on the temperature at various different layers of the atmosphere. All precipitation starts as minute particles of condensed water high in clouds. If the temperature is above freezing or only slightly below freezing, then these particles will take the form of minuscule droplets of water. If, on the other hand, the temperature is substantially below freezing, then the particles will take the form of microscopic ice crystals. These ice crystals gather together to form snowflakes. These snowflakes will reach the ground as snow only if there is a continuous column of subfreezing air all the way down to the ground. But where warm air is moving aggressively up the slope of a wedge of cold air it is often the case that there is a tongue of air warmer than 32 degrees overlying the subfreezing air at the surface. Snow that falls through this tongue of warmer air melts to some degree before continuing its fall into the subfreezing air below. What sort

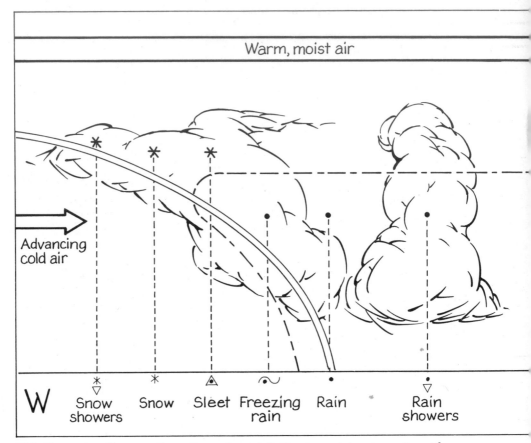

Warm, moist air

Advancing
cold air

W   Snow   Snow   Sleet Freezing   Rain   Rain
     showers   rain   showers

*This illustration diagrams the pattern of precipitation in a winter storm, in a side
view as seen from south of the storm.*

of precipitation is experienced at the ground depends on the thickness of the
overlying tongue of warm air and the thickness of the underlying layer of cold
air. If the warm layer is thin, the snow does not have time to melt very much
before it reenters subfreezing air. It comes to the ground as snow-grains or
sleet. But if the warm layer is thick and the underlying cold layer is also thick,
then the snow is transformed first into rain as it falls into the above-freezing
layer and then into ice pellets as the raindrops fall into the subfreezing air
below. If the tongue of warm air is very thick, and the underlying cold layer is
very thin, then the rain falling from the warm layer does not have time to
congeal before it hits the ground. It therefore falls as rain, and freezes as soon
as it hits the ground.

When a storm advances on a particular location all the various forms of
winter precipitation may be experienced in succession. As the high clouds
approach, they may overrun a region where the day's heating by the sun has
produced a narrow band of above-freezing air near the surface of the earth.

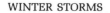

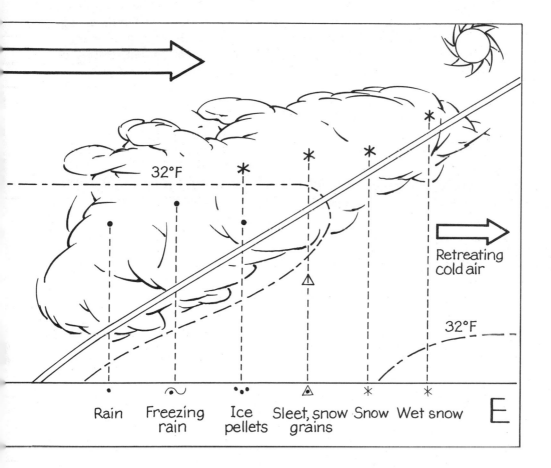

Rain   Freezing   Ice   Sleet, snow Snow Wet snow   E
         rain   pellets   grains

Thus, when the precipitation begins, it falls from freezing layers above into a melting layer at the surface. The storm begins as a cold rain. Shortly, however, the fall of all these freezing particles into the lower atmosphere cools it and the rain becomes first wet snow and finally, just plain snow, as the surface layer of air is finally cooled to below the freezing point. For a few hours, the snow continues. But all the time, the warm air is advancing overhead and the cold air is retreating. As this process continues, the injection of warm air aloft brings some part of the air aloft above the freezing point. On the ground we can tell this is happening because the snow first changes to sleet, then perhaps to ice pellets, and finally to freezing rain. Finally, the advancing warm air penetrates to the surface, the temperature rises quickly and the weather becomes showery and mild.

Although we think of winter storms as snowstorms, heavy snow (i.e., enough snow to accumulate and be a nuisance) occurs over a relatively small part of a cyclone's whole precipitation area. The production of heavy snow requires a precise balance in the amount and temperature of the air being carried aloft. If too much warm air is carried aloft, then rain forms at high levels and the precipitation at the ground falls as rain, freezing rain, or sleet. If too little warm air is carried aloft, then there is an inadequate moisture supply aloft to support heavy snow. Thus, the zone of heavy snow in a "snow" storm is likely to be confined to a comma-shaped area with its fat part just north and west of the cyclone's center and its tail extending out in front of the warm front. West and north of this region, the precipitation is likely to fall as very light snow or snow flurries. South of this region, precipitation is likely to be falling as rain, freezing rain, or sleet. Given this typical structure of "snow" storms it is not surprising that even in the winter months and even in places with a bad reputation for snowstorms, much of the winter's precipitation falls as rain.

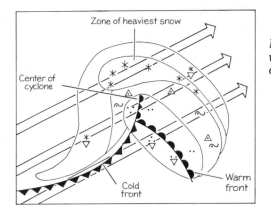

Here is the pattern of precipitation in a winter storm as it would appear if you could look down on it from above.

    Because of the structure of winter storms and because of the way these storms bring contrasting air masses into proximity, your position with respect to the storm track can have a tremendous effect on what sort of weather you get. If you live right in the path of the center of the storm you might expect to get an hour of light snow or snow flurries, a half an hour of heavy snow, two hours of mixed precipitation, and a few hours of steady rain. After the storm center passed, you might expect an hour of mixed precipitation and three hours of light snow or snow flurries. At the end of the storm you would have frozen ground with a dusting of snow on it.
    If you live a hundred miles southeast, then you would have even less of a snowstorm. The initial period of snow flurries and snow would be down to an hour; the mixed precipitation period and rainy period would be about the same. You would experience two to three hours of mild showers, perhaps even with sunny breaks. Finally, the storm would end with a cloudy, blustery period but with not much in the way of snow flurries.
    A hundred miles northwest of the storm's track, however, the picture would be entirely different. Here, you would have an hour of light snow

followed by four hours of heavy snow followed by an hour of snow flurries. When the storm was over you might be left with several inches of dry snow on the ground, and the cold winds around the back of the storm would be pushing that snow into drifts. In a winter storm, a few hundred miles can make the difference between a minor inconvenience and a life-threatening calamity.

Because of the way in which precipitation is distributed in a "snow" storm, large snow accumulations are a comparatively unusual event in places that don't get lake effect or orographic snow. Most parts of the United States can expect less than three feet of snow in a season. Spread over a snow season of twenty weeks, three feet per season means that people can expect an average of less than two inches a week. Much of this fall is taken up with frequent little snows of one to two inches, which are often washed away immediately. Little is left to be accounted for by the rare colossal snowstorms. Thus, a dangerous snowstorm is an unusual event, even in parts of the country where snow is expected every winter.

Winter Storm Hazards

To say that big snowstorms are rare events is not to discount their hazards. A meteorological event does not have to be frequent to be calamitous. In fact, as we have seen with hurricanes and tornadoes, rare meteorological events are relatively more dangerous because so many people do not prepare for them. Everybody knows that if you travel in open country in winter, you should have a good car radio and appropriate emergency equipment. But if you are like me, between blizzards, the car's antenna gets snapped off in a carwash, the shovel that you keep in the back of the car migrates to the gardening shed, and the

(continued on page 216)

The hazards of a winter storm and where to find them.

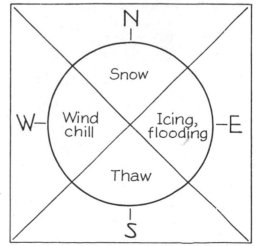

Traveling in Winter

Most of the deaths that occur in winter storms have something to do with traveling. The interstate highway system has been a wonderful thing, in many ways. But it has also exposed many people to hazards for which they are ill trained, ill prepared, or both. If you are planning a trip through open country during a northern winter, there are several rules to keep in mind.

1. Approach winter travel philosophically. If you do travel regularly in the winter, you should adopt a philosophical attitude. Make all your travel plans conditional upon the weather. A philosophical attitude is often most difficult to maintain when one is headed home. When people are caught up in a calamity, they experience a powerful desire to get home. Not only are they seeking shelter for themselves, but they are worried about their families at home. This powerful homing instinct will lead the most sensible people to do dangerous things.

Since maintaining a philosophical attitude may be more difficult than you anticipate, the best program is to take great pains to see that you are where you want to be when the storm begins.

2. Stay informed. As with all weather hazards, your safety lies in staying well informed. When a winter storm is likely to occur in your area, the NOAA will issue a "winter storm watch." When the storm is imminent, the watch will be upgraded to a "winter storm warning." The warning will delimit a particular region to be warned and particular hazards to be guarded against. These include heavy snow, blizzard, severe blizzard, ice storm, and high wind warnings. According to the NOAA, heavy snow is snow that accumulates at a rate of four or more inches in a twelve-hour period. An ice storm warning warns of a condition in which rain or drizzle freezes onto environmental surfaces making roads and bridges slick and bringing down tree limbs and power lines. A blizzard is a combination of high winds and falling or blowing snow sufficient to obscure visibility and obstruct travel for several hours or more. If a blizzard is accompanied by gale winds and near-zero temperatures it is termed severe. Blizzard or high wind warnings will be accompanied by a prediction of wind chill temperature. The wind chill temperature gives you an indication of the capacity of cold, moving air to

rob heat from your body. In general, wind chills below 0 degrees are dangerous. If you are outside in such weather you should not only dress warmly, you should also cover exposed surfaces of skin to prevent frostbite.

As with thunderstorm and hurricane warnings, it is important that the weather information you get is fresh. Radio stations and newspapers may occasionally provide you with forecasts that are stale. If you plan travel, your best bet for a forecast is from a television broadcast, a NOAA weather radio, or one of those recorded messages which you can get by telephoning a special weather number in most large cities.

3. Be prepared. The NOAA suggests that you carry with you a "winter storm car kit," including blankets or sleeping bags, matches and candles, facial tissues, paper towels, extra clothing, high-calorie, nonperishable food, compass, roadmaps, knife, first-aid kit, shovel, sack of sand, flashlight or signal light, windshield scraper, booster cables, two tire chains, fire extinguisher, catalytic heater, and an axe. Somehow, as I look at this list, I know that most people will not carry all that equipment in their car no matter what I say. I think if I had to do much winter travel in blizzard country I would give up all the rest of the stuff for an arctic sleeping bag and a CB radio: the CB radio to call for help, and the arctic sleeping bag to stay alive until help arrived.

4. Know what to do. If you do get trapped in your vehicle in a blizzard, it is important to know what to do. The first thing is to realize that your situation is pretty grave. You have to think carefully and preserve your energy for staying warm and performing a few crucial life-sustaining activities until rescue can come. The worst thing you can do is to leave your car and go running around in the cold looking for help. Stay in the car. Run the engine sparingly to keep warm. Turn on the dome light so that rescuers will know you are inside. Beware of carbon monoxide gas; keep the car ventilated by opening a downwind window a bit, and make sure the exhaust pipe of your car is not fouled. Do exercises, sing, wrestle, do anything to keep moving. Somebody in the car should always be awake. If you do all these things you are sure to be cold, bored, and frightened, but you will probably survive.

safety flares in the trunk soak up the residue from a punctured milk carton. The bag of tire chains, the sack of sand, and the blankets get heaved out onto the garage floor to make room for the Christmas presents as you set out on a holiday excursion. When the big storm finally does come, you are not prepared for it.

Winter storms provide hazards to gardener and nongardener alike. Each of these hazards is localized in a characteristic part of the storm, so that if you have an idea of how the storm is going to pass you by, then you can make a reasonable guess about what sort of difficulties it is likely to make for you. For the purpose of speaking about hazards, a winter storm can be divided into four quadrants. The north quadrant is usually the snow quadrant, the east quadrant the icing and flooding quadrant, the south quadrant the thaw quadrant, and the west quadrant the wind chill quadrant. These designations are approximate and their accuracy for any particular storm will depend on its direction of movement and degree of development.

The North Quadrant

Of the four, the snow quadrant gets the most attention. It is here that the snow accumulation records are set, and television camera crews can find images of pedestrians bucking drifts in city streets. Most of the hazards of north quadrant weather are obvious: you can skid into something or you can get stuck somewhere you do not want to be. The most deceptive hazard of north quadrant weather is shoveling snow. People who have not lifted anything heavy for years, rush out with snow shovels and try to clear their walks of the damp, heavy snow that often falls in the north quadrant. Heart attacks are a frequent cause of snowstorm deaths.

North quadrant weather may be hard on the gardener, but it is easy on the garden. There is nothing better for a garden in winter than a foot of snow. Snow is an excellent insulator. In winters when the snow is deep on my garden, I know that the frost will not go deep into the ground. If I mulch before snowfall, I can dig root crops all winter long. In spring the melting snow and the early spring rains soak into the ground instead of running off. In such winters the soil seems to warm up quickly in the spring and soil life seems more vigorous from the start. Last winter (1981–82) was a snowy winter on my garden. In fact, the snow was so deep it buried some Brussels sprouts before the zero-degree temperatures got to them in December. In January, I was out digging carrots and noticed the top of one of the sprouts plants peeking out of the snow. I dug it up and the sprouts were still green. So we had fresh carrots and sprouts for dinner. The soil under the snow was moist and warm and I came across several worms who seemed to be hard at work getting my garden ready for the following spring.

The East Quadrant

It is in the east quadrant of a winter cyclone that the most precipitation usually falls. The precipitation often starts as snow but changes over rapidly to various forms of freezing precipitation—sleet, ice pellets, and freezing rain. It is in this quadrant of the storm that the most dangerous driving is often found. In hilly regions with deep valleys, the cold air is slow to depart as the warm air overruns it, and there may be many hours of freezing rain before the surface temperature finally gets above 32 degrees. When finally the precipitation changes to "wet" rain a different set of hazards present themselves. Because the ground has been cold and subjected to several hours of freezing precipitation, it won't accept any water. The rain and melted snow run off as fast as the rain falls, and streams and streets rapidly flood.

East quadrant weather can be particularly hard on people with fruit orchards or ornamental trees. The wet snow and freezing rain that often fall in the east sector of a storm pile up on the boughs of trees and can damage them, sometimes severely. Evergreens are particularly vulnerable because their fronds provide so much more surface area for the snow and freezing rain to cling to. If nature is determined to give me a serious ice storm, there is not a lot I can do to protect my trees. Sometimes, if a small tree looks particularly overburdened, it helps to go out with a garden rake and try to knock some of the snow and ice off its branches. Very small shrubs can be protected with wooden tents and burlap wrappings. Beyond that, all I can do is hope that the freezing rain changes back to rain and the icing stops.

The South Quadrant

The south quadrant is the kindest to the gardener, but is hardest on the garden. Frequently, the south quadrant of a winter storm is subjected to unseasonably mild weather. The sun may come out, the temperatures rise, the snow may melt, and the top surface of the ground may thaw. If the storm is a slow-moving one and the thaw continues for a few days, plants may be prodded into premature activity. But sooner or later, the thaw must end. The wet ground freezes up hard again. Expanding as it freezes, it often heaves and cracks, separating shallow-rooted plants like strawberries from the subsoil and lifting bulbs up to the surface. Tissues of trees and shrubs that have become prematurely engorged with fluid freeze, winterkilling the trees. Fruit tree buds that began to swell are damaged or killed when the cold returns, and some or all of the crop may be lost.

I feel ambivalent about these thaws. Winters are long and hard where I live and these occasional jolts of warm weather are a great help in getting me through. We have a sheltered, sunny, southern deck on our house, and just as soon as the weather warms up even a little, we are out there at lunchtime,

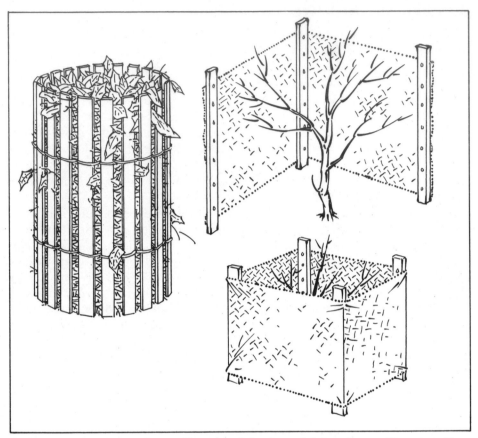

Snow protection devices for small trees and shrubs. At left is a plant well protected by a snow fence cylinder loosely filled with dry leaves or straw. At right are two simple structures you can make from burlap and wooden stakes to keep blowing or wet snow from piling up against shrubs or young trees.

trying to raise our color and our spirits just a bit. But oh, what these thaws can do to the orchards! My fruit-growing neighbors across the valley paint the trunks and lower branches of their trees white, to reduce the amount of heat absorbed during a winter thaw. This is often enough to keep the trees dormant during a brief warm spell. But with each day of the thaw, my neighbors become more and more worried. About all I can do at my place is enjoy the warm weather and keep adding to the mulch around my trees and shrubs, hoping to hold the frost in the ground until the thaw passes.

The West Quadrant

Of all the parts of a winter storm, the nastiest and the most dangerous to people is the west quadrant. The danger here is wind chill. Cold air entering the storm from the north surges around its west side. Here, typically there is a powerful pressure gradient between the low-pressure center and the arctic high-pressure center that inevitably tags along behind a big winter storm. With very cold temperatures, dry air, and powerful winds, wind chill factors are usually below 0 degrees in the western quadrant of a strong winter storm. While less snow falls in this quadrant, snowsqualls and blowing snow may reduce visibility to nothing, and drifting snow may block roads just as fast as plows can clear them.

The west quadrant is where the winter hardiness of your trees and shrubs will be severely tested. West quadrant weather is particularly hard on livestock. Large animals do not need to be under cover, but they do need to be out of the direct wind and they do need food and water or they may fail to survive west quadrant wind chills.

Wind Chill

Temperature (°F)

Wind Speed (mph)	40	35	30	25	20	15	10	5	0	−5	−10	−15	−20	−25	−30	−35	−40
5	35	30	25	20	15	10	5	0	−5	−10	−15	−20	−25	−30	−35	−40	−45
10	30	20	15	10	5	0	−10	−15	−20	−25	−35	−40	−45	−50	−60	−65	−70
15	25	15	10	0	−5	−10	−20	−25	−30	−40	−45	−50	−60	−65	−70	−80	−85
20	20	10	5	0	−10	−15	−25	−30	−35	−45	−50	−60	−65	−75	−80	−85	−95
25	15	10	0	−5	−15	−20	−30	−35	−45	−50	−60	−65	−75	−80	−90	−95	−105
30	10	5	0	−10	−20	−25	−30	−40	−50	−55	−65	−70	−80	−85	−95	−100	−110
35	10	5	−5	−10	−20	−30	−35	−40	−50	−60	−65	−75	−80	−90	−100	−105	−115
40	10	0	−5	−15	−20	−30	−35	−45	−55	−60	−70	−75	−85	−95	−100	−110	−115

Frostbite a   Considerable Danger   Grave Danger of Frostbite
Possibility   of Frostbite

Did you know that you can get frostbitten when the temperature is 35°? You can . . . if the wind is blowing hard enough. Frostbite danger depends on wind speed as well as temperature. So be sure to check for wind as well as cold temperatures when you dress yourself or your children for the outdoors on a cold winter morning. And if wind chill temperatures are below 0°, make sure that exposed skin surfaces are covered if you are going to be out for more than a few minutes.

Winter Weather-Watching: The Off-Season Hobby for Gardeners

Hard as winters are, I need them as a gardener. My gardening enthusiasm is like a fruit bud that needs a few weeks of winter chilling in order to blossom in the spring. I need winter's fallow period to mull over the seed catalogs and scheme about new techniques and new varieties that will make my garden even better and earlier than last year. And in between these off-season gardening reflections, watching the weather is definitely the best of winter hobbies. In winter, there is more weather to watch than at any other time of year. If only for this reason, gardening and weather-watching make ideal companion enthusiasms, since the high season for one is the low season for the other and vice versa.

Winter Protection for Evergreens

For evergreens like holly and rhododendron, one of the worst winter hazards is a spell of dry, cold, windy weather. Evergreens, because they have much more surface area than deciduous plants without their summer foliage, are very susceptible to dehydration of their leaves or needle tips during prolonged periods of low humidity and steady wind. They may suffer extensive tissue damage, which becomes evident in late winter as pale brown or grey-green blotches, usually on the plants' windward side.

To reduce the threat of this type of injury, the plant's resistance to evapotranspiration must be increased. In other words, water from leaves or needles that is normally transpired through the leaf surface must either be replaced, or kept within the plant. One tactic is to try and keep the soil from drying out. Watering can help if you have no snowcover, even though the roots are only minimally effective in frozen ground. Or you could spray the plants with a commercial wilt-preventive product in late fall. These products put a slowly degradeable coating on plants, which resists the passage of water vapor. By spring, the coating is gone and the leaves can transpire normally again.

17

BOOKS, GADGETS, AND OTHER SOURCES OF INFORMATION

We are coming to the end of this gardener's guide to the weather. If you have been reading this book carefully and I have written it well, you may feel just the slightest sense of panic. Only a few days ago, when you began to read, you had just a few questions about the weather and 250 pages of book ahead of you to answer them. Now, it may seem, you have a hundred questions to ask and only a few pages of book ahead of you. How are you to get your questions answered?

This chapter is designed to help you carry on your study of the weather beyond the pages of this book. It tells you some books you can read to understand better the principles I have been describing, some useful sources of weather information, and some gadgets you may want to buy to help you carry out your own observations of the weather.

Books and Other Sources

Into every program of self-education in a scientific field must inevitably come an encounter with an introductory textbook. Dreary as such books often are, they serve the function of teaching the reader the technical jargon that professionals use, so that the reader can read technical publications without being mystified. Fortunately, for people who want to learn about the science of meteorology, there is an excellent introductory textbook. I strongly recommend **221**

Joe R. Eagleman's *Meteorology, the Atmosphere in Action* (New York: Van Nostrand Reinhold, 1980). Dr. Eagleman's text is lucid and marvelously illustrated with satellite photography and imaginative diagrams. The book is most helpful in two areas where Dr. Eagleman has been an active scholar. Particularly full and useful are the discussions of water balance and of severe local storms—thunderstorms, hailstorms, tornadoes, lightning, and the like. Eagleman's book was an invaluable reference for me in preparing my own. If you want to learn more about the terms and concepts that modern meteorologists use in their work, you will find this book especially helpful.

The British have long been in the forefront of weather study. Consequently, some of the best general works on weather originate in Britain. Reading about foreign weather isn't quite as much fun as reading about one's own, but the general principles of weather are the same everywhere, and some of these books are so interesting that they are enjoyable to read even though the examples they present are from an alien geography. The best is James A. Taylor and R. A. Yates' *British Weather in Maps* (London: Macmillan & Co., 1958). It is a very carefully assembled book which takes pains to explain terminology so that a reader can follow along, even if you do not have a technical background. The book uses carefully prepared versions of British Weather Office charts to illustrate warm, cold, and occluded fronts, and high-pressure and low-pressure areas. When you are done studying this book you will have a very clear picture of what the weather is like on both sides of a cold front or near the center of a big cyclone, or anywhere else on a weather map for that matter. The book's only weakness is that it was written too long ago to include any upper-air information. Still, if you liked chapter 2 of this book, you will like *British Weather in Maps*.

Another good British weather book is Alan Watts' *Weather Forecasting* (London: Coles, 1975). The title is a bit misleading, since the book deals more with the analysis of weather than with forecasting in the narrow sense. It is a chaotic book that pays comparatively little heed to what terms a reader may or may not already understand, as the discussion develops. But it is full of ingenious illustrations and contains many good ideas and clever ways of looking at things.

Many of Watts' cleverest ideas are assembled in his more recent book, *Instant Wind Forecasting* (New York: Dodd, Mead, 1975). This forecasting handbook is organized around twenty color photographs of clouds. Along with each photograph is listed a variety of wind, barometer reading and precipitation events that might accompany such a sky, and what each would portend for future weather. The concept is a nifty one, but I found his forecasting rules too complicated for my patience. Readers with more perseverance might find the book useful. Watts is the first writer I know of to encourage nontechnical readers to collect and make use of upper-air observations in their study of the weather. His books deserve consideration for your library, if only for that reason.

One of the most recent general books on American weather is *A Field Guide to the Atmosphere* by V. J. Schaefer and John A. Day (Boston: Houghton Mifflin Co., 1981). Like many of the entries in the distinguished Peterson Field Guide series, this is a wonderfully well-illustrated guide. It contains a particularly useful set of cloud illustrations which are all presented in the same format to facilitate comparison. Many are supplied with detailed keys so that the reader can pick out and interpret the salient features of each cloud. The text is carefully written but limited almost entirely to the presentation of properties of the atmosphere. Little information is presented about climates or large-scale weather systems.

Several excellent books have been written on local or regional weather in the United States. If your garden is along the seashore, you may want to buy a book that helps you decode the weather information that waves and tides can provide. The period of a wave (the time between wave crests) and the height and direction of a wave are all directly related to the direction of the wind that generated them. The waves often betray the approach of a storm several hours or even days ahead of its arrival. A book which presents some of this information nicely is W. J. Kotsch's *Weather for the Mariner*, 2d ed. (Annapolis, Md.: Naval Institute Press, 1977). It is a well-illustrated presentation of the principles of meteorology with an emphasis on the kind of weather that happens over oceans.

People who garden next to the Great Lakes will want to own Val Eichenlaub's *Weather and Climate of the Great Lakes Region* (Notre Dame, Ind.: University of Notre Dame Press, 1979). It is a very thorough and well-organized presentation of the general principles of meteorology and of the special features of Great Lakes meteorology. For gardeners living on the lake shore it is a must; for gardeners with friends who live on the lake shore, it would make an excellent gift.

David Ludlum and the editors of *Country Journal* magazine have assembled a weather book for the Northeast, *The New England Weather Book* (Boston: Houghton Mifflin Co., 1976). It is more a compendium of weather information than an instructional book. It is full of historical weather information and statistics about the weather of the New England region. I think its best feature is a month-by-month calendar that presents dire meteorological events that have occurred over the years in New England on each day. It has some good text here and there and some excellent illustrations. It is a first-rate book to have on a night stand or side table for reading in odd moments.

If you have been gardening on the West Coast you are probably already familiar with Harold Gilliam's book on the weather of the California coast: *The Weather of the San Francisco Bay Region* (Berkeley, Calif.: University of California Press, 1962). His description of the mechanisms of ocean upwelling and fog production on the West Coast is unforgettable. The Sierra Club has also published a book on mountain weather, *Weathering the Wilderness: The Sierra Club Guide to Practical Meteorology*, by William Reifsnyder (San

Francisco: Sierra Club Books, 1980), which is designed for backpackers. If you hike as well as garden, you might like to own it.

Several books about the weather have been written specifically for gardeners. Each has its good points, but I find them all a bit ill organized and frustrating to read. James J. Rahn's *Making the Weather Work for You, a Practical Guide for Gardener and Farmer* (Charlotte, Vt.: Garden Way Publishing Co., 1979), contains a lot of useful information about how temperature, sunlight, and other factors affect plant growth. But also, it contains a lot of information recycled from general gardening books. Depending on what books you already have in your gardening library, you may or may not want to own this one.

Tim Campbell's *Do it Yourself Weather Book* (Birmingham, Ala.: Oxmoor House, 1979) is directed toward large-scale farmers with a lot of decisions to make about which crop to plant in what fields and when. The book emphasizes on-farm weather observation techniques and interpretation. It makes the important point that even within relatively small areas of a farm, precipitation and temperature can vary dramatically with features of the landscape such as hills, groves of trees, or bodies of water. The book does some things very well, but most are beyond the scope of a backyard gardener. Look it over before you buy it.

In addition to the many fine books about weather, there are numerous periodicals and information services that will increase your knowledge and understanding of the weather.

Daily Weather Maps: Once a week, the NOAA will send to subscribers a booklet of daily weather maps covering each day of the previous week. These maps include a seven A.M. surface weather map, a 500-millibar chart, and maps showing the high and low temperatures and the precipitation totals for each day. Because these maps come more than a week late, they are of no use in making your own forecasts. But if you like to understand the weather after the fact, they can have a variety of interesting uses.

I sometimes have used my weather maps in a way that might interest some readers. Each day, I write down what the weather is like around my garden: the winds, the barometer, the movements of the clouds, and the sequence of weather changes over the last twenty-four hours. Then, I make a little sketch of what I think the weather map is like. I use these weather maps to make my own weather forecast. Several days later, when the weekly weather maps come, I compare the actual weather map for that day with the sketch map I made. When my homegrown forecasts do not work out, I can figure out what went wrong: did I misunderstand the weather situation at the time, or did I understand the situation correctly and make a bad forecast on the basis of it? Each error teaches me something new about the weather.

The daily weather maps, weekly series, are available from the Superintendent of Documents, United States Government Printing Office, Washington DC 20402. A year's subscription costs $40.

Weekly Weather and Crop Bulletin: The NOAA and the USDA collab-
orate to produce a newsletter called the *Weekly Crop and Weather Bulletin.*
Every issue includes a national weather summary for the preceding week, with
maps showing rainfall and temperature distributions. It includes a national
agricultural summary with descriptions for each significant crop and for each
state of the agricultural practices going on and the impact of weather events
upon those practices. Are farmers able to get on their fields in Ohio, or has
there been too much rain? Have Florida orange-growers had to use their
smudge pots? Have cranberry-growers in Massachusetts had to flood their
bogs? Is dry weather holding back the corn crop in Iowa? The bulletin tells all.
It also includes weekly weather statistics for more than 200 recording stations
in the United States, and a regular summary of world weather events and their
effect on crops around the world. These summaries are sometimes quite
detailed, and incorporate discussions of such matters as the progress of
monsoon rains in India and the effects of too much (or too little) moisture on the
strawberry crop in Mexico.

The bulletin has several seasonal features, too. In winter, the heating
degree-days are provided for more than a hundred cities. In the growing
season are provided such statistics as the soil temperature, the accumulations
of growing degree-days, drought severity, and the progress of planting, seeding, and harvesting by comparison with a normal year.

The *Weekly Weather and Crop Bulletin* is an extraordinarily interesting
document. You may not want to subscribe to it every year of your life, but one
year's subscription is a must. It will give you a tremendous sense of the
relationship of your own gardening efforts to those of other farmers and
gardeners all over the world. The bulletin is available for $25 from the
NOAA/USDA Joint Agriculture Weather Facility, USDA South Building,
Room 5844, Washington, DC 20250.

NOAA Weather Radio: The National Oceanic and Agricultural Administration operates a system of transmitters which continuously broadcast recorded weather information over a special frequency. The broadcasts include
typical weather forecasts, the kind you can get from dialing weather numbers
on the telephone. In addition, they may provide five-day forecasts, a summary
of weather conditions in the region, and other information of interest to
growers or other special interests. Local NOAA forecasters can also break into
the recorded broadcasts at any time with emergency weather bulletins. These
might warn of imminent severe weather: tornadoes, flash flooding, and the
like.

Considering the possibilities of the NOAA system, its operation has been a
big disappointment to me. Mostly, it seems designed for those people who want
quick, superficial weather broadcasts, the same people who could readily
listen to an AM radio. The broadcasts could be much more informative. With a
longer tape cycle, the broadcast could include information relevant to a variety
of special interest groups, including gardeners. Granted, members of each
group would have to wait a few seconds to get their particular bit of

information, but the number of people helped by the service would be greatly increased at very little additional cost to the government. The NOAA weather radio system is planned to become the core of the government's weather information services into the next decade and policies are currently being established. A concerted effort by gardeners and farmers to get more high-quality agricultural weather information in these broadcasts would probably be effective.

The special radio that you need to receive the NOAA broadcasts can be purchased for under $50. For a few extra dollars, you can buy one that will sound an alarm to announce any special weather bulletins, such as a severe thunderstorm or a flood warning. Be sure to purchase your set on approval. You'll want to decide if the information you get is really worth the price. In addition, the frequency of the transmission is very high, and reception is often very spotty. If your retailer will not let you buy and try the set out at home, go to another retailer.

"AM Weather" on PBS: Public Television has a program called "AM Weather" which is broadcast in the early morning on more than 200 stations of the Public Television Network. Broadcast times vary from the early hour of 5:45 A.M. in Phoenix, Arizona, to the very civilized hour of 11:45 A.M. in New York City. This program provides the most complex dose of weather information ever assembled into a fifteen-minute experience. The behavior of the North American atmosphere is described and predicted for three days in advance and at several different levels of the atmosphere. Luxurious graphics support the spoken text. Satellite loops and stills from both the East Coast and the West Coast stationary satellites are presented in a very leisurely manner so that a viewer can look for particular features and draw his own conclusions.

"AM Weather" is a very high-quality weather broadcast, probably the weather broadcast to end all weather broadcasts. The format of the program is a bit odd and you may have a tough time explaining to your family why you are up at the crack of dawn watching these two funny men bark at each other about the weather. Never mind your family's ribbing, the program is well worth it. What do families know about weather, anyway?

The American Meteorological Society: This group publishes journals and books that are often informative. Its least technical journal, *Weatherwise,* is a rather dowdy publication which seems somehow halfway stuck between an academic journal and a magazine. Still, it has some interesting features from time to time, and you may want to subscribe. If I were going to subscribe to a meteorological journal, however, I would get the *Bulletin of the American Meteorological Society.* The language of its articles is more technical than *Weatherwise,* but the articles are interesting and the writing is surprisingly crisp for an academic journal. Both are available from the American Meteorological Society, 45 Beacon Street, Boston, MA 02108.

The American Meteorological Society also publishes books from time to time. It has, for instance, published a series on the history of American weather, edited by David Ludlum. These are compendia of historical accounts of significant weather events from colonial times on into the nineteenth century. They are fascinating. Some of the early colonists were accurate observers of the weather scene and they felt acutely the effects of weather upon their agriculture. Reading selections from their diaries about coping with all the same sorts of weather calamities that I cope with in my garden makes history come alive for me as effectively as anything I have ever read.

The National Climatic Center: Finally, if all these sources of information fail you, and you still want more, you can apply to the National Climatic Center. The center has the responsibility to organize and store all the vast quantities of information about weather that are daily being collected. The time will no doubt come soon when it will be strictly a computer-to-computer operation, but right now the organization consists of people whose job it is to help you locate important information. If you want to know what kinds of information are available, send for their *Selective Guide to Climatic Data Sources*, a 140-page book *about* information. Write to the Director, National Climatic Center, Federal Building, Asheville, NC 28801.

One of the jobs of the Climatic Center is to gather up data from time to time and put it in a readily accessible form for the public. One such publication is the *Climatic Atlas of the United States*. For only $6 you get 480 square feet of maps and charts describing American weather. The information is presented both by year and by month, so that you can compare the weather in different parts of the country in different months. All the data I expected are depicted in these maps, along with a few kinds I had never heard of. For instance, from this publication you can learn about regional and seasonal differences in insolation (the amount of energy received from the sun), and in pan evaporation (the amount of water sopped up from a standard pan of water by evaporation). This atlas is a real prize for people who love the weather and wonder what weather is like in other parts of the country.

Canada has no single clearinghouse of weather data like the NOAA. Weather information for Canada can be obtained from several different government agencies, such as the Department of Environment and the Department of Oceans and Fisheries. Weather maps and general information on weather systems for different areas can be obtained from *Canadian Weather Review*, Department of Environment Supply and Services Canada, Publishing Center, Hull, Quebec, Canada K1A 0S9.

Weather Gadgets

If you are the sort of person who likes to buy gadgets, a lifetime of amateur weather study is sure to delight you. You can spend anywhere from $100 to $3,000 outfitting a home weather observatory. But only a few of these devices are really essential to amateur weather observations and forecasting. I will try to give you some idea which are really useful and which are downright frivolous. Those readers who want to browse through a selection of weather instruments of all costs and sophistication may do so right in their own armchairs. Just write WeatherMeasure, a Division of Qualimetrics, Inc., P.O. Box 41257, Sacramento, CA 95841 and ask for their free catalog.

Barometer: A barometer is absolutely essential even to the most casual program of weather observation. Of all weather instruments, only the barometer measures something that human beings cannot directly sense. You can *feel* temperature and you can *feel* humidity, and you can *see* the effects of wind, but you cannot feel the changes in the barometer. So far as I know, no manufacturer has ever produced a bad barometer. I have had three in my lifetime, and every one has always worked just fine. You should expect to pay $30 to $40 for a good barometer.

Most home barometers are aneroid barometers. The key element in an aneroid barometer is a little metal device that looks like a concertina. It collapses as the pressure of the air outside it increases, and expands when the pressure decreases. Attached to the device are various levers and linkages that translate its movements to movements of a needle or a recording pin.

There are simple dial barometers and recording barometers to choose from. In a recording barometer, or "barograph," a pen makes a permanent tracing on a piece of paper. The advantage of a recording barometer is that you do not have to keep checking your barometer every hour to see if it is rising or falling. The disadvantage is that it needs to be serviced periodically; its paper and ink need changing and its clock needs to be wound. The only person I know who owned one stopped maintaining it years ago and it sits on his mantel gathering dust.

For most gardeners a simple dial barometer will be more than adequate. The faces of dial barometers differ. You can get barometers marked in inches, or in the metric unit, millibars, or both. I recommend a barometer calibrated both in millibars and in inches. Every year, metrication intrudes into more and more of our activities, and I suspect that the days of "inches of mercury" are numbered. Professional weatherpeople already work and think in millibars. If you have a millibar scale on your barometer then you, or your children, won't have to go out and buy a new one when meteorology finally goes 100 percent metric. The forecasting indications written on the faces of so many home barometers—such as "stormy" and "fair"—are not very useful, and I would suggest getting a barometer without them. Where the needle is on the face of the barometer is not nearly as important as which way it is moving. Manufacturers put the indications on more for decoration than for functional purposes, and I get tired of being told by my barometer that the weather is fair when it is pouring outside!

Be sure when you get your barometer home to follow carefully the manufacturer's instructions for adjusting it. Barometers are very sensitive to altitude. In fact, altimeters are just barometers calibrated in thousands of feet, rather than inches of mercury. A difference in altitude of 1,000 feet from the store where you purchased the barometer to your house where it will be installed will have a greater effect on your barometer than many severe storms. To compensate for altitude, set your barometer to the same reading as a nearby NOAA office or television station. Do it on a day when there is not any wind. (Wind indicates a pressure gradient, and if there is a pressure gradient, even a nearby NOAA office or television station may actually have a different pressure from yours.) If a barometer has once been set to the correct sea-level pressure, than it should always read correctly thereafter unless it is moved. If you are ever in doubt, wait for another still day and check it again.

Thermometer: Cheap, serviceable thermometers are plentiful, so there is almost no reason to do without one. For years I used an inexpensive thermometer that I bought at the nearby farmers' store. I dropped it while mounting it and it always read 10 degrees too low. But we just added 10 degrees to the temperature and used it that way for years. It worked just fine.

More recently, I gave myself a treat and bought one of those maximum/minimum recording thermometers. It not only tells me the present temperature, it also tells the lowest and highest temperatures that have occurred since the thermometer was last reset. To mount the new thermometer, I prepared a stake out of a three-foot length of 1 × 2. One end of the stake I sharpened, and in the other end I drilled a hole, so that the stake could either be stuck in the ground or hung on a wall. I then attached the thermometer to the hole end of the stake. When I want to use the thermometer as a wall thermometer, I hang it on a nail in the north wall of the woodshed. When I want to use it as a garden thermometer—for instance, to check the low temperature in the garden overnight—I take it down from its hook, stake and all, and plant the thermometer out in the garden. A maximum/minimum thermometer like mine need not be expensive. Models with plastic cases sell for under $30; fancy models with metal cases sell for up to $40.

Weather Vane and Anemometer: A rooftop weather vane is a great convenience. The little bit of altitude that a rooftop gives a weather vane increases its reliability and sensitivity considerably, compared with observations from the ground. I would recommend a weather vane for every gardener's roof. An anemometer or wind-speed indicator, on the other hand, is only for the most gadget-prone of weather enthusiasts. Adequately accurate estimates of wind speed can be made by watching the wind's effects on trees. (See the Beaufort wind scale chart in chapter 11.) An error of 10 miles per hour in a wind speed is not likely to significantly affect a weather forecast. However (where I live anyway), a difference of 30 degrees in the wind *direction* can sometimes make the difference between the prediction of a blizzard or a rainstorm. Of the two instruments, a well-placed weather vane is by far the more important.

If you are determined to measure wind speed, however, there are a few devices that will perform this task for you at not too great a price. The simplest is a hand-held plastic instrument that costs around $10. It is not very glamorous but it does the job. More complicated is an instrument that you mount on your rooftop. It is essentially a hollow plastic cylinder with a "tail" on it to keep it pointed toward the wind. The wind blows into the cylinder, increasing the air pressure inside it, and this change is transmitted by a hollow rubber tube to a simple indicator on your living room wall. The indicator consists of a hollow plastic vial filled with red fluid, so that as wind speed increases, the red fluid creeps up the tube in a very dramatic fashion. This gadget is an excellent conversation piece for parties on stormy nights and has a lot of boast value. ("How fast was the wind blowing at your place last night? At my place. . ." etc.) It is durable enough, but the snow tends to clog it up in winter and the wasps build nests in it in the summer, so that you can come down to your living room on a peaceful morning and find the indicator reading "Hurricane!" In short, wind-speed indicators are pleasing toys, but they are not essential to forecasting from the end of your garden.

Hygrometer and Psychrometer: Of all the measures of air properties, humidity is the most difficult to come by. Two instruments make the measure possible. One, the hygrometer, is based on the principle that animal hair—human hair, actually—expands when it is wet and contracts when it's dry. In the hygrometer, a bundle of hair is attached to a level system and the whole device is calibrated so that a dial gives readings from 0 to 100 percent relative humidity as the bundle of hair contracts and lengthens.

A psychrometer permits you to make a different measure of humidity, the wet-bulb depression. This term does not refer to something that goes wrong with your daffodils in damp weather, but rather to the difference between the temperatures recorded on two types of thermometers. One of these thermometers has a little bit of wet muslin wrapped around its bulb and is called (predictably enough) a "wet-bulb" thermometer. A current of air blows over the muslin and the evaporation of the moisture in the muslin cools the bulb of the thermometer. The drier the air, the greater the evaporation, and thus, the greater the cooling. The second thermometer is just a conventional thermometer without the muslin, hence, a "dry-bulb" thermometer. The difference between the reading on the dry-bulb thermometer and the lower reading on the wet-bulb thermometer is called the wet-bulb depression and is a measure of the dryness of the air: the greater the depression, the drier the air.

The psychrometer consists of the wet- and dry-bulb thermometers mounted together and some sort of device for blowing a current of air on the wet-bulb thermometer to aerate it.

Although you can buy devices to measure the wet-bulb depression and the relative humidity, these measures do not by themselves tell you what you want to know: how much potential energy there is in the air in the form of water vapor.

The problem is that both of these humidity measures vary with temperature. For instance, the relative humidity of a warm, humid air mass in summer may start out near 100 percent around dawn and fall to 50 or 60 percent during the course of the day, even though the amount of moisture in the air remains absolutely the same. Thus, if you were using relative humidity to assess the amount of potential energy in the atmosphere for making thundershowers, you would expect that the thunderstorms would occur in the morning, rather than in the afternoon. To assess the moisture content of the air you need to measure the dew point, and no handy home instruments are available for directly measuring dew points.

Fortunately, it is possible to compute dew point depressions if you know the current temperature of the air. The computation involves the use of some pretty complex tables which should be supplied with the instrument if you buy one. Before you go out and spend $20 or $30 on a psychrometer or a hygrometer, I would urge you to sit down with the instructions and make sure that you are the sort of person who is going to want to fuss with conversion tables and all the other complexities of humidity measurement.

Rain Gauge: For a gardener, a rain gauge of some sort is absolutely indispensable. The amount of rain that has fallen on a garden is very difficult to estimate without some sort of collection arrangement. The weather can be drizzly for a whole weekend and not accumulate half an inch of rain. Or it can unload a shower while you are in the basement stacking wood and accumulate an inch in twenty minutes. Getting readings from a nearby NOAA office is a risky substitute for making your own observations. Rainfall is often spotty, particularly during the growing season when so much of it comes from local showers.

You don't have to spend a lot of money on a rain gauge: a coffee can will do quite nicely. As long as the coffee can is on a flat surface and the rain falls fairly vertically, an inch of rain in the can means an inch on the garden. But there are several attractive and inexpensive devices available that make measuring rainfall, particularly small amounts of rainfall, more accurate and convenient. These collectors are tapered toward the bottom so that small accumulations do not get lost in the bottom of the collector. Pick a collector with a smooth inside surface. Algae and dirt inevitably get into rain gauges and one without seams or bumps inside is easier to keep clean. Remember to empty and store your gauge before freezeup occurs in the fall; freezing rainwater can crack it.

Soil Thermometer: For gardeners who are always tempted to try to beat the season, there is nothing so sobering as a measurement from a good soil thermometer. A soil thermometer is an ordinary thermometer with a sharp metal shield that makes it possible to insert the thermometer into the ground. Where I garden, hot spells in the early spring happen almost every year, and it is awfully tempting to go rushing out and plant the garden in April. The classic instructions to plant "after the soil has thoroughly warmed and all danger of frost is past" are subject to interpretation, but when my soil thermometer reads 45°F, I know I would be a fool to put my beans in the ground, no matter how warm the air is. Since I was given my soil thermometer several years ago, I have been planting my tomatoes later and harvesting them earlier. Moreover, I have saved myself a lot of effort dreaming up fancy frost protection devices for bedding plants that shouldn't be out in the garden yet. Frost or no, the plants will not grow well unless the soil is warm enough.

If you can't afford to buy a soil thermometer, try a meat-testing thermometer. Most meat thermometers have a metal probe, just like a soil thermometer. You will have to take a few minutes to calibrate the low end of the scale, which usually isn't marked on an oven thermometer, but you will save half to three-quarters of the price of a soil thermometer.

Keeping a Garden Diary

Now that you have bought all the gadgets you want and read all the books and subscribed to all the publications, you may want to start your own program of observation. A weather, garden, and natural history diary takes just a bit of discipline to keep, but it is a joy to read years afterwards. Only one year of my gardening life did I have the stick-to-it-iveness to keep such a diary, and I treasure it. One of the most amusing aspects of rereading this diary is discovering the things that I once knew and then forgot. I am constantly doing little experiments in the garden, testing little techniques, exploring how things work. Usually the results get lost. But the year I kept the diary, nothing got lost.

I recommend that every gardener keep such a diary, at least for one year. Don't set your standards too high. Even if you only make entries once a week, you will be amazed at how interesting the information is a year later. Quickly note down the weather observations I suggested in chapter 11: cloud types and motion, wind direction and speed, precipitation, temperature, barometric pressure, and your best guess at the humidity. Then note any premonitions you may have about tomorrow's weather. Finally, record any notable natural history or gardening events: the birds you saw in your garden that day, the crops you may have planted or harvested. Record any experiences with fertilizers or planting arrangements you may have tried that day. If you manage to keep up the diary, you will be surprised at how much you learn from it.

Gardeners who keep a daily diary of weather and natural history events might want to subscribe to the NOAA daily weather maps and include them in the notebook. When you get a week's booklet of maps, snip its spine, so that the pages separate. Each page will be just about the right size to put in a looseleaf notebook. Now if you write your weather or garden diary on notebook pages, you can alternate pages of diary with pages of weather map so that you always have the diary page and the weather map for a given day facing one another. The combination of the weather maps with a diary is unbeatable for remembering the weather. The maps remind you of what was going on on a national scale, and the diary reminds you how it affected your garden.

Good luck with your program of observations and your diary. I have no doubt that if you keep it up, you will make significant observations: significant not only for yourself but for others as well. The essence of good science, after all, is attentive observation by a person who loves nature. As a gardener, you certainly qualify.

CONCLUSION
ONE GARDENER'S VIEW OF THE WEATHER

By now you should have made your first successful weather forecast and be wondering why you never tried it before. You should be watching the television weatherpeople as a colleague, not as a spectator. You are sharing in their forecasting triumphs and gaffes. As you go about your day, you frequently squint at distant horizons, hoping to gauge the moisture content of the air. You often peer upward, hoping to catch a glimpse of a high cloud that will give you a sign of the movements of the upper-air westerlies. You see the sky a bit differently—not as a flat painting of white blobs on a blue background, but as a three-dimensional stage with high clouds that are up to twenty times as far away as low clouds. Your garden thrives, safe from frost, drought, and other forms of meteorological mayhem. You are no doubt perceived around the neighborhood as something of an expert. You are expected to provide timely warning of blizzards and squalls. Neighbors deferentially solicit forecasts from you. Spouses and children blame you when the weather goes bad. You have become a weather-lover.

I am glad for you. I think that amateur weather study is a good thing for the same reasons I think backyard gardening is a good thing. The more of us who are involved with nature and the more of nature's aspects we are involved in, the less likely we are to take nature for granted. People are prone to assume that nature has always been and will always be the way it is today. But nature is always changing. As our environment changes, we labor to insulate ourselves against the change. If the air becomes smoggy in our cities, we build shopping malls and condition the atmosphere. Inside we put fountains and plastic foliage as emblems of the nature we used to know firsthand. The more we insulate ourselves from nature, the less we are aware of how fragile it is and how much we are altering it. We must not be so blasé. No matter how ingenious

234

we are, the forces of nature will inevitably seek us out in our shopping malls and high-rise havens. Natural forces are patient and will not be denied.

The atmosphere, the oceans, and the land surfaces of the world form a system. The weather we experience, day by day, year by year is the result of the operation of this system. Each component makes its contribution, and a change in any one of the components will ultimately bring about some change in the system as a whole.

As human populations increase and industrial technology becomes more complex and widespread, human activities have begun to make changes in the various components of the earth/air/water system. The atmosphere has become more turbid from pollution and it traps more heat within the system. The oceans become less clear, and light and heat penetrate less deeply into them. Tropical rainforests are cut down and the land surface is slower to receive water and quicker to dry out and heat up in the absence of rainfall. Instance after instance, we can point to ways in which human beings are making little changes in the components of the earth/air/water system that determines our weather.

Too often we assume without evidence that the relationship between changes in the components and changes in the system as a whole is a simple one. We expect that small changes in the components will only result in changes of comparable size in the system as a whole. Many familiar systems are like this. When we press an accelerator a bit harder or turn a faucet a bit farther, the car increases in speed and more water pours into the sink. Since the changes we are making in the components of our earth/air/water system are small, why should we expect that anything but gradual changes should take place in the activities of the system as a whole. Why should we fear for our climate and for our weather?

But not all systems respond gradually to subtle changes in their components. In fact, many of the comforts of living in an industrialized society depend on this principle. If you push very gently up on your thermostat, nothing will happen for a while until suddenly, the little drop of mercury in the glass vial inside the thermostat rolls from one end of the vial to the other, making the electrical contact and sending current to the starting mechanism of your furnace. Then, suddenly, the furnace will spring into life, oil or gas will start to flow, the fire will burn, and the furnace will begin to heat your house. The thermostat/furnace/house system is one in which a tiny change in one of the components can trigger a dramatic change in the behavior of the system.

Another such system is one of those tiny click toys we all got in our Christmas stockings as children. These toys consist of a little piece of metal, one end of which is immobilized in a metal or wooden shell of some sort—usually made to look like a cricket or a frog. If you hold the shell steady and press on the metal spring, nothing happens for a while except that the spring pushes back at you a little harder. As you press harder and harder, the spring suddenly gives way with a loud "click." The same thing happens as you let up on the spring. The spring releases very slowly at first, and then all of a sudden it jumps back to its original position with a loud "clack." Thus, a small change may produce gradual response from a system up to a point, and yet, beyond that point, a small change may produce a catastrophic reaction.

It is important to know which kind of a system the earth/atmosphere/ocean system is. If it is a system like the automobile accelerator or a faucet, where changes in the components always make gradual changes in the system, then we are correct to be reassured that all the little changes we are making in the components of the earth/air/water system have so far provoked only minor responses from the system itself. But if the earth/air/water system is like the clicking toy or like the thermostat, then the absence of a major reaction may only indicate that the atmosphere has not "clicked" yet. The "click" may occur, and it may occur soon. Some little additional thing we do to the atmosphere may be the last straw and the atmosphere may react in a most dramatic way.

One of the most glamorous worries of this type has to do with glaciers. The last million years has seen alternations in the world climate between cold periods called ice ages or glacials, in which permanent snow and ice spread out from high altitudes and high latitudes, and warm periods called interglacials, in which the ice and snow retreat. Scientists have considered the possibility that the shifts from glacial to interglacial periods and back are like clicks and clacks of our click toy. Right now we are in the midst of a profound interglacial period. In fact, one has to look a long way back into geological history to find a thousand years as warm as the last millenium, and a long way back in the millenium to find a period of thirty years in which the climate was better than the period from the 1950s to the present.

If the earth/air/water system is like a click toy, then the end of the interglacial might be at hand and we would have no way of knowing it. Some steady change in the atmospheric system which may have been going on for thousands of years and to which we may have been contributing by our activities may suddenly bring the system to its "clicking point." The system may then snap over from the present interglacial state to a glacial state. The climate will swiftly become colder, moisture will be locked up in the ice caps and human populations will be reduced to a squalid remnant scratching out a living around the margins of great ice mountains.

Devoting time to thinking about the return of the glaciers has its good points and its bad. The good points are that it makes us aware that the earth/air/water system is a very dynamic one and that we live at a very special time in its history. We should not expect that system to remain in its present state for very long or to expect it to be particularly resilient in the face of the various changes we are making in its components. The bad part of thinking about the return of the glaciers is that there are many other more imminent calamities that are much more likely to affect us in our lifetime than glaciers. Even if reglaciation came on very swiftly indeed, it would take a century or two to get started. There are other drastic atmospheric consequences of human activities that could come about in decades.

Human-induced changes in the atmosphere wouldn't have to bring back the glaciers to substantially affect the way we live our lives. Minor differences in the operation of the earth/air/water system can have profound effects on things that are important to people. The rainfall pattern left by a weak cyclone crossing the country in the summer is narrowly confined. Some areas get heavy downpours, while others only a few miles away get only a trace of rain. Similarly, in winter, the line between dangerous snowstorms and balmy southerly winds is only a few dozen miles wide. The fact that our North American weather is as bearable as it is depends mostly on the fact that the pathways traveled by weather systems vary from week to week. But sometimes, weather systems get stuck, and when they do, disastrous consequences can occur.

We tend to think of deserts as places where there is no water. We forget to inquire why there is no water in these places. Most of the world's deserts are located where they are because they stand under immovable high-pressure areas. The Sahara, the Kalahari, the Sonoran deserts, the Great Sandy Desert of Australia, the Empty Quarter of Saudi Arabia are all places where high-pressure areas are "stuck." Weather patterns would only have to get stuck a little farther north or a little farther south, and many very important agricultural regions of the earth would become deserts. For instance, it would not take very much to transform the Great Plains of the United States into a desert. As we saw in chapter 13, much of this region already experiences a soil water deficit of around twenty inches a year. Agriculture is possible here only because of irrigation and because crops like winter wheat are up and out before the hot summer sun depletes soil moisture reserves.

To imagine the dire consequences of weather patterns getting stuck in the wrong place, you need only recall the bicentennial year of 1976–77. For reasons that nobody quite understands, that year the Pacific Ocean near the equator remained warmer than usual. Perhaps because of this oddity, the California Subtropical High parked itself off the coast of California for nearly a year, refusing to recede southward during the winter. Consequently, all winter the westerlies had to make landfall hundreds of miles farther north than usual, crossing the mountains in Canada and then plunging southward to the central United States. This pattern held rigid through most of the winter. It brought a legendary series of cold outbreaks to the Midwest and the Northeast, and an equally legendary drought to the Sierra Nevadas.

It does not take much meteorological expertise to project what would have occurred if the weather had remained stuck in the bicentennial pattern from that time to the present. The energy demands of the eastern United States during the Iranian oil crisis would have been much greater. Winter plant and school closings would by now be an annual tradition. The economy might well have slid into decline several years earlier than it did. Severe and permanent damage would by now have been done to the grain-growing regions of the northern Plains. The water supplies for Southern California would have been long since exhausted and California agriculture destroyed. Grain prices around the world would have shot up, with resulting political turmoil. Populations within the United States would have been uprooted as people fled blighted agricultural regions. By now, the United States would be a very different place to live, and all because of a little shift in the position of the westerlies.

Fortunately, the westerlies did not stay in the bicentennial pattern. There were meteorological flashbacks, when the pattern was reestablished for a month or six weeks or even two months, but always the pattern broke and allowed warm air to penetrate to the East and moisture to penetrate to the West.

Because scientists know so little about how weather systems get stuck in one place or another they can give us no idea about how human activities affect the likelihood of such disasters. Grit in the atmosphere could accumulate and reflect sunlight, cool the oceans, and bring on a series of cold, dry springs that could devastate the grain belt. Carbon dioxide in the atmosphere may ultimately enclose the earth in a greenhouse so warm that the California and the Bermuda highs expand northward, turning the southern third of the United States into a desert in a few decades. Or cutting the forest in the Amazon basin could weaken the trade wind circulation in the eastern Pacific and give us a series of years like the bicentennial year. Farfetched, you say. But the fact is we cannot rule out any of these possibilities because we simply have no idea how the changes in the position of the westerlies come about. Until we have some idea, no sane scientist would rule out any possibility.

But there are calamities even more likely than major climate changes. All of us who live in the Northern Hemisphere live at the shores of the same giant river. This river, the river of the upper-air westerlies, is a strange sort of a river, because each of us is both upstream and downstream of everybody else. Each thing that we do to the river, each pollutant that we pour in it, not only harms the people downstream but eventually returns to affect us.

The acids and heavy metals disgorged into the upper-air river by the great smokestacks of the industrial Midwest aren't eliminated any more than the contaminants thrown in the Ohio River were a generation ago. Throwing airborne industrial sewage into the westerlies only inflicts that sewage on the people and ecology of the Northeast and Canada. The Ohio River may be a bit cleaner nowadays, but acid rain and heavy metals may ultimately destroy the recreation and forest products industries of the northeastern forests.

We cannot trust the experts to protect us from such calamities. Experts have their commitments as experts—their special languages, their conventions, their ambitions to be the first to discover this or patent that. The only protection against our own self-destruction is a citizenry that is aware of what is going on in nature. In this sense, we gardeners and weather-lovers may be the Paul Reveres of the ecological revolution. We will ride our tillers and our garden tractors into the shopping malls of America, leap up on the parapets of the indoor waterfalls, steady ourselves by grasping the trunks of the potted trees, and shout our warning to all who will hear.

As I write these closing words, winter is about over and the planting of my peas is a few short weeks away. The time has come to set aside my winter hobby, the weather, in favor of my summer hobby, the garden. For several weeks, now, I will think of the weather mostly as it serves my gardening. I will worry about frost, and soil temperatures, and moisture supplies, and I won't think much about the drama of weather. But when June rolls around, and the garden is in and growing, then there will be time again to watch the sky and ponder. Looking up from the spinach that I am harvesting or the carrot row I am weeding, I will study for a moment the froth of cirrus on the jet stream, five miles over my head. It is flotsam borne on a river of air, a river that girdles the globe. All around the globe—in England, in Germany, in Russia, in Japan—are gardeners and farmers who draw their weather from this same river. To me, it is an awesome thought and one that gnaws at me whenever I become aware of that procession of cirrus parading silently and steadily across my sky.

INDEX

Page numbers in italic indicate illustrations.